VIEWS
FROM THE
WATER'S
EDGE

Abundant Blessings,

Patricia

Romans 11:36

VIEWS
FROM THE
WATER'S
EDGE

A DAILY DEVOTIONAL

PATRICIA VAN GORDER

DEDICATION

To my loving husband, Larry. His continual quiet expressions of love have encouraged me. His involvement with everyday obligations and household chores allowed me the time to be in the scriptures and writing. Most of all, he shares in my love of God, a partnering that binds us together as husband and wife and best friends, "a cord of three strands is not quickly torn apart" Ecclesiastes 4:12 (NASB). It includes God.

To my mother. She doesn't talk about patience and endurance; her life reflects these and many more qualities of her strong Christian faith. Her grace and wisdom have influenced me and all those who love her in the trials and uncertainties of life.

To my precious children, grandchildren, and those to come, who gave birth to the inspiration for this book.

INTRODUCTION

The Blue Pacific is awesomely beautiful and powerfully inviting. Everyone from the beach dweller to the occasional visitor is welcomed to her shores. The ocean is possessed by all yet owned by none.

Here, God's Word has come alive for me. I seek His lessons in the vibrant life of the sea and its surrounding environment. Rarely have I come away from time at the beach without some newfound inspiration. It is on these shores that I am content to reflect on people, events, and things that have influenced my life.

It is impossible for me to capture with a pen the sights and sounds of the mighty Pacific, but I have certainly enjoyed the exercise. These are some views from where I live: at the water's edge.

> I will sing of the loving kindness of the LORD for-
> ever; to all generations I will make known Your
> faithfulness with my mouth.
>
> Psalm 89:1 (NASB)

JANUARY 1

WRITE-ERASE

So you shall keep His statutes and His commandments which I am giving you today, that it may go
well with you and with your children after you, and
that you may live long on the land which the Lord
your God is giving you for all time.

Deuteronomy 4:40 (NASB)

In school I looked forward to my time at the blackboard. If
it was Monday and I was called upon first, there were long
pieces of white chalk, clean erasers, and a coal black board.
As the week wore on, we were down to stubby pieces of
chalk, dusty erasers, and a smeared black and white board.

New Year's Day reminds me of Monday, new chalk,
clean erasers, and an unused blackboard. It is a brand-new
year; we can write what we want!

In Deuteronomy chapters 1 through 4, Moses recalls
what God had done for His people and the mistakes they
had made since leaving Egypt. They continually disobeyed
God. What should have been an eleven-day journey had
taken forty years. It seems they were slow learners.

But in today's reading, he is telling them they can learn
from their mistakes, keep the commandments, and live
long on the land the Lord was giving to them.

We too can look ahead with anticipation and hope. We don't need to let past mistakes influence the future. We can begin writing with new chalk. It's Monday!

Lord, thank You for a new year in which I can write and erase.

JANUARY 2

RESOLVE

> Not that we are adequate in ourselves to consider anything as coming from ourselves, but our adequacy is from God.
>
> 2 Corinthians 3:5 (NASB)

Resolution is the buzz word at the start of a new year. Each one is made with a determination that this year will be different. We begin with resolve; but the battle is difficult, and after a while we find our resistance wears down. We give in to old habits.

Nehemiah is the picture of resolve. He set out to rebuild the walls of Jerusalem. Even though he held a position of influence and trust with the Persian King Artaxerxes, he left the security of job and home to accomplish the task. He faced ridicule, slander, and threats from enemies.

But Nehemiah was determined, and in just fifty-two days the walls were completed. A seemingly impossible task was accomplished because Nehemiah relied on God.

We live in a world immersed in the pursuit of pleasure and self-satisfaction. Our resolve can seem almost impossible when we consider the roadblocks. But resolutions don't work without God's grace. We are inadequate to cope. He is our adequacy. Like Nehemiah, we can rely on Him.

Plan to trust in Him for your willingness to follow through on New Year's resolutions.

Lord, I can do nothing without You. Please help me.

JANUARY 3

I WAIT

Psalm 37:4-11

Dear Father,

I will delight myself in You, humbled by Your promise that You will give me the desires of my heart.

I will commit my way to You and trust in You; knowing You will do it.

You will bring forth my righteousness as the light, and justice will be served.

I rest in You, Father, and wait patiently.

I don't fret about one who prospers, or one who is wicked.

I am not angry or concerned about the evil around me for I know they will cease.

Yes, I wait on You, knowing that all of us who trust in You shall inherit the earth.

I wait Father, knowing I will be delighted in Your abundance.

I wait.

JANUARY 4

FOLLOW ME

As Jesus passed on from there, He saw a man, called Matthew, sitting in the tax office; and He said to him, 'Follow Me!' And he arose, and followed Him.

Matthew 9:9 (NASB)

How did Jesus decide whom He would call to follow Him for the three years of His earthly ministry? Some were fishermen; most of them uneducated. Matthew was a Jew and held a lucrative position as a tax collector for the Romans. Most collectors overcharged and received a commission from the taxes they collected. They kept the profits. This was no small matter to the Jews. They hated collectors, such as Matthew, for robbing them and for siding with the Romans against their own people.

Matthew was cheating his fellow Jews. Why did Jesus call him? And how amazing that when He did, Matthew quit what he was doing and accompanied Jesus. He left a life to which he could never return to pursue an unknown future. All with the words "Follow Me."

He called Matthew, and He changed him. He calls us. "Today if you hear His voice, do not harden your hearts" (Hebrews 4:7 NASB).

I want to follow You, Jesus.

JANUARY 5

INTERCEDE

Do not cease to cry to the Lord our God for us.

1 Samuel 7:8 (NASB)

The holidays are over. Decorations are coming down and being stored away for another year.

But what are you going to do with those Christmas cards you received? I have a basket in which I put Christmas season correspondence. Each day I draw out a card or letter and pray for that person and/or family.

The apostle James tells us that the effective prayer of a righteous man can accomplish much. It is said that James spent so much time on his knees in prayer that they became hard and calloused like those of a camel.

In these verses the Israelites were coming up against the Philistine army. They were afraid and urged Samuel to cry to the Lord God for them. Samuel prayed, and the Lord answered him.

There are many who need our prayers. We may be the only ones who pray for them. We can pray for strangers we meet, for our doctor, our employer. The list is endless.

One has said, "Intercessory prayer might be defined as loving our neighbor on our knees."

Make this a year of prayer. Pray unceasingly for others. Keep a basket of prayer.

Lord, please bring to mind those who need my prayers.

JANUARY 6

GIFTS

Opening their treasures, they presented to Him gifts of gold, frankincense, and myrrh.

Matthew 2:11 (NASB)

As a youngster, I could not understand what those three wise men were thinking. Why would they bring such gifts to baby Jesus? What possible use would He have for gold, frankincense, and myrrh? They wouldn't be on my Christmas list!

But that list eventually changed, along with my understanding of the significance of the Magi's gifts. They were gifts worthy of a King; Jesus, King of the Jews. It was customary for people of the east to always approach persons of such distinction with a present. These expensive gifts were the most valuable that the country of the Magi produced; they revealed their high regard for Him and their belief that He was to be an illustrious King.

I no longer have a list of what I want but instead a list of what I can give—gifts worthy of a King—which are dearest to me and hopefully most valuable to Him. A few on the shopping list of valuable gifts fit for our King might include patience, time in His service, and precious time with Him in His Word.

May my gifts be pleasing to You, my King.

JANUARY 7

IF

See, I am setting before you today a blessing and a curse: the blessing if you listen to the commandments of the Lord your God, which I am commanding you today; and the curse, if you do not listen to the commandments of the Lord your God…

Deuteronomy 11:26-28 (NASB)

"Young man, if you don't clean your room, you'll be grounded this weekend," his mother said emphatically.

It is a familiar scene played out in many households—parents issuing ultimatums. From toddler to teenager, a child learns that conditions must be met to receive privileges and rewards. We could say it is an incentive program, of sorts.

God, our Father, gives us ultimatums. Many of His promises are filled with ifs and come attached with stipulations. In this instance, the covenant between God and Israel had been established, both agreeing to the terms. If Israel obeyed, they would be blessed with land, have abundant crops, and defeat their enemies. And if they broke their end of the agreement, a curse would ensue. They had a choice.

Jesus, in the New Testament, offers us choices. One which fills us with hope is found in John 14:23 (NASB):

> …if anyone loves Me, he will keep My word; and My Father will love him, and We will come to him and make Our abode in him.

If is a two-letter word filled with volumes of consequences and rewards.

I love You, Lord Jesus, and choose to obey You.

JANUARY 8

NATURE'S LESSON

Wait for the Lord; be strong and let your heart take courage; yes, wait for the Lord.

Psalm 27:14 (NASB)

I was on my early-morning beach walk when I saw a Great Blue heron standing on a bed of rocks lining the water. He stood immobile, watching the easy rolling waves lapping at his feet.

Great Blue herons look majestic with their long legs and S-shaped neck stretched outward and forward while fishing. They snare their prey by either standing motionless or wading slowly through the shallow water until a fish comes close. Then quick as lightening, they nab it, swallowing it immediately. They can wait hours for that moment. I tarried for a few minutes absorbed in this grand display of nature and then hurried on. I couldn't wait; I had too much to do.

Waiting is a learned discipline. We rush only to wait in checkout lines, traffic lights, doctor's offices, and more. Stress mounts and attitudes sour when circumstances force us to wait. Waiting becomes a virtue when practiced with patience.

Waiting on the Lord develops our dependence on Him, cultivating in us the fruit of the Spirit: love, joy, peace, patience, kindness, goodness, faithfulness, gentleness, and self-control (Galatians 5:22).

Have you been waiting on the Lord for the answer to an urgent request? Are you praying for loved ones and friends with special needs or illnesses, only to see the situation remains the same or worsens? Do you ask, "Why, Lord?" If you think about it, you may recognize some of the fruits of the spirit growing in you. Are you more loving, joyful, patient? Are you more filled with a gentle and kind spirit? Because these fruits bring us in harmony with God's will, we experience His peace. We are able to be strong and take courage in spite of the circumstances.

I wait on You, Lord.

JANUARY 9

MANIPULATIVE

Only obey My voice.

Genesis 27:13 (NASB)

Why would a woman such as Rebekah (blessed by God) be so manipulative in deceiving her husband, Isaac? She favored her son Jacob over his brother Esau. When their father called for Esau that he might give him the blessing, Rebekah quickly took advantage of Isaac's old age and his impaired vision.

She got what she wanted; Isaac gave the blessing to the younger son, Jacob. But when it was all done, she had to send her precious son away so Esau would not kill him. Rebekah never saw Jacob again.

Rebekah had waited for children, and God blessed her with twins. He told her that Jacob would be the family leader. With this in mind, Rebekah might have thought she would help God to make that happen. For her, the end justified the means.

She was a "take charge" woman, and she got things done. But there can be a fine line between taking charge and manipulating—controlling a situation. It can happen without our being aware of it, maybe in our marriage or workplace. We need to examine our motives, especially when we think we are following God's will.

Father, help me see when I am manipulative.

JANUARY 10

ALONE OR LONELY

I have set the Lord continually before me; because He is at my right hand, I will not be shaken.

Psalm 16: 8 (NASB)

Being alone doesn't necessarily mean being lonely.

When I was in my midforties, I was living alone for the first time in my life. It was an emotionally difficult time, and I was fearful about my future. Although I had support of family and friends, there were times I felt alone—days when despair nearly engulfed me and I was overwhelmed with loss.

But with perseverance I engaged in simple pleasures that might cheer me. For instance, each evening I set the table for one although I didn't have much of an appetite. Even when the menu was tomato soup, I used a pretty place-mat with matching cloth napkin and lit a candle. At first this was simply a discipline, but gradually I began looking forward to that time of day. I was becoming comfortable with myself.

It was surprising that although I was alone, I experienced moments of joy. How is that possible? Because God promises that He will make known a path of life for us. In His presence we will find fullness of joy, and in His hand we will find pleasures. Eventually I realized that I didn't need to fear the future, for He would show me the way. And with time I knew that I really wasn't alone. God lived with me.

If you are feeling lonely, find a way to enjoy simple pleasures. Happiness is fleeting, but joy based on God's presence is lasting.

Lord, thank You that I can know I am never alone because You are with me.

JANUARY 11

NUMBER OF DAYS

So teach us to number our days that we might present to You a heart of wisdom.

Psalm 90:12 (NASB)

Dear Father,

Life is brief.

This body will return to dust.

Please help me to number my days.

I want to use my time for eternal good, not earthly satisfaction.

I want to use it wisely, and for Your glory, that Your will might be fulfilled in my life.

JANUARY 12

OPPORTUNITIES

Going on from there He saw two other brothers, James the son of Zebedee, and John his brother, in the boat with Zebedee their father, mending their nets; and He called them. Immediately they left the boat and their father, and followed Him.

Matthew 4:21-22 (NASB)

It is not necessary to strive to make opportunities to serve God. If we live for God, He will make the opportunities. He will provide the work.

Think of the disciples. Two of them—James and his brother, John—were doing what they had been doing all their lives when Jesus called them. Fishing was a major industry around the Sea of Galilee, and they were part of their father's fishing business. It says they left the boat immediately and followed Him. *Immediately*! He called, and they knew it was time to serve.

While I was writing this devotional, I received a phone call from someone in the ministry in which I serve. She invited me to write devotionals for the ministry leadership teams. I had been praying that God might use me in His service. I was awed by His answer; here was my opportunity.

In our desire to serve, we might move ahead of His timing, motivated by love but misguided by our instincts. We can pray for the opportunity to serve. Then wait on His call. When He does call, we will know it is His will and His perfect timing.

Make me aware of Your opportunities for me, Lord.

JANUARY 13

RENEWED LIFE

> But for you who fear My name, the sun of righteousness will rise with healing in its wings; you will go forth and skip about like calves from the stall.
>
> Malachi 4:2 (NASB)

The calf is frisky, leaping and running! The spirited youngster has been released from the stall. Freedom! He kicks his hind legs, racing across the grassy field. It is a celebration of youthful joy.

And so it will be when Christ comes again. Those of us who know Him, who revere and fear His name, will be as that calf—quickened and invigorated, feeling the vigor of His love and the joy of His presence.

> For the Lord God is a sun and shield; The Lord gives grace and glory; no good thing does He withhold from those who walk uprightly.
>
> Psalm 84:11 (NASB)

Whatever trials we endure, what suffering we are going through, we can look to the day when Jesus returns. We will be full of new life. We will be healed; leaping and joyous as a new calf released from the stall.

Praise You, God, for this promise of renewed life.

JANUARY 14

HUNGRY FOR THE WORD

How sweet are Your words to my taste! Yes, sweeter than honey to my mouth.

Psalm 119:103 (NASB)

I was a young mother when I began the discipline of reading the Bible. It was a struggle for me to understand. The Old Testament was particularly confusing. I wondered how it could possibly apply to my life and what the ancient cultures have to do with me. I would become discouraged and stop reading it altogether. But I would try again from time to time. I began attending Bible studies and continued to search.

Since my initial decision to discipline myself in reading the Bible, my spiritual life has matured. I will never understand all there is to know about His Word. But I am not frustrated by that, nor do I struggle to comprehend everything. I am content just to hear or read scripture. I have a deep appreciation of the Old Testament and make it part of my daily readings.

Do you struggle to understand the Bible? Attending Bible studies gives the opportunity to learn and share with others who have a hunger to learn more about God. Feeding on God's Word is filling and satisfying. We grow spiritually as we feed on His Word as regularly as we feed ourselves physically.

Thank You, God, for giving me an appetite for Your Word.

JANUARY 15

OVERWHELMINGLY

> But in all things we overwhelmingly conquer through Him who loved us.
>
> Romans 8:37 (NASB)

I read this scripture, and I ask myself,

Why are you such a slow learner?

When will you be absolutely calm in every circumstance, no matter what happens?

Nothing will ever separate you from Him.

Nothing will ever put a wall between you and Jesus—

not tribulation or distress; poverty or hunger; not even life or death.

Not angels;

Not anything present in your life.

Nothing that will come your way can separate you from Him; nothing!

You are conqueror of all things because of Him.

You don't merely get through or get by, but you over-whelmingly conquer any hardship or pain.

So why question, worry, or fret?

Lord, I am a slow learner. Help me realize that I am totally secure in You.

JANUARY 16

LIST OF QUESTIONS

Then the Lord answered Job out of the whirlwind.

In his suffering, Job had a list of questions for God. Instead of answering him directly, God questioned Job with a list of questions to which no human can answer, "Yes."

> Have you ever in your life commanded the morning, and caused the dawn to know its place, that it might take hold of the ends of the earth, and the wicked be shaken out of it?
>
> It is changed like clay under the seal; and they stand forth like a garment.
>
> From the wicked their light is withheld, and the uplifted arm is broken.
>
> Have you entered into the springs of the sea
> or walked in the recesses of the deep?
> Have the gates of death been revealed to you,
> or have you seen the gates of deep darkness?
> Have you understood the expanse of the earth?

Tell Me, if you know all this.

Job 38:1-18 (NASB)

Lord, I cannot comprehend Your mighty power!

JANUARY 17

A SERVANT'S HEART

But whoever wishes to become great among you shall be your servant.

Matthew 20:26 (NASB)

What is a servant's heart? While I was recuperating at home from surgery, my husband became my caregiver—a role I would not have willingly assigned him. But I saw his servant's heart. His heart had been prepared for the task long before he was called upon. It was a task that demanded humility, not superiority. He is a humble man.

The Mother of James and John asked Jesus if her sons might sit at His side in His kingdom. His reply was, if you want to become great, you must first be a servant. Here, Jesus gives the formula of being a servant: if you want to be first, you must be a slave. He said, "Just as the Son of Man did not come to be served, but to serve…" (v. 28 NASB).

Jesus is the perfect example of a servant. We are told that he made Himself nothing, taking the very nature of a servant. At the Passover Feast, Jesus washed the feet of His disciples.

Look for those who have a servant's heart. You will recognize them by their love and humility.

I like the saying, "Not 'til the life is broken is it ready for the Master's use."

Break my heart, O Lord, and give me one of a servant.

JANUARY 18

FEELINGS ARE UNIVERSAL

The water I give him will become in him a spring of water welling up to eternal life.

John 4:14 (NIV)

We had just met, but I could see the pain in her eyes. I invited conversation, and as we visited, I learned that her husband had died less than two years before. Since his death she had moved to a new city and purchased a much smaller home. She was struggling in her adjustment to the changes.

I understood the pain. The end of a twenty-five year marriage brought tumultuous change in my life. I moved to a different city, and the downsizing process was painful. As I listened to her, I recalled the saying, "Feelings are universal; events are not." Although our circumstances were different, the feelings of loss, grief, and loneliness were the same.

Today we read that Jesus was alone with the woman at the well when she came to draw water. He was weary yet took time to listen. *Springs in the Valley* gives some touching examples of Jesus's awareness and compassion for others.

> The most faithful cannot compare with Jesus in lowliness of manner: He taught only one woman at Jacob's well; He noticed a finger-touch on the hem of His garment; He stooped to take little children up in His arms and bless them; even so small a thing as a cup of cold water, He said, would yield its recompense of a heavenly reward.[1]

When we take time to listen, we may find our lives bound in empathy with others. We may not have experienced the same situation, but we can recognize the feelings.

Lord Jesus, I pray that I will live by Your example. Help me to be aware of the needs of others, and realize that although the circumstances might be different, our needs and feelings may be the same.

JANUARY 19

EMPTY ME

May the God of hope fill you with all joy and peace
as you trust in Him, so that you may overflow with
hope by the power of the Holy Spirit.

Romans 15:13 (NIV)

Dear Father,

Empty me.

Empty me of all thoughts, feelings, and emotions.

May there not be even the slightest glimmer of me.

I wait to hear only You.

My voice is silent.

I want to feel only You.

It is in the emptiness of self that I can be truly full and
brimming with Your grace and love.

I ask for nothing.

I think of nothing.

I am empty.

Fill me.

JANUARY 20

PERSISTENCE

So it came about when Moses held his hand up, that Israel prevailed, and when he let his hand down, Amalek prevailed. But Moses's hands were heavy. Then they took a stone and put it under him, and he sat on it; and Aaron and Hur supported his hands, one on one side and one on the other. Thus his hands were steady until the sun set.

Exodus 17:11-13 (NASB)

It was time to fight. The Amalekites, a fierce nomadic tribe who lived in the desert, and who killed for the pleasure of it, were determined to kill the Israelites. Joshua prepared the troops, and Moses headed to the top of the hill with the staff of God in hand. He held it in the air, and Israel prevailed; he let his hand down and Amalek prevailed. When it got too much for him, two friends came along side. They gave him something to sit on, got on either side of him and held up his arms.

Jesus talked about the same kind of persistence when He told about the widow who made a complete pest of herself before a judge that really wasn't at all concerned about her needs. But he gave into her because he knew if he didn't, she would keep coming back until he couldn't stand it anymore.

What about God? He loves us; won't He be willing to grant us our petitions if we persist? Jesus says that He will.

And like Moses, it is good to enlist our friends and family to help us lift our prayers to God. When we get weary, they can come along side and join in the prayer.

It is written, "We might believe that God can and may do all. But do we believe that He will do all?"

Lord, thank You for hearing my prayer and thank You for those who come alongside to pray with me.

JANUARY 21

HIS THOUGHTS—HIS WAYS

> For My thoughts are not your thoughts, nor are your ways My ways," declares the Lord. For as the heavens are higher than the earth, so are My ways higher than your ways and My thoughts than your thoughts.
>
> Isaiah 55:8-9 (NASB)

We are unable to comprehend the magnitude of God's thoughts and ways.

We often attempt to use natural limitations in an attempt to measure the supernatural, but it can't be done. We try to fit God into an image we have created, endeavoring to conform His ways and thoughts to ours.

Wouldn't it make more sense to strive to fit into His plans for us? And how do we know His plans? We have His Word and His guarantee that the Word will accomplish what He desires. There is no mention that it will accomplish what we desire.

God says,

> For as the rain and the snow come down from heaven, and do not return there without watering the earth and making it bear and sprout...so will My word be which goes forth from My mouth; it will not return to Me empty, without accomplishing what I desire, and without succeeding in the matter for which I sent it.

Isaiah 55:10-12 (NASB)

Using our human reasoning, we might ask, "Why wouldn't I read His Word knowing that it will accomplish what He desires in my life? I may not comprehend His ways or thoughts, but I can surrender my will for His."

I want to trust Your way for my life, Lord.

JANUARY 22

DON'T GIVE UP

Even Simon himself believed; and after being baptized, he continued on with Philip, and as he observed signs and great miracles taking place, he was constantly amazed.

Acts 8:13 (NASB)

Phillip was a Jew and a leader in the early church. Yet he went to Samaria, a region despised by the Jews, and preached about Jesus. He exorcized demons and healed the sick in the name of Jesus. People in the city were amazed when they saw this; many believed and were baptized.

Simon, a magician, listened to Phillip. Simon was quite popular with the Samaritans because of his magic. Magicians were numerous and very influential in those days. Many believed Simon himself could be the Messiah since his powers were so great. We might be able to say that Simon would be so full of himself, there would be no room for God. But he too came to believe, was baptized, and began to follow Phillip.

Is there someone you are convinced will never believe in God? Does their lifestyle or philosophy seem to be a barrier to accepting Christ? Remember, Phillip let nothing stop him from preaching the Word. His courage and commitment brought Simon and countless others to believe in Jesus.

If we are committed to tell others about Jesus, we too may bring others to believe in Him.

Lord, I want to tell others about You.

JANUARY 23

OUR OLD WAYS

> Now when Simon saw that the Spirit was bestowed through the laying on of the apostles' hands, he offered them money, saying, "Give this authority to me as well, so that everyone on whom I lay my hands may receive the Holy Spirit."
>
> Acts 8:18-19 (NASB)

Yesterday we read that Simon believed Jesus was the Messiah. Yet when he saw the people receiving the Spirit through the laying on of hands by the apostles, he wanted that same power. Was he jealous? He even tried to bribe Peter and John that they would give him the authority to do likewise.

Probably some of Simon's old ways still lingered. The magician in him was fascinated by what the disciples could do. He wanted that! But Peter rebuked him, telling him his heart was not right before God. Yes he had accepted Christ, but he had not shed old habits and desires. Peter told him to repent and ask the Lord to forgive him. Simon could have left right then, but he didn't. He asked Peter to intercede for him (v. 24).

We need to get rid of our old ways. There are habits to which we still cling. It is a process. Jesus called Peter from a fisherman's life and gradually changed him forever. He can change our life just as He did Simon and Peter if we are willing to shed the sins of the past and get our hearts right with Him.

Give your heart to Christ. He will help you resist old ways.

Lord, I want to change my life. Help me recognize the old ways that I must surrender.

JANUARY 24

IN SONG

But as for me, I shall sing of Your strength; Yes, I shall joyfully sing of Your loving kindness in the morning, For You have been my stronghold and a refuge in the day of my distress. O my strength, I will sing praises to You; for God is my stronghold, the God who shows me loving kindness.

Psalm 59:16-17 (NASB)

I have always wanted to sing. It is not one of my gifts. I did sing in the church choir as a youngster, and I joined the Glee Club in high school. I wasn't very good at it, but I think they had to take whoever wanted to join. But God isn't interested in our talents. He is interested in our hearts and the desire we have to worship Him. When we sit in His presence and tell Him of our praise, I believe He hears our voice.

I sing of Your praises, O Lord. May it be pleasing unto You.

JANUARY 25

DISPOSITION OF SPIRIT

> And do not be conformed to this world, but be transformed by the renewing of your mind, so that you may prove what the will of God is, that which is good and acceptable and perfect.
>
> Romans 12:2 (NASB)

I have a favorite daily devotional book that has been a source of renewal for over twenty years; its pages are tattered, its binding worn. Some of the readings have made quite an impact on me. I was particularly drawn to this one by St. Catherine of Siena and have taken it to memory.

> Use your utmost endeavor to attain such a disposition of spirit that you may become one with Me, and your will may become so entirely conformed

to My all-perfect will, that not only will you never desire that which is evil, but not even that which is good, if it isn't according to My will; so that whatever befalls you in this earthly life, from whatever quarter it might come, whether in things temporal or things spiritual, nothing shall ever disturb your peace, or trouble the quietness of spirit; but you shall be established in a firm belief that I, Your omnipotent God, love you with a dearer love and take more watchful care of you than you can for yourself.2

Lord, may I always seek a disposition of spirit that will bring me to the full knowledge of Your perfect love. May I be transformed by the renewing of my mind so I might be aligned with Your all-perfect will.

JANUARY 26

MASTERING THE DIFFICULT

Ah Lord God! Behold You have made the heavens and the earth by Your great power and by Your outstretched arm. Nothing is too difficult for You.

Jeremiah 32:17 (NASB)

The first time I snow-skied was in Crested Butte, Colorado, a few hours from where I lived. Some of my family and I were taken to one of the highest ski runs in the resort.

We stepped out of the gondola into the eerie silence of the clouds, broken only by the crunch of the snow beneath our boots. We wordlessly began strapping on the skies, all the while staring at the sheer rugged slopes that lay before us.

"What are we doing?" I asked. "We will never make it down this mountain." No one answered; they were entertaining their own thoughts of dread. It took three hours of tumbling and falling to get to the bottom. I was exhausted and humbled.

But I was persistent, and the more I skied, the less threatening the slope. Eventually, I was able to make it down that mountain in one hour.

There have been more days than I care to remember when I felt as though I were on that mountain again, facing difficult challenges. I don't want to expend the effort to tackle them. If I had a choice, I wouldn't try. I feel like that today.

But I will persist. There are obligations. Others need me, and there are everyday mundane tasks that need to be accomplished.

O Lord, nothing looms ahead that I can't handle as long as You are with me. I believe that nothing is too difficult for You. Today we can master the difficult.

JANUARY 27

WHERE THE WAVES STOP

God spoke to Job. I read with awe as He answers this man—one who had suffered beyond anything I can imagine. Here, where the waves stop at ocean's edge, I stand and ponder the mighty works of His hand.

> Who enclosed the sea with doors when, bursting forth, it went out from the womb; when I made a cloud its garment and thick darkness its swaddling band, and I placed boundaries on it and set a bolt and doors, and I said, "Thus far you shall come, but no farther; and here shall your proud waves stop?"
>
> Job 38:8-11 (NASB)

He who created the sea and all that is in it, is our Creator. We must submit to Him even as the waves obey. We must remember during the most difficult times, His ways are not our ways. But He knows what is best for us.

Praise You, God, that You know what is best for me.

JANUARY 28

AFFLICTION

Is anyone among you suffering? Let him pray.

James 5:13 (NKJV)

When we get sick and are confined to the house, we can get restless and impatient. We want to be well.

But I've come to believe that it is in suffering that we draw nearer to God, and is one of His designs to lead us to the throne of grace. David wrote in Psalm 119,

Before I was afflicted I went astray…

(v. 67).

It is good for me that I have been afflicted…

(v.71).

…in faithfulness You have afflicted me.

(v.75).

When our health returns, we appreciate those things we had begun to take for granted. For instance, just stepping outdoors seems to be a privilege.

I agree with the psalmist, and recognize that unless I am brought under the ruling hand of suffering, I cannot appreciate the blessings I have been given.

Suffering. May I offer all to You, O God.

JANUARY 29

LOVING KINDNESS

Dear Father
Your loving kindness extends to the heavens;
Your faithfulness reaches to the skies.
Your righteousness is like the mighty mountains;
Your judgment like a great deep.
O Lord, You save both man and beast.
How precious is Your loving kindness.
I take refuge under the shadow of Your wings.
I drink my fill of the abundance of Your house.
You give me to drink of the river of Your delights.
With You is the fountain of life.
In Your light I see light.
Continue Your loving kindness to those of us who
love You.
Continue Your righteousness to the upright in
heart.

Psalm 36:5-10 (NASB)

David's psalm of praise speaks to my heart, Lord. Thank You for Your loving kindness.

JANUARY 30

SUNSHINE

Turn to Me with all your heart.

Joel 2:12 (NKJV)

The fern hanging in the kitchen is bare where it gets no sun. The other side is profusely full with delicate green leaves cascading down the white ceramic pot. We have to turn it occasionally so that both sides receive the benefit of the sun's soft rays through the window.

It reminds me of my own life when I turn away. It is then that I lack the healthy nourishment provided by God. I need to expose it to His sunshine found in His Word.

Do you need to be turned to His light?

JANUARY 31

REPENT

He did right in the sight of the Lord.

2 Kings 22:2 (NASB)

Josiah is remembered as Judah's most obedient king. He was eight years old when he became king, and he reigned for thirty-one years.

One day, Hilkiah, a high priest, found "the book of the law in the house of the Lord" (v. 8). Evil kings had ruled in Judah for many years, and the book had been lost. The excited Hilkiah gave it to the scribe, Shapan, to read, who in turn gave it to the king, now about twenty-six years old. He was overwhelmed with what he read. He immediately instituted God's law in Judah and literally cleaned house. He did away with idol worship and the priests who practiced it. He reinstated the Passover, which hadn't been celebrated since the day of the judges.

It only took one young king committed to God to clean up the kingdom that had strayed so far from God's law. He called on the people to repent.

Repent means to acknowledge our sin and turn away, changing the direction of our life from rebellion against God's laws. We can pray that God would acquit us of hidden faults and keep us from presumptuous sins. When we refuse to repent, we place a barrier between us and God.

Lord, help me to respond with action when I recognize sin in my life. Help me to repent and to remove any idols that keep me from worshiping You.

FEBRUARY 1

A CLEAN HEART

Create in me a clean heart, O God, and renew a steadfast spirit within me. Do not cast me away from Your presence and do not take Your Holy Spirit from me. Restore to me the joy of Your salvation and sustain me with a willing spirit.

Psalm 51:10-12 (NASB)

David's heart was grieved, and he cried out to God for forgiveness. He was truly sorry for the adultery he had committed with Bathsheba, and for his role in the murder of her husband. David confessed to the prophet Nathan and told him that he had sinned against the Lord. Nathan replied,

The Lord has taken away your sin. You are not going to die. But because by doing this you have made the enemies of the Lord show utter contempt, the son born to you will die.

(2 Samuel 12:13-14 NIV)

His sin was grievous, and there were consequences, but God forgave His servant.

There are things we have done that we are certain could never be forgiven. We zero in on the transgression and not on God's mercy. But there is no sin we have committed that is too great for God to forgive. If we truly repent, we can seek His mercy and plead as David did, offering to our Holy God a broken spirit and contrite heart.

O God, please create a clean heart in me. Do not cast me away but bring me into Your presence, forgive me, and have mercy on me.

FEBRUARY 2

DISCIPLINE OF MEDITATION

May my meditation be pleasing to Him, as I rejoice in the Lord.

Psalm 104:34 (NIV)

I've struggled with the discipline of meditation for years. It is difficult to subdue the activities of the mind, but we must try. We will find that with practice, silent worship will grow for us and will bring a peace and rest to our day. Stillness from the world is challenging, but stillness from ourselves and our energy is doubly difficult.

Meditating means to read His Word and ponder what we have read. If we invite the Holy Spirit to help, He participates in our understanding of God's Word. Jesus told His followers that the Holy Spirit will teach us all things.

Whenever Moses had been in the presence of God, his face shone. He put a veil over it because the people were afraid to come near him. Does your face reflect when you have been with Him?

I still struggle with meditation, but I continue to try with His help.

Lord, please help me to grow in meditating on Your Word.

FEBRUARY 3

HIS PLANS

It is best when making our plans that we first confer with the coordinator of all, the Almighty God. He is completely trustworthy and will counsel and guide us. Plan to trust in Him before making any plans.

Almighty God,
By Your word, the heavens were made,
And by the breath of Your mouth all their host.
You gather the waters of the sea together into a heap and lay up the deeps in storehouses.
All the earth shall fear You and stand in awe of You.
For You spoke and it was done.
You commanded and it stood fast.
You nullify the counsel of all nations.
You frustrate their plans.
But Your counsel stands forever.
Your plans from generation to generation.

Psalm 33:6-11

FEBRUARY 4
IMITATORS

> Therefore be imitators of God, as beloved children; and walk in love, just as Christ also loved you and gave Himself up for us, an offering and a sacrifice to God as a fragrant aroma.
>
> Ephesians 5:1-2 (NASB)

"I'm the mom," Jessica asserted as she filled our plastic teacups with water. I smiled as my granddaughter went about preparing our tea party. Just three years old, Jessica was already playing out the example set by her parents. She could only do this by being with them and absorbing what they said and did. She was a reflection of them.

Watching our children imitate us is like looking in a mirror. I have a make-up mirror that is ten times the normal view. Every flaw is glaringly revealed. When our children imitate us, we can see our faults as if looking in a mirror.

Paul tells the Corinthians to "Be imitators of me, just as I also am of Christ" (1 Corinthians 11:1 NASB).

Is this an arrogant statement by the apostle to ask others to imitate him? The gospels weren't written yet, and these new Christians didn't know much about Jesus. So Paul was merely telling them to follow his example so they could ultimately follow *Christ's* example.

If we want our children to know about Jesus, can we tell them to follow our example? Do we imitate Him?

Lord, help me to imitate You.

FEBRUARY 5

CHOOSE

> But you have forsaken Me and served other gods, so I will no longer save you. Go and cry out to the gods you have chosen. Let them save you when you are in trouble!
>
> Judges 10:13-14 (NIV)

When things are going well, we seldom think of God. Once in a while something might trigger a "God Memory." But mostly we are absorbed in things or people that have taken God's place. They are the "other gods" in our lives.

When life delivers a blow of disturbing or grievous hardship, we often call out to God. In our scripture verse today, God sounds pretty harsh as He tells us that when these things happen we can call on those gods whom we have chosen to save us. He will not save us.

But God is compassionate; ready to receive us when we repent and return to Him. When the Israelites repented, got rid of the foreign gods, and served the Lord, He could bear their misery no longer. It is important to note that they admitted their sinfulness and got rid of their foreign gods. They acted, and God responded.

We can repent now and choose to serve God. We shouldn't wait until we're trapped in a corner or when tragedy strikes. We can call upon God now and choose to serve only Him.

Thank You, God, that you are merciful and forgiving. Today, I choose to serve only You and to honor and worship You in all my ways.

FEBRUARY 6

FREE TIME

For whoever has, to him more shall be given, and he will have an abundance; but whoever does not have, even what he has shall be taken away from him.

Matthew 13:12 (NASB)

Are there times you want to be left alone? I remember that while raising my family, demands on my time left few opportunities to shut out the world. It seemed everyone had needs more urgent than mine. Occasionally I was able to steal a few quiet moments before someone came looking for me.

Children are gone now, and there is more time for me. The use of my time is the important issue. With what do I fill my days? I know that God

> Will render to each one according to his deeds.
>
> (Romans 2:6 NASB)

We can ask ourselves each day, "What have I done for You, Lord?"

When we have been given the precious commodity of time, we can use it for the good or for the frivolous.

Thank you for the free time I have been given, Lord. May I use it for Your honor and glory.

FEBRUARY 7

KNOWING HIM

> I am the good shepherd; and I know My sheep, and am known by My own.
>
> John 10:14 (NKJV)

A common superficial greeting for those we see once in a while is, "How are you?" Most of the people in our lives are just passing through. We probably know something about a lot of people, but we don't know them. The circle of our close personal friends is small. We become intimate with only a few.

To know someone, we need to spend time with them. We most likely talk with them or see them at least two or three times a week; phone calls and emails keep us in touch with those we truly care about.

We can know about God, but to be intimate with Him we need to spend time with Him. Just to know some things about Him doesn't mean we know Him. But He knows us and longs to have genuine communication with us.

I want to spend more time with You, Lord. I am Yours and long for a more intimate relationship with You. I want to know You.

FEBRUARY 8

DEATH

Precious in the sight of the Lord is the death of His saints.

Psalm 116:15 (NIV)

Sometimes I think of the mystery of death, knowing that I will experience its sting. Death, as described in God's Word, should be a welcome journey for us. God has conquered death, which means that we cannot be destroyed by it.

When a popular nightly news anchorman died, the news media carried his life story with pictures on the internet, TV, and in the newspaper. Most of us probably won't go out like that. We're not news material.

But that should not concern us. What does it matter if the world remembers us? We are accountable only to God. We are His children and will receive more of a welcome in heaven than a send-off on earth. I want that.

I want a chorus of angles singing "Hosanna" and "Alleluia" upon my arrival. I want to stand in God's holy presence and hear the words, "Well done, good and faithful servant."

Lord, help me not to fear death. Instead, fill me with the knowledge that I will see You face-to-face.

FEBRUARY 9

IT'S OUR DUTY

Which of you, having a slave plowing or tending sheep, will say to him when he has come in from the field, 'Come immediately and sit down to eat'?

Luke 17:7 (NASB)

Obeying God is not based on a point system. When we obey Him, we have only done what is expected of us. We have done our duty. Do you ask hired help to join you for dinner, or do you give them their just pay for the labor performed? Jesus asked this question of His disciples.

But will you not say to him, "Prepare something for me to eat, and properly clothe yourself and serve me while I eat and drink; and afterward you may eat and drink? He does not thank the slave because he did the things which were commanded, does he? So you too, when you do all the things which are commanded you, say, "We are unworthy slaves; we have done only that which we ought to have done.

(v. 8-10)

We might think that we should get credit for obeying God. We may even be proud of ourselves and believe God is proud of us also. But that is not what Jesus said. When we do the things, which God has commanded, we are to recognize that we are unworthy and only doing what we are suppose to do.

Lord, help me to recognize that obeying Your commandments is a duty, not an option.

FEBRUARY 10

DELIGHT

But the blameless in their walk are His delight.

Proverbs 11:20 (NASB)

Years ago, I watched an experiment on TV. A child in her highchair was alone in a room and absorbed in the colorful plastic toy on the tray. Her mother walked in with an animated smile and obvious delight at seeing her child. She didn't say anything, nor did she touch her. The baby could hardly contain herself, forgetting about the toy and enthusiastically responding to her mother.

Then mother walked out of the room for a brief time. Upon her return, the child began to smile, moving about in her high chair, kicking her feet and waving her hands. This time, mother just stood there; no smile, no response to the child's excitement. Only minutes passed before the child's demeanor became one of inactivity, no smile or watching her mother. She returned to play with the object on the tray.

I was touched by this display of a child's response to her parent and the demonstration of communicative interaction that brings such a response. Children are influenced by just knowing of a parent's delight in them.

Likewise, what a thrill it is for us to know that we are His children; we are His delight! I love this Proverb!

Father, as I delight in my children, so You delight in me. Thank You.

FEBRUARY 11

HIGHER PLACES

And makes me walk on my high places.

Habakkuk 3:19 (NASB)

Habukkuk lived in Judah during a time of oppression and persecution. Wicked, evil kings had been on the throne; the country was in a state of lawlessness and immorality. The prophet couldn't understand why God continued to allow such evil to exist.

After agonizing over the devastating results such evil would do to his country, he recognized his limitations in contrast to God's unlimited power over all things.

> Though the fig tree should not blossom and there be no fruit on the vines, though the yield of the olive should fail and the fields produce no food, though the flock should be cut off from the fold and there be no cattle in the stalls, yet I will exult in the Lord, I will rejoice in the God of my salvation. The Lord God is my strength, and He has made my feet like hinds' feet, and makes me walk on my high places.
>
> (v. 17-19)

We live in a world of evil and injustice. Yet, like Habukkuk we can rejoice that we are not controlled by events surrounding us but by faith in a just God. God is alive; He is in control. We can't see all that He is doing, but we can be assured that if we place our trust in Him and not in man, we will be surefooted in these difficult times. We will walk on high places.

Oh Lord God, help me to take my eyes off the events around me and look only to You.

FEBRUARY 12

INFIRMITIES

My flesh and my heart may fail; but God is the strength of my heart and my portion forever.

Psalm 73:26 (NASB)

I am really hard on myself when my body is fatigued and I don't feel well. I am discouraged by the desire to get things done and the lack of energy to do it. But I know I need to listen to what my body is telling me: take some time for rest.

When a child becomes ill, a parent cares for him or her. She doesn't scold the child for being sick but patiently and lovingly embraces her in her weakened condition. So, too, our Lord cares for us He scoops us up in His arms and assures us that we can rest on Him, giving our body time to recover.

Father John writes,

When you feel ill and indisposed, and when in this condition your prayer is cold, heavy, filled with despondency, and even despair, do not be disheartened or despairing, for the Lord knows your sick and painful condition. Struggle against your infirmity, pray as much as you have strength to, and the Lord will not despise the infirmity of your flesh and spirit.3

Lord, You are my strength when I am weak.

FEBRUARY 13

OUR PULPIT

If possible, so far as it depends on you, be at peace with all men.

Romans 12:18 (NASB)

I waited patiently for the space in an unusually crowded supermarket parking lot. She finally backed out. Suddenly from the other direction, a woman came speeding up and darted into the vacant space. My first instinct was to honk the horn. My second was to wait until she got out of the car and give her a piece of my mind. After considering both, I reluctantly drove away. She may have been in a hurry with a lot on her mind and just didn't see me, I rationalized. It was some time before I was able to reconcile my feelings with those thoughts.

I once read, "make a pulpit of every circumstance." How do we do that? It's difficult when we rely on ourselves. Our human reaction often sends a poor message. But the Bible says we can be conformed to the image of God's Son.

The verse says "if possible, so far as it depends on you, be at peace with all men."

It takes determination, but we can meet each challenge with graciousness and patience.

We don't need a platform, pulpit, or microphone to tell others about God. We can show them.

Lord, when I encounter a situation that leaves me frustrated, help me turn it over to You.

FEBRUARY 14

THE TEETER-TOTTER

Do not fear, for I am with you; do not anxiously look about you, for I am your God. I will strengthen you, surely I will help you, surely I will uphold you with My righteous right hand.

Isaiah 41:10 (NASB)

The teeter-totter was fun, until one day my friend on the other side jumped off, and I slammed to the ground. I never trusted anyone on the teeter-totter again. I was always ready to jump if I had any inkling the other was going to. I could never enjoy the ride. It takes two to teeter-totter, and I had to trust the one on the other side not to jump.

Relationships are much the same—to function properly, it takes two. Once we've been hurt when the other one jumps off, it takes time to trust again. Our caution level rises.

But unlike earthly relationships, we can, and should, feel completely secure in a relationship with Jesus. If we trust in Him, nothing can shake us. He promises to strengthen us and help us. We need not fear that He will abandon us and allow us to fall.

Security and trust are the essence of this relationship. Once we are secure in Him, we can risk trusting others. No matter who fails us, He will uphold us with His right hand.

Have you been hurt by someone you trusted? Today is Valentines Day, a day to celebrate relationships. Make Jesus your most important relationship. Put your trust in Him.

Lord, I am secure in You.

FEBRUARY 15

MY WORDS

"The one with whom you find your gods shall not live; in the presence of our kinsmen point out what is yours among my belongings and take it for yourself." For Jacob did not know that Rachel had stolen them."

Genesis 31:32 (NASB)

I think of the times when I have been so sure about someone or something and emphatically defended that opinion, only to find that I was wrong.

Today's reading gives a vivid example of times when we should hold our tongue even when we feel certain we are right. Jacob was so sure that Rachel, the love of his life, would not have taken her father's idols that he vowed to Laban that the offender would die. But she did take them, and his promise put her life in jeopardy. Whatever her motive, Rachel was clever enough to hide them when her father searched her tent; she was not found out.

We can never really know about anyone or anything. The only one of whom we can be certain is God. We can be certain that He is who He says He is.

In loving relationships, we put our trust in others. But even when we feel absolutely sure about someone or something, it is best to avoid rash statements.

Teach me to choose my words carefully. Help me to be faithful to those whom I love with my trust and confidence, but cautious with my words.

FEBRUARY 16

A PESKY CHILD

Will not God bring about justice for His elect who cry to Him day and night, and will He delay long over them?

Luke 18:7 (NASB)

This story that Jesus told His followers about an unrighteous judge and a persistent widow has always interested me. Was I to be as a pesky, persistent child begging a parent for my needs? It didn't align with my perception of my Heavenly Father and His loving child. Persisting in prayer isn't an endless repetition or an endless prayer session, is it?

On the other hand, just telling Him my wants and desires and never mentioning them again didn't seem at all sincere.

I lost a special bracelet and couldn't find it after several weeks of cursory searches. I didn't panic but instead prayed about it frequently. One day I had an idea to look where I hadn't before, and there it was. I couldn't quit praising Him!

He knows our heart and mind. Without verbal (and sometimes *with* verbal) expression of our petition, we lay them before Him, casting our desires and needs at His feet. Does that make us persistent? Maybe so. It also makes us faithful to cry to Him day and night with a sincere and loving heart, knowing He hears and will answer.

I come before You, Father, Your pesky child.

FEBRUARY 17

RESISTING TEMPTATION

No temptation has overtaken you but such as is common to man; and God is faithful, who will not allow you to be tempted beyond what you are able, but with the temptation will provide the way of escape also, so that you will be able to endure it.

1 Corinthians 10:13 (NASB)

In Matthew chapter 4, we read of three times that Satan tempted Jesus, and each time our Lord quoted scripture. When He became hungry, He said in Deuteronomy 8:3,

Man shall not live on bread alone, but on every Word that proceeds out of the mouth of God.

When the devil told Jesus to stand on the pinnacle of the temple and throw Himself off, Satan quoted Psalm 9:11-12:

He will command His angels concerning You; and on their hands they will bear You up, so that You will not strike Your foot against a stone.

But Jesus said to him,

On the other hand, it is written, "You shall not put the Lord your God to the test" Deuteronomy 6:16.

From a very high mountain, Satan offered Jesus all the kingdoms of the world. But Jesus said, "Go Satan! For it is written, 'You shall worship the Lord Your God and serve Him only.'"

(v.13)

Christ knew the scriptures well enough to ward off Satan. But the enemy used scripture himself. It is good to remember that he is a powerful enemy.

It was only by the Father's grace that Jesus was able to resist. In the world, there are attractive and convincing arguments for us to try something that is wrong. There may even be scriptural verses that support such a viewpoint.

We need to study the Bible and be armed with God's Word that we too, like our Lord, can use this powerful weapon against Satan. Memorize scripture. Arm yourself for the fight.

O Father, I want to store Your Word in my heart that I may resist temptation.

FEBRUARY 18

REWARDS

The woman conceived and bore a son at that season the next year, as Elisha had said to her.

2 Kings 4:17 (NASB)

This prominent Shunammanite woman could not have conceived the rewards of her generous hospitality to Elisha.

She knew of his need for a place to stay, and she and her husband prepared a room for him in their home. With no selfish motive, she gave from her heart, and her kindness was rewarded beyond her wildest dreams. Elisha asked how he might repay her. Childless, she had longed for a son. Elisha said to her, "At this season next year, you will embrace a son" (v.16).

It came to be.

Doing good without any thought of reward seems unnatural. Little do we endeavor to accomplish without thoughts of receiving positive reward. Study brings good grades; hard work can bring promotion; regular exercise can mean good health; planting a garden could reap an abundant crop.

> So let each one give as he purposes in his heart, not grudgingly or of necessity; for God loves a cheerful giver.
>
> (2 Corinthians 9:7)

Practice acts of kindness without one thought of reward.

I have read, "It is possible to give without loving, but it is impossible to love without giving."

Lord, help me to give without thoughts of getting.

FEBRUARY 19
IT WILL BE WELL

It will be well.

2 Kings 4:23 (NASB)

The Shunammite woman in yesterday's reading had been given a son by God, as promised by Elisha. When the child was grown, he became ill and died. She laid him on the bed that she and her husband had provided for Elisha. Anxious but determined, she and a servant hurried to find Elisha. When she found him, she cast herself at his feet, begging for his help. Elisha returned with her and restored her child to life.

Was she really expecting this miracle when she sought out Elisha? We don't know. But she told her husband as she left, "It will be well." Abandoning all fear, she came to the man of God, falling before him, knowing that no matter the outcome, all would be well.

Could we do that? Could we believe all will be well under such grievous trial? Only by God's grace, for He assures us,

> "My grace is sufficient for you, for power is perfected in weakness."

(2 Corinthians 12:9 NASB)

O Lord, may I trust you so completely that no matter what happens to me or those I love, I might say, "It will be well."

FEBRUARY 20

I AM HERE

I am with you always, even to the end of the age.

Matthew 28:20 (NASB)

Dear Father,

I linger here this morning, reluctant to leave.

My time in Your Word has fed me richly.

I am full but want more.

However, duties beckon me.

I am so grateful that when I leave this place of sweet communion that I don't leave You.

I know You abide in me all through my day.

You are here and everywhere.

Thank you!

FEBRUARY 21

BANDAGED

Come, let us return to the Lord. For He has torn us, but He will heal us; He has wounded us, but He will bandage us.

Hosea 6:1 (NASB)

God had allowed His beloved people to be held captive by the Babylonians for seventy years because they had rejected and disobeyed Him. But He assured them if they would turn to Him, repent, and seek Him, He would welcome them.

I cling to God's promise that when we return to Him, He will heal us. I have been torn and wounded by some of the events of my life. Those times that I have done things my own way, I was taken captive by the world, and held in slavery by what it offered.

There was no one moment that I can remember when I returned to Him. It was a gradual process, one of mistakes and severe consequences. But I did return. He has welcomed me as His precious child and bandaged my wounds. I was torn, but now I am healed.

It is never too late for us to turn to Him. God longs for a relationship with each of us.

Father, I am sorry for having rejected and disobeyed You. I return repentant and seeking You with all my heart.

FEBRUARY 22

IMPOSTER

But you have received a spirit of adoption as sons by which we cry out,
   "Abba! Father!"

Romans 8:15 (NASB)

I was an imposter. As a novice, I had enrolled in an advanced writing course. I'll just be quiet and learn, I vowed.

But the first day, the instructor's soft English accent stung my relaxed composure. "We'll have ten minutes of writing. 'My Perfect Day' is the topic." It took only a few experienced writers sharing their ideas of a perfect day for me to recognize my inadequacy.

After attending a few classes, I felt more comfortable. Working with advanced writers increased my desire to be a better writer.

It reminded me of the first Friendship Bible Coffee I attended. I had never read the Bible. There were women who were more spiritually advanced than I. Their knowledge of the Bible and their obvious close relationship with God increased my desire to read His Word and know Him better. I listened and I learned.

Do you feel as though you are a novice in your faith? Remember, the Holy Spirit will lead you. We are all God's children; we can call Him "Abba, Father."

If you want to know Him better, join a Bible study. Don't be intimidated by the more mature Christians. Learn from them.

Teach me Your Word, O Lord.

FEBRUARY 23

ORDER OF THINGS

Thus the heavens and the earth, and all the host of them, were finished. And on the seventh day God ended His work which He had done, and He rested on the seventh day from all His work which He had done.

Genesis 2:1-2 (NKJV)

When I was young, every Monday was laundry day. Before the sun came up, the washing machine was rolled off the screened-in back porch onto the blue flowered linoleum kitchen floor. The four-legged machine worked compatibly with two metal washtubs—one filled with rinse water, the other with bluing.

The clothes were hung on the five long lines that stretched across the grassy area just outside the back door. When they were dry, we used a coke bottle with a sprinkler on the end to dampen those that needed to be ironed, rolled them up, and put them in a pillowcase. Tuesday was ironing day. I learned at a young age if there is an order of things, the work can be accomplished.

God is a God of order. He created the heavens and the earth in an orderly fashion. From the first day that He separated the light from the darkness to the seventh day when He rested, there was order. Order brings harmony and tranquility. Chaos brings confusion.

God is not a God of confusion but of peace.

1 Corinthians 14:33

Check the order of things in your life. Do you find chaos or tranquility?

Lord, help me to live my life with order.

FEBRUARY 24

IMMERSEDINPRAYER

I gave my attention to the Lord God to seek Him by prayer and supplications, with fasting, sackcloth, and ashes.

Daniel 9:3 (NASB)

When you pray, can it sometimes be a struggle to give your full attention to God? I can say a prayer and at the same time be thinking of other things. The words are there but my mind is not.

Today's scripture says that Daniel gave his attention to God, seeking Him in prayer, supplication, fasting, sackcloth, and ashes. In every way he surrendered to God. He spoke openly and directly to Him.

...O Lord, the great and awesome God, who keeps His covenant and loving kindness with those who love Him, and who keep His commandments...

Daniel 9:4

In his prayer, Daniel pleads with God for mercy for his nation and his people. Having given God his full attention, he immersed himself in prayer,

"O Lord, hear! O Lord, forgive! O Lord, listen and act!"

Daniel 9:19

O Lord, I want to pray as Daniel prayed, totally immersed in You, surrendering my heart and mind to You.

FEBRUARY 25

HELPLESSNESS

But You have seen, for You observe trouble and grief, to repay it by Your hand. The helpless commits himself to You; You are the helper of the fatherless.

Psalm 10:14 (NASB)

Helplessness. Have you faced the challenge of trying to control or change a person? Have you experienced a situation that you desperately want to change but are helpless to do so?

Our lives can spiral down, whirling out of control. It can be gradual or in an instant—an unfaithful spouse or rebellious child, coping with illness and being totally dependent on others, death of a loved one. Where can we go when circumstances seem to control us instead of our controlling the circumstances?

I have found myself in many an unwanted life situation over which I have no control. My first inclination is to make it work out in the way that I know is best, only to realize it isn't going to happen that way. Human nature dictates, but God changes. He doesn't necessarily change the situation, but He changes us. With His grace, we cope with what we can't control but control that with which we can cope.

There are times, Lord, that I feel helpless. The psalmist reminds me that I must commit myself to You, my Helper.

FEBRUARY 26

FICKLE FEELINGS

And God is able to make all grace abound toward you, that you, always having all sufficiency in all things.

2 Corinthians 9:8 (NKJV)

Dear Father,

I am fickle.

My feelings are unreliable from moment to moment.

My world can be fairly settled, all in order.

I feel close to You—grateful, joyful.

Then routines are interrupted. I'm ill, the words or actions of another irritate me, the car won't start, I'm stuck in traffic, a major appliance needs repair, or my flight is delayed or cancelled.

My world is fragile, Father, and so are my feelings.

In an instant, my pious attitude that all is well changes to one of frustration and disappointment.

Help me to realize that Your unfailing love is not dependent on circumstances, moods, or my fickle feelings.

Only by Your grace can I have sufficiency in all circumstances, rough or smooth.

I am fickle.

You are Constant!

FEBRUARY 27

INTRUSIONS

Let my cry come before You, O Lord; give me understanding according to Your word.

Psalm 119:169 (NKJV)

There are days when everything seems to be an intrusion. Demands on our time leave us drained and weary. Laundry piles up; yesterday's dishes are still in the sink. In the children's room there are more clothes on the floor than in the closet.

We are encouraged to read the Bible and pray. And when we don't, we feel guilty. But these are often last on the "to do" list. The more the pressure, the more inadequate we feel. So what do we do?

There was a Carmelite monk, Brother Lawrence, who served in the monastery kitchen. He was in continual conversation with God. He addressed Him every moment, asked for His assistance in knowing His will, and thanked Him when a task was done. He had a habitual sense of God's presence.

In his book, *Practicing the Presence of God*, he writes:

> The time of labor does not with me differ from the time of prayer, and in the noise and confusion of my kitchen, while several persons are at the same time calling for different things, I possess God in as great tranquility as if I were upon my knees at the Blessed Sacrament.4

If life's demands leave no time for secluded prayer, converse with Him. Tell Him about it. Even a kitchen can be a sanctuary.

I give You all my concerns and cares, O Lord.

FEBRUARY 28
READING GOD'S WORD

The Word of God is alive and active, sharper than any double-edged sword. It cuts all the way through, to where the soul and spirit meet, to where joints and marrow come together. It judges all desires and thoughts of man's heart.

Hebrews 4:12 (NASB)

Reading God's Word, the Bible, is a necessary spiritual discipline. Like me, you may have grown up hearing the gospels in your home, church, or Sunday school. But the Bible can become head knowledge and not heart response. Have you read the gospels enough that they slip through your mind without affecting your heart?

Do you read with casual belief that Jesus was talking only to the crowds that gathered and not to you when He gave the Beatitudes? Have you read about the crucifixion for so many years that no longer does it grieve your heart when you read what Christ endured for you?

Reading the Bible is essential for us to grow. Fifteen minutes a day devoted to reading the Bible and it can be read through in less than a year. We probably spend that much time reading the newspaper. Five minutes a day takes us through in less than three years. Most churches can provide a daily reading guide.

It's helpful to read at the same time and same place each day—maybe before getting out of bed in the morning, or with morning coffee or when going to bed at night.

When I began the spiritual discipline of reading the Bible, I got up about five to ten minutes earlier in the morning before waking my children for school Eventually this wasn't enough time, and I began getting up at least a half hour before them. I still find my best time to be first thing in the morning.

Help me to be spiritually disciplined in reading Your Word.

FEBRUARY 29

FAITH

All things are possible to him who believes.

Mark 9:23 (NASB)

Faith isn't like opening a bank account and making deposits. Faith is a gift from God. That means we don't have to do anything at all to earn the gift of faith. But we do have to accept the gift or it isn't ours.

> Faith is a grasping of Almighty power;
>   The hand of man laid on the arm of God;
>   The grand and blessed hour

In which the things impossible to me
Become the possible, O Lord, through Thee.

Anna E. Hamilton5

Thank You, Father, for the gift of faith.

MARCH 1

DISPLAY OF POWER

Praise the Lord!

Psalm 148:1 (NASB)

My Mother and I sit here at the oceanfront pool of her rented condominium. She reads while I write my devotionals. It is a cool, breezy early March afternoon, but the sun spreads its blanket of warmth. The ocean roars below, treating us to a splendid display of its power. I pray,

> I praise the Lord.
>
> I praise the Lord from the heavens; praise Him in the heights.
>
> I praise Him with all His angels and all His hosts.
>
> I praise Him as do the sun and moon and stars; the highest heavens and the waters that are above the heavens.
>
> All praise the name of the Lord for by His commandment, we were created.

He has established us forever and ever, and made a decree which will not pass away.

Psalm 148

I praise You, Lord for this precious time and the visible display of Your power in all creation and in my life.

MARCH 2

JOY OF FORGIVENESS

How blessed is he whose transgression is forgiven, whose sin is covered!

Psalm 32:1 (NASB)

David writes this psalm filled with the joy of knowing he had been forgiven. What had he done? He had taken another man's wife who became pregnant with his child and deviously planned the death of her husband. He was a powerful king, and all was at his command.

He writes:

When I kept silent about my sin, my body wasted away through my groaning all day long. For day and night Your hand was heavy upon me; my vitality was drained away as with the fever heat of summer.

(v. 3-4)

He knew what he had done. He was overwhelmed with guilt, agonizing over the consequences of his actions. And then he writes:

> I acknowledged my sin to You, and my iniquity I did not hide; I said 'I will confess my transgressions to the Lord,' and You forgave the guilt of my sin.
>
> (v. 5)

He acknowledged his sin, confessed it to God, and knew he was forgiven. He was overwhelmed with joy.

When we are burdened with knowing our sin and trying to suppress it without confessing it as sin, we too will suffer the consequences.

David ends his Psalm with

> Be glad in the Lord and rejoice, you righteous ones; and shout for joy, all you who are upright in heart.
>
> (v. 11)

He knew he was forgiven. Do you feel his joy?

Father, I am a sinner. I confess my sin knowing that forgiveness is Your promise.

MARCH 3

HEALING

He entered the temple with them, walking and leaping and praising God.

Acts 3:8 (NASB)

We don't know his name. We know he had been lame from birth and had to be carried to the gate of the temple. He was a beggar and dependent upon the worshipers to support him. Peter and John were still new in their miracle working, having received the power of the Holy Spirit at Pentecost. When the beggar asked them for money, Peter said, "I do not possess silver and gold, but what I do have I give to you: In the name of Jesus Christ the Nazarene, walk!" (v. 6).

The people were amazed by what they saw. But Peter gave the glory to God, not himself. He told them that Jesus is the Holy and Righteous One, the Prince of Life and the Risen One (v. 14-15). It is recorded that about five thousand heard Peter, and many came to believe in Jesus as the Messiah (Acts 4:4).

Peter had seized the opportunity to proclaim the gospel. Jesus, God's Son, was crucified, died, and was raised from the dead. We too are empowered by the Holy Spirit to proclaim the gospel. We must take every opportunity to tell others of the healing, saving power of Jesus.

Lord, You are the Risen One. May I seize the opportunity to tell others.

MARCH 4

CINDERELLA COMPLEX

Whatever you do, do your work heartily, as for the Lord rather than for men... It is the Lord Christ whom you serve.

Colossians 3:23, 24 (NASB)

I had a Cinderella complex when I was young. My sisters and I had routine chores, but I always felt I was doing most of the work. "I feel just like Cinderella," I would grumble. But complaining did not lighten my workload, and feeling like the martyr made me miserable at times.

Martha and Mary had a similar problem. Martha felt she had to do everything while Mary did nothing but sit at the Lord's feet. Agitated with her sister, Martha complained to Jesus. "Tell her to help me," she insisted. Jesus gently told Martha that Mary had chosen the good part, the only necessary and lasting thing. He knew Martha saw things that needed to be done but reminded her to set priorities.

We probably all have our "Martha" times—times when we seem to have to do it all. Our attitude turns bitter, but it is the attitude of our heart that the Lord sees. He places little value on the obedience of a discontented heart. Having experienced the unpleasant Cinderella complex in my youth, I find it helpful to frequently examine the attitude of my heart. David's prayer in Psalm 139:23 becomes my own: "Search me, O Lord, and know my heart."

Jesus knew that Martha loved Him as Mary did. But Martha missed out because she didn't take time to sit with Him. Carve out time in your day to be alone with the Lord in prayer. From this, tranquility and cheerfulness will spring up and be evident to those with whom you serve.

Help me Lord Jesus to do all my work with a cheerful heart, accepting all as an act of worship.

MARCH 5

HE HEALS

And large crowds came to Him, bringing with them those who were lame, crippled, blind, mute, and many others, and they laid them down at His feet; and He healed them.

Matthew 15:30 (NASB)

Jesus,

They brought their loved ones to You, laid them at Your feet, and You healed them.

The mute spoke,

the crippled were restored,
the blind could see.
You healed their physical disabilities.

But ever greater than this, when the paralytic was brought to You, You demonstrated the power of forgiveness of sins.

Oh Lord, what good is a healthy physical body if my soul is sick with sin?

Doctors can treat my physical ailments and disabilities, but only You can
forgive my sins,
restore my broken life,
and make me whole again.
Heal me, Lord.

MARCH 6

AN APPETITE FOR SYMPATHY

Jesus declared, "I am the bread of life. He who comes to me will not hunger."

John 6:35 (NASB)

An appetite for sympathy can devour a person. It seems to take on a life all its own and needs constant nourishment. Instead of feasting at a table of joy and abundance, there are those who would rather sit at a secluded table where they can feed on ills and cares. There's no one to join them, and they find themselves alone.

> The art of life consists in taking each event which befalls us with a contented mind, confident of good. This makes us grow younger as we grow older, for youth and joy come from the soul to the body, more than from the body to the soul. With this method and art and temper of life, we live, though we may be dying. We rejoice always, though in the midst of sorrows; and possess all things, though destitute of everything.
>
> James Freeman Clark6

When trials overwhelm us, we can feed on an appetite for sympathy, feeling sorry for ourselves and certain no one understands what we are going through. But we will never satisfy such an appetite, and it can isolate us from those who love us. Jesus is the bread of life, and He will provide what we need. He says, "Blessed are you who hunger now, for you will be satisfied" (Luke 6:21 NIV).

Lord, help me to overcome an appetite for sympathy. I want to sit at Your feast table with those who know You and are fed by Your Word.

MARCH 7

BOTHERSOME THINGS

…with patience, showing tolerance for one another in love.

Ephesians 4:2 (NASB)

Why do I let those things bother me? I ask myself. My list includes grocery carts left in the parking space, drivers who cut in front of me, stores that play loud music, and dogs on the beach when the sign says, "No dogs on the beach."

I would like to think that while minor distractions may annoy me, they do not affect me. However, that's not always true, and I must rely on God to help me rise above them.

Do you share my limited ability to cope with such things? In my experience, when I allow petty conflicts to influence me, I am away from God. After all, I want to do His will, and if there is someone or something that distracts me from my goal, I need to take a hard look at myself and study my motives. I need to remember Paul's words when he says that we must tolerate one another in love. That's the bottom line, isn't it? Love. For where there is love, there is God.

I have read, "Gaze at God, glance at all other things." When I keep my eyes on Him, I barley notice the distractions.

I rely on You, Lord, that I might overcome the bothersome things in my life.

MARCH 8

SWEET SLEEP

When you lie down, you will not be afraid. When you lie down, your sleep will be sweet.

Proverbs 3:24 (NIV)

Dear Father,

Sometimes an army of thoughts stomps through my mind, robbing me of precious sleep. None of them seem that important; even if they are, there is certainly nothing I can do about them.

I long for what You have promised me in Your Word—sweet sleep. In the still darkness while struggling to rid myself of pesky thoughts, teach me to pray. Help me to seize the opportunity to be alone with You and experience the peace and tranquility of a sleep-filled night.

> On my bed I remember You; I think of You through the watches of the night.
>
> Because You are my help, I sing in the shadow of Your wings. My soul clings to You; Your right hand upholds me.
>
> Psalm 63:6-8 (NASB)

MARCH 9

LUXURY BATHS

Now to Him who is able to do exceedingly abundantly above all that we ask or think, according to the power that works in us.

Ephesians 3:20 (NKJV)

I still marvel at the luxury of having three bathrooms in our home. The master bath has his and hers sinks!

I think of the days when I was a young girl and we didn't have a bathroom in our home. On Saturday evenings we set the aluminum washtub on the kitchen floor, and each of us took our turn to bathe. Seniority wasn't a factor—youngest to the oldest was the rule.

When I was a senior in high school, we were all thrilled with a bathroom addition. The first bath I took is still a sweet memory. We were each allowed to take a bath by ourselves. Just watching the water gushing from the faucet was a treat—a luxurious feeling indeed. I could never have imagined the luxury I enjoy today.

Today's scripture reminds us that God's blessings exceed anything we can ask for or even think of. Are we grateful?

Oh Father, I marvel at the luxury of the many blessings You have bestowed on me. They are more than I could ever think or ask.

MARCH 10

A GLIMPSE

Who establishes the mountains by His strength, being girded with might; Who stills the roaring of the seas, the roaring of the waves.

Psalm 65:6-7 (NASB)

The eight-foot window over our kitchen sink offers a majestic view of the blue Pacific. Neighbor's red tile roofs sculpture an outline for the picturesque view. Gray colored sand welcomes lazy rolling white caps as the sea sweeps onto the shore. Oftentimes I can do nothing more than just stand at the window, staring in wonder at such a sight.

I treasure this miniscule glimpse of an ocean so vast that my mind cannot comprehend its scope. I am humbled by its beauty, awed by its power. And yet, I can only partake in the smallest glance of its overall majesty.

Sometimes in my quiet time, when I'm alone with God, I am granted a miniscule glimpse of His beauty and His power—indeed, His majesty. It is a glimpse of a God so vast and mighty that my mind cannot comprehend Him.

But oh, for that smallest glance, my heart rejoices; my pulse quickens. I am humbled that He sculptures for me a brief encounter of Himself from His Word.

Great is our Lord, and abundant in strength.

Psalm 147:5

MARCH 11

DEEDS

He saved us, not on the basis of our deeds...but according to His mercy.

Titus 3:5 (NASB)

There are times when we do something that makes us feel good about ourselves. There's nothing wrong about feeling good about deeds that benefit ourselves or others, as long as we remember that it is not us but the Spirit living in us who does good.

We must be mindful that it is not the deed that will save us, for there is nothing we can do that can save us. It is God's mercy that saves us. We are justified only by His grace, and as His children, we inherit His kingdom.

So what are good works to me? Why do I bother? It is not I, but the Spirit living in me who does good works. How can I do any good? I am full of sin. Paul recognizes this in Romans 7:24-25 (NKJV) when he says of himself,

> O wretched man that I am! Who will deliver me from this body of death? I thank God through Jesus Christ our Lord! So then, with the mind I myself serve the law of God, but with the flesh the law of sin.

I do good not of my own power or pleasure but because He lives in me.

You are Abba, my Father. May any good deed I do please only You.

MARCH 12

LISTENING

But the Lord was not in the wind. And after the wind an earthquake, but the Lord was not in the earthquake. After the earthquake a fire, but the Lord was not in the fire; and after the fire the sound of a gentle blowing.

1 Kings 19:11-12 (NASB)

Sometimes I close my eyes and just listen, surrendering my mind to the rhythm of the ocean. On certain days, it sounds like a roaring wind. Other times I hear it lapping gently to shore like a lazy lake.

Elijah was on the run from Jezebel who had threatened his life. He was so terrified that he had even asked God to take his life. He had been brought along to the cave by God's guidance. Elijah didn't find God in the strong wind, earthquake, or fire but in the gentleness of a soft breeze. He listened.

Sometimes, when we are confronted with tragedy or turmoil, we also yield to fear's tenacious, powerful grip. We're afraid. So afraid we may be like Elijah, begging God to end it all. But God longs to reveal Himself to us.

When we fail to hear His voice, maybe it's because we're not listening. We need to be quiet. We can't listen if we're talking. God tells us, "Be still, and know that I am God" (Psalm 46:10 NASB).

Oh, that we would just listen when confronted with fear. God is there for us just as He was for Elijah.

Be still. Listen.

Heavenly Father, teach me to listen. I want to hear.

MARCH 13

INJUSTICE

> I also noticed that throughout the world there is evil in the courtroom. Yes, even the courts of law are corrupt! I said to myself, "In due season God will judge everyone, both good and bad, for all their deeds."
>
> Ecclesiastes 3:16-17 (NLT)

We can't escape injustice. One of the greatest examples of injustice is the arrest and crucifixion of Jesus.

When I was jolted by an injustice in my family, I wanted to jump in and make it all okay. I was struggling with God's Word that He would judge everyone for their deed in due season. I wanted justice now.

It was time for me to be submissive as our Lord Jesus was in the garden when they came to arrest Him, and Peter drew his sword and cut off the ear of the High Priest. Peter, maybe angry, confused, and scared wanted to jump in and make it all okay. But Jesus said, "The cup which the Father has given Me, shall I not drink it?" (John 18:11 NASB).

Even if we are not personally affected by injustice we see it. When we submit to God, it doesn't mean we understand it or are passive about it. We are trusting Him that one day He will bring justice for all.

Father, trusting You helps me deal with the evil that I can do nothing about.

MARCH 14

MY VIEW FROM HERE

They who dwell in the ends of the earth stand in awe of Your signs; You make the dawn and the sunset shout for joy.

Psalm 65:8 (NASB)

The glory of God the Creator is reflected in nature. My view from here at the water's edge is a reminder of His lavish generosity.

It is seen in the vibrant sea action as white caps scramble for the shore's edge; the pelicans as they cruise the waves. The dolphins feeding on a school of fish, and sea gulls soaring on wind currents.

We can all respond to creation wherever we are, no matter the view. The psalmist says that God makes the dawn and the sunset shout for joy. Our view of His glory is everywhere inviting us to participate.

O thank You, Father, for the wonder of Your creation.

MARCH 15

MY PROMISE: ASK

> Ask and it will be given to you; seek and you will find; knock and the door will be opened to you. For everyone who asks receives; he who seeks finds; and to him who knocks, the door will be opened.
>
> Matthew 7:7-8 (NIV)

Dear child,

What would you ask of Me?

You know the world can offer you opportunity, wealth, possessions, earthly happiness and reward.

But what would you ask of a Father who can give you anything? Would you ask for knowledge, wisdom, understanding, and love for all? And what of discernment, peace, and tranquility?

Ask.

I will give them to you.

Your Father

MARCH 16

RECEIVE

But when the kindness of God our Savior and His love for mankind appeared, He saved us, not on the basis of deeds which we have done in righteousness, but according to His mercy, by the washing of regeneration and renewing by the Holy Spirit, whom He poured out upon us richly through Jesus Christ our Savior, so that being justified by His grace we would be made heirs according to the hope of eternal life.

Titus 3:4-7 (NASB)

I stood on the shores of Kaanapali, Maui, on my first visit to Hawaii. The warm, turquoise, clear water was substantially different from the March conditions at home in San Diego. It is the same ocean but a different climate.

The ocean reminds me of God's grace. It is the same for everyone, available to all. But just as the ocean climate differs, so do our hearts. We respond differently. Some long for and seek God. Others go about their daily tasks, ignoring God's presence and His grace.

God saved us all, not because of anything we have done, but by His kindness and mercy. "For by grace you have been saved through faith; and that not of yourselves, it is the gift of God" (Ephesians 2:6).

Check the climate of your heart. Is it ready to receive God's grace?

Father, may I be receptive to Your gift of grace.

MARCH 17

PERSONALLY SPEAKING

> You formed my inward parts; You wove me in my mother's womb.
>
> Psalm 139:13 (NASB)

God speaks to us personally. He expresses His tenderness and love for us through His Word.

I love You. I know everything about you (Psalm 139:1).

I created you; you are fearfully and wonderfully made (Psalm 139:14).

I have made you in My image (Genesis 1:27).

I have numbered every hair on your head (Matthew 10:29).

I want to lavish My love on you (1 John 3:1).

You will receive gifts today, but every good gift comes from Me (James 1:17).

I am Your Father; your perfect Father (Matthew 5:48).

I meet your every need (Matthew 6:31).

Always remember; all your days are written in my book (139:16).

Lord, You formed me and know me. Thank You for Your words of reassuring love and care for me.

MARCH 18

JOY

David, wearing a linen ephod, danced before the Lord with all his might, while he and the entire house of Israel brought up the ark of the Lord with shouts and the sound of trumpets.

2 Samuel 6:14-15 (NASB)

I watched as the buoyant six-year-old charged into the oncoming waves. With complete abandonment, she shouted with delight, engaging the surf in joyful fun; the ocean was her playmate.

It reminded me of David, the distinguished king of Israel, leaping and dancing through the streets of Jerusalem when the ark was brought to the city. He celebrated with all the people shouting and sounding the trumpets. David's display of emotion must have been pleasing to God.

In his book, *Crossing the Threshold of Hope*, John Paul II wrote,

> We need the enthusiasm of the young. We need their joie de vivre. In it is reflected something of the original joy God had in creating man. The young experience this same joy within themselves. This joy is the same everywhere, but it is also ever new and original. The young know how to express this joy in their own special way.7

We, too, can abandon ourselves to God's love and charge trustingly into His care. Think of coming before Him with total surrender. Give no thought to self, seek no request; just praise His majesty, His holiness.

Sing joyful noises unto Him. Just praise Him for who He is.

Father, I shout with joy that You are my God! May my praise be pleasing to You.

MARCH 19

DOUBT

> But he must ask in faith without any doubting, for the one who doubts, is like the surf of the sea, driven and tossed by the wind.
>
> James 1:6 (NASB)

Dear Father,

I know I've asked for things I consider important enough that You need to attend to them immediately. When You don't answer either right away, or in the right way, I doubt. Then I realize that because of my lack of faith, I am the one James refers to when he writes about being driven and tossed by the wind.

I want to persevere in trials, to be so anchored in You that no matter how severe the storm, it cannot toss me around. Help me to surrender my will to You, assured of peace and tranquility when I trust You in every situation.

I admit my sin of doubt. I want to be like Daniel. When he was thrown to the lions, did he doubt? No! He knew You were with him, and if it be Your will, he would not perish.

I will rely on the saying, "The faith that will shut the mouths of lions must be more than a pious hope that they will not bite."

MARCH 20

FORGIVENESS

He kissed all his brothers and wept on them.

Genesis 45:15 (NASB)

Joseph's brothers hated him, threw him in a pit to die, and when Medianite traders came by, they sold him into slavery. He was only seventeen. Taken to Egypt, he served in the home of an Egyptian officer, Potiphar. Wrongly accused of seducing Potiphar's wife, Joseph was thrown into prison. But through a series of God-planned events, he rose in status to become second in command only to Pharaoh.

Joseph was in charge of all of Egypt's food distribution during a great famine, which forced his brothers to come to him seeking grain. Joseph was now thirty years old, and had been enslaved for thirteen years. His brothers didn't recognize him; they were certain he hadn't survived. They believed he was dead.

When he revealed to them who he was, they were dumbstruck. He told them not to be grieved or angry with themselves for what they had done. He said it was God's plan that he be brought to Egypt. And then he kissed them, weeping and hugging them.

What an incredible display of forgiveness! I can find excuses for lack of forgiveness. Joseph certainly had a case for it. But he didn't think about it; he just felt it and did it.

When we want to cling to petty wrongs, we need only remember Jesus on the cross when He asked forgiveness for His executioners. We need only remember, "Father, forgive them," and then we can let go.

Lord Jesus, may I always forgive others as You have forgiven me.

MARCH 21

PRESS ON

But whatever things were gain to me, those things I have counted as loss for the sake of Christ.

Philippians 3:7 (NASB)

Can we say this with Paul?

Furthermore, he goes on to say,

> More than that, I count all things to be loss in view of the surpassing value of knowing Christ Jesus my Lord, for whom I have suffered the loss of all things, and count them but rubbish so that I may gain Christ.

> (v. 8)

Do we believe that every relationship, material possession, health—all are nothing compared to the surpassing value of knowing Christ as our Lord? Any hardships or suffering that we have endured, can we consider them as rubbish compared to knowing Him?

I pray with the apostle that I might know in my heart that all that has been gain for me I have counted as loss for the sake of Christ. And as this scripture penetrates my mind, heart, and soul, I pray with Paul,

> Not that I have already obtained it or have already become perfect, but I press on so that I may lay hold of that for which also I was laid hold of by Christ Jesus. I do not regard myself as having laid hold of it yet; but one thing I do: forgetting what lies behind and reaching forward to what lies ahead, I press on toward the goal for the prize of the upward call of God in Christ Jesus.

> (v. 12-14)

Lord, I haven't obtained it yet, but I will press on for the goal—forgetting what's behind and looking ahead. The goal is that of Your call.

MARCH 22

HE LONGS FOR US

The Lord longs to be gracious to you, and therefore
He waits on high to have compassion on you. For
the Lord is a God of justice; how blessed are all
those who long for Him.

Isaiah 30:18 (NASB)

Dear Father,

You are gracious and just.

You shower us with compassion,

Loving us so much that You call us blessed in that we
long for You.

Such a great and mighty God You are!

You sent Your Son to earth longing to draw all men
to You.

He healed the sick, gave sight to the blind, and raised
the dead.

In the end, He shed His precious blood that we might
have eternal life.

Such love we cannot comprehend.

You know the longings of our hearts, Father.

You know we long for You.

MARCH 23

THE GREATNESS OF GOD

And they were all amazed at the greatness of God.

Luke 9:43 (NASB)

Peter, James, and John had just had a mountain top experience with Jesus. They had seen His glory in the Transfiguration.

But the next day, when coming down from the mountain, they were met with evil. A demon had possessed a young boy; the sight of it was appalling. He was running around wildly, screaming, convulsing, and foaming at the mouth. The evil in him was so invasive, it was difficult to witness. But then they watched in amazement as Jesus, with authority, ordered the spirit out of the boy, and he was healed.

I pray constantly for a young man whose battle with the evil one is ongoing. It breaks my heart, for I love him very much. Jesus can order the evil spirits out of him; He can heal him.

Are you praying for someone who needs the all-powerful healing of the Lord? Read this account in Luke. God can order Satan out of their life. We know the greatness of the Lord.

Lord, You are a great and mighty God. You can do all things.

MARCH 24

WHY

And while He was being accused by the chief priests and elders, He did not answer.

Matthew 27:12 (NASB)

Why didn't God skip the horrendous crucifixion of His Son and just take Him up when His ministry was finished? After all, didn't Enoch and Elijah escape death? Elijah's exit was spectacular in a fiery chariot drawn by horses of fire and a whirlwind, which swept him out of this life and into the next.

Rather than enduring the mocking and derision, Jesus could have been taken up in the clouds with miraculous display while hosts of angels proclaimed Him to be the Son of God. All those who saw would believe Him to be the Messiah they had long awaited.

But Jesus's mission had not been fulfilled. He needed to be the final perfect sacrifice, unblemished and pure. He would need to die to show His power over death. He conquered death by His resurrection. And by His resurrection, we have the assurance that we will also be resurrected. Death need not be feared, for Christ overcame death, and so will we.

Death has been defeated, and we will live forevermore with You, our Resurrected Lord.

MARCH 25

MOMENT TO MOMENT

The Lord will guide you always; He will satisfy your needs in a sun-scorched land and will strengthen your frame. You will be like a well-watered garden, like a spring whose waters never fail.

Isaiah 58:11 (NIV)

By always mapping out tomorrow instead of resting in today, we are tempted to be fearful and anxious. Although we possess God now, we think of Him as something to be attained. Heaven is a goal, and we must earn it. Not so!

We can be determined to exercise small practices of looking to Him throughout the day. Fear and anxiety flee when confronted with trust and confidence in our Lord.

God knows and controls the future; He is our hope and security. Moment to moment we are secure if we trust Him. "And my God will supply all your needs according to His riches in glory in Christ Jesus" (Philippians 4:19, NASB).

O Lord. I want to be free of all fear and anxiety and as a well-watered garden. Help me to look to You, who will meet all my needs moment to moment.

MARCH 26

GRACE

For by grace you have been saved through faith; and that not of yourselves, it is the gift of God; not as a result of works, so that no one may boast.

Ephesians 2: 8 (NASB)

As Christians we know grace to mean the free gift of unmerited favor of God. I have always identified it with the song "Amazing Grace." To me, that's what it is—amazing. Grace speaks of the saving activity of God in giving His Son to die in place of sinners.

So can we build up a storehouse of grace that can be drawn upon when needed? Can we accumulate grace as we might accrue points in a merit system? Can we earn it? No, but instead we rely on God to supply the grace sufficient for every need at the moment we need it.

In Hebrews, Paul writes that it is grace that allows us to come boldly to God for help in time of need. And James says grace is given to the humble to resist the devil.

Father, I praise You for Your free gift of grace.

MARCH 27

CIRCUMSTANCES

My brethren, count it all joy when you fall into various trials, knowing that the testing of your faith produces patience.

James 1:2-4 (NKJV)

Oh that we could learn to trust God, not circumstances. They cannot hurt us if we hold fast. Can we trust Him about everything, for every need? Yes! Hold on to Him.

Difficult circumstances do not have to be unbearable. It depends on the way we look at them—through faith or unbelief. Do we know without a doubt that God permits trials to come our way for our own good? If we are not convinced of that, we anticipate our trials with fear, helplessness, and hopelessness.

If we see all through faith, we will occupy ourselves with God and not the circumstances.

I see Your hand in all the circumstances of my life, Lord. I trust You.

MARCH 28

FILTHY RAGS

Now Joshua was clothed with filthy garments and standing before the angel. He spoke and said to those who were standing before him, saying, "Remove the filthy garments from him." Again he said to him, "See, I have taken your iniquity away from you and will clothe you with festal robes."

Zechariah 3:3-4 (NASB)

Joshua appeared before God representing the Jewish people who were filthy with sin. Their merciful God loved them beyond measure and chose to save them in spite of their sins. He ordered Joshua's filthy clothes to be removed from him, replaced with rich robes. He would restore His people and blot out all their iniquities.

God wants to forgive us as He forgave the Israelites.

If we confess our sins He is faithful and righteous to forgive our sins and to cleanse us from all unrighteousness. If we say that we have not sinned, we make Him a liar, and His Word is not in us.

1 John 1:9-10 (NASB)

Christ has taken our filthy, ragged garments of sin, replacing them with His righteousness. We can stand before His throne and ask God to remove our sins. He will dress us in His goodness and mercy.

Forgive me, Father.

MARCH 29

MY PROMISE: CALL TO ME

> Call to Me and I will answer you and tell you great and mighty things which you do not know.
>
> Jeremiah 33:3 (NASB)

Dear child,

I am as close to you as the breath you take.

In everything I hear you.

If you will just call to Me, I will be listening.

Would you deny your child anything if he/she called to you?

Never!

Nor shall I.

Call Me, and I will answer.

Your Father

MARCH 30

REJECTED

If You do these things, show Yourself to the world.
For even His brothers did not believe in Him.

John 7:4-5 (NKJV)

Jesus's own brothers must have thought, "What is He thinking, claiming to be the Messiah?" They didn't believe Him. The Feast of Tabernacles would be held in Jerusalem, one of the three feasts that every Jewish male was obliged to attend. They told Jesus to go because there would be large crowds; it was the perfect opportunity for others to see His works.

Jesus was a controversial figure. It was believed that the Messiah would simply appear one day. He would come from nowhere, free the Jews from Roman rule, and set up His earthly kingdom. But the people knew this man Jesus, and where He was from-He didn't just appear. He grew up among them. Yes, many knew He was a good man, but the Christ, the Son of God?

Many who believed in Him argued with their neighbors, "When the Christ comes, He will not perform more signs than this man has, will He?" But there were those who just weren't buying it, and they looked for ways to discredit Him. Even when He healed a man who had lain by the pool at the Jerusalem sheep gate for thirty-eight years, they ignored the miracle. Instead, they blasted Jesus for telling the man to get up and carry his pallet. They looked past the healer to the law.

Jesus was rejected by His family and by those He came to save. It was only by His death and resurrection that many came to believe in Him. We have the advantage of the scriptures revealing who He really is, the Son of God. And we are promised that if we confess Him as Lord and believe that God has raised Him from the dead, we will be saved and spend eternity with Him. Don't reject Him.

I know You are the Son of God, Lord Jesus. I accept You as my Savior.

MARCH 31

OBEDIENCE

And being found in appearance as a man, He humbled Himself and became obedient to the point of death, even the death of the cross.

Philippians 2:8 (NKJV)

It is impossible for us to imagine subjecting ourselves to death on a cross. But Christ did that for us. He was obedient to the point of death.

I may not be asked to humble myself in obedience to the point of death, but God expects me to obey. Do I really desire to obey God? I strive to obey with the exercise of small acts, attending to details of everyday duties, thinking of myself as a child who matures in obedience by learning what is expected of her. She experiences the rewards of obedience and the consequences of disobedience.

I try to recognize a sin in my life to which I give in or one I practice with regularity. I diligently begin to uproot it; just as I might pull a weed that invades a beautiful garden.

Attention to the most menial duties with love and submission will bring gradual strength to achieve higher degrees of conformity to His Will. Simple practices can form good habits of obedience. More steadfastness is involved in these little acts than what we think. Because of their reoccurrence, they require a strict watchfulness against any thought, word, or act that seeks our will and not God's. Knowing that Christ died for us, how can we do anything less?

I long to be obedient, Lord.

APRIL 1

AS A CHILD

Assuredly, I say to you, whoever does not receive the kingdom of God as a little child will by no means enter it.

Luke 18:17 (NKJV)

I was staying at my daughter's home while she and her husband were away. I sat at the kitchen table with my eleven-year-old grandson and ten-year-old granddaughter. We had been talking about Jesus. They were attentive and sat quietly as I explained the meaning of His invitation to ask Him into our lives. They were excited and began to ask questions. It wasn't long before they eagerly asked if they might do that.

With heads bowed and hands folded, I led them in a simple prayer. When we finished, I suggested they get their Bibles and write the date in them. I watched as they carefully wrote, "Today, I invited Jesus into my life."

They were beaming.

My grandson said, "Grandma, when I asked Jesus into my life, I felt a burst of happiness and energy."

Oh that we could all receive the kingdom of God like a child.

I come to you as a child, Lord, seeking You with all my heart.

APRIL 2

TIME

Bless the Lord, O my soul! O Lord my God, You are very great; You are clothed with splendor and majesty, covering Yourself with light as with a cloak, stretching out heaven like a tent curtain. He lays the beams of His upper chambers in the waters; He makes the clouds His chariot; He walks upon the wings of the wind; He makes the winds His messengers, flaming fire His ministers. He established the earth upon its foundations, so that it will not totter forever and ever.

Psalm 104:1-5 (NASB)

Daylight Saving Time has been used on and off in the United States since World War I. Twice a year we manipulate the clock, moving the hands forward and backward to fit our needs.

But no matter what we do to take charge, the Creator is the timekeeper. His perfect timing is revealed in nature. One example of God's precision is the tide. Every day it rises fifty-five minutes later than it did the day before. The timing has to do with the moon's revolution around the earth. It's incredibly fascinating, as are so many of God's wonders.

Considering the lavish detail God spends on the management of the universe, how much more does He tend to us? We are His masterpiece, a work of art. "Then God said, 'Let Us make man in Our image, according to Our likeness'" (Genesis 1:26).

He loves us so much that in His time, He sent His only Son to die for us. And in His time, the Lord will come again. We can surrender to His timetable. As believers, it is exciting to know that our time will be spent eternally in His presence.

Lord, I look for Your perfect timing in my life.

APRIL 3

REFINING

He will sit as a refiner and purifier of silver.

Malachi 3:3 (NASB)

I was intrigued by this account of refining on the web site virtueonline.com:

This verse from Malachi 3:3 puzzled some women in a Bible study; they wondered what this statement meant about the character and nature of God. One of the women offered to find out the process of refining silver and get back to the group at their next Bible Study. That week, the woman called a silversmith and made an appointment to watch him at work. She didn't mention anything about the reason for her interest beyond her curiosity about the process of refining silver.

As she watched the silversmith, he held a piece of silver over the fire and let it heat up. He explained that in refining silver, one needed to hold the silver in the middle of the fire where the flames were hottest as to burn away all the impurities. The woman thought about God holding us in such a hot spot; then she thought again about the verse that says: 'He sits as a refiner and purifier of silver.' She asked the silversmith if it was true that he had to sit there in front of the fire the whole time the silver was being refined. The man answered that yes, he not only had to sit there holding the silver, but he had to keep his eyes on the silver the entire time it was in the fire. If the silver was left a moment too long in the flames, it would be destroyed. The woman was silent for a moment.

Then she asked the silversmith, "How do you know when the silver is fully refined?" He smiled at her and answered, "Oh, that's easy—when I see my image in it."

> So if today you are feeling the heat of the fire, remember that God has His eye on you and will keep watching until He sees His image in you.

> Unknown

Refine and purify me, Lord.

APRIL 4

HOSANNA

On the next day the large crowd who had come to the feast, when they heard that Jesus was coming to Jerusalem, took the branches of the palm trees and went out to meet Him, and began to shout, "Hosanna! Blessed is He who comes in the name of the Lord, even the King of Israel." Jesus, finding a young donkey, sat on it; as it is written.

John 12:12-14 (NASB)

As a child, I loved the Bible story read in church on Palm Sunday of Jesus's entrance into Jerusalem. It was such a visual! But it is no longer just a story to me. I am moved by the reality this was Jesus's last week on earth, and the people were hailing Him as their king.

That day, the city of Jerusalem was bursting with crowds who had come for the weeklong Passover festival. Many had heard of Jesus and were anxious to get a look at Him.

A warring king would have ridden into Jerusalem on a horse or in a chariot. Jesus rode in on a colt, as was foretold in the Old Testament.

Behold, your King is coming to you; He is just and endowed with salvation, humble, and mounted on a donkey, Even on a colt, the foal of a donkey.

Zechariah 9:9 (NASB)

People were jubilant, for they knew deliverance was near. The Messiah had arrived! As the humble King passed by, shouts of "Hosanna!" resounded from the multitudes.

Jesus is King. He is God Himself, come to earth to die and free us from the bondage of sin.

We bow before His Majesty and claim Him as Lord, Messiah.

Make Jesus the King of your life.

Blessed are You, O Lord. You are King! Hosanna in the Highest.

APRIL 5

DISCIPLINE

> Make every effort to add to your faith goodness; and to goodness, knowledge; and knowledge, self-control and to self-control, perseverance, and to perseverance, godliness; and to godliness, brotherly kindness; and to brotherly kindness, love.

2 Peter 1:5-7 (NIV)

Often when I go to the beach I would prefer to plop down on my beach chair, gaze at the water, or read. But I know I need to walk. We're told 30 minutes a day helps keep the weight off, gives us a fit body, lowers cholesterol, and much more.

These verses speak to us of discipline. Through God's divine power, we become partakers of His divine nature (v. 3). What a magnificent promise. But it's much more than just believing.

The qualities given aren't automatically ours. We must earnestly practice them so we don't stumble, "discipline yourself for the purpose of godliness" (1 Timothy 4:7, NASB).

When I return from my brisk walk, I recline and enjoy. So it is when we apply all diligence in our faith. We derive moral excellence, knowledge, self-control, perseverance, godliness, kindness, and love. To possess such qualities is worth the discipline. Most of all, we are promised that eternal life will be abundantly ours.

I will discipline myself in reading Your word.

APRIL 6

A MIGHTY GOD

I am the Lord, and there is no other; besides Me there is no God…

Isaiah 45:5 (NASB)

We serve a Mighty God. His voice is heard, His message sent. When we read these words, spoken by the God who created us, we need not ask what He is doing. For He says no one is to quarrel with his Maker. His words are mighty and powerful.

> I am the Lord, and there is no other; besides Me there is no God.
>
> I will gird you, though you have not known Me; that men may know from the rising to the setting of the sun that there is no one besides Me.
>
> I am the Lord, and there is no other, the One forming light and creating darkness, causing wellbeing and creating calamity; I am the Lord who does all these. Drip down, O heavens from above, and let the clouds pour down righteousness; let the earth open up and salvation bear fruit, and righteousness spring up with it. I, the Lord, have created it.
>
> Woe to the one who quarrels with his Maker—an earthenware vessel among the vessels of earth! Will the clay say to the potter, "What are you doing?" Or the thing you are making say, "He has no hands?"
>
> (Isaiah 45:5-9).

Oh, Lord, maker of all, I have been made by Your hands. You are a Mighty God.

APRIL 7

A FATHER'S RESPONSE

At that moment the curtain of the temple was torn in two from top to bottom. The earth shook and the rocks split. The tombs broke open and the bodies of many holy people who had died were raised to life. They came out of the tombs, and after Jesus' resurrection they went into the holy city and appeared to many people.

Matthew 27:51-53 (NIV)

When His Beloved Son died on the cross, God responded with colossal gestures in nature. He blanketed the land in darkness, tore the temple veil in two, raised the dead, and shook the earth. The agony was over; Jesus's work was finished. The Father responded. It is fitting that creation should have trembled; mankind, whom God had created, crucified Him.

Seven hundred years before Christ was born, Isaiah had written about what would happen that day. Crucifixion hadn't even been heard of then. It would later become a Roman form of execution. It was a slow and painful death.

Christ died for us that we might be reconciled to God. He was a man of sorrows-scourged, afflicted, pierced, and crushed.

Father, all the earth felt Your response at the death of Your Beloved Son. I cannot comprehend the suffering He endured to redeem me. I am grateful for His sacrifice that has brought me reconciliation with You, my Creator.

APRIL 8

REJOICE

Jesus said to her, "Mary." She turned toward Him and cried out in Aramaic, "Rabboni! (which means Teacher)."

John 20:16 (NASB)

Mary Magdalene watched as they crucified her Lord. His last words, "It is finished," pierced her heart. Later, she looked on as the stone was rolled against the tomb.

Now it is the first day of the week. A stillness falls over the garden. Mary stands weeping, distressed, and confused, for she has found an empty tomb. She had been an early follower of the Master. He had cast out seven demons from her. Jesus, her Beloved, is gone.

"Mary." She hears her name. "Mary!"

Without hesitation, she cries out, "Rabonni!" She knows the voice. She knows Him. He is alive!

Jesus had told His followers, "Therefore, you too have grief now, but I will see you again and your heart will rejoice" (John 16:22).

Just as Jesus had freed Mary of the demons, He has freed us from the bondage of sin. He is our Redeemer. Do you know Him? When He tenderly calls your name, do you recognize your Risen Savior?

> And He is the radiance of His glory and the exact representation of His nature, and upholds all things by the word of His power. When He had made purification of sins, He sat down at the right hand of the Majesty on high.
>
> Hebrews 1:3

Our Savior lives! Listen. He calls your name.

I shall rejoice! You are the Risen Lord!

APRIL 9

BELIEVE

> He was buried… He was raised on the third day according to the Scriptures, and… He appeared to Cephas, then to the twelve…
>
> 1 Corinthians 15:4 (NASB)

When Jesus was arrested and crucified, His disciples scattered. Their faith crumbled as they watched Him die. They had wanted so much to believe that He would establish an earthly kingdom, yet now He hung on a cross.

What must their days have been like between Jesus's death and His resurrection? At first they were hiding out for fear they too would die. For Peter it was agonizing. He had denied even knowing Jesus, and his days were filled with remorse and grief.

When he learned from the women that Jesus's body was gone from the tomb, he raced to the garden in disbelief. As he stared into the empty tomb where only discarded linens lay, reality was slowly setting in. The tumultuous events of the past few days had erased what Jesus had told them; He would be put to death, and three days later He would rise again.

He appeared to Peter and then to the twelve. What a reunion it must have been for Peter when he first saw Jesus. I imagine he was overwhelmed with emotions, wanting desperately to tell Jesus how unbearable was his grief and shame that He had denied Him. "O Master, forgive me." But perhaps he was speechless with awe in the presence of the Risen Lord.

Do you waver in your belief of Jesus? The disciples believed in Jesus, but did they believe Him, believe in what He said and who He is, the Son of God? Do you believe Jesus?

Lord Jesus, I believe You are the Son of God, that You died and rose from the dead.

APRIL 10

THE ROOM

Very early the next morning, long before daylight, Jesus got up and left the house. He went out of town to a lonely place, where He prayed.

Mark 1:35 (NASB)

When our children were little, we had a living room that was off limits. The family room was their TV and play-room. If the doorbell rang, there was a room to which we could usher our guests—a room free of clutter and furniture stains. Our daughters didn't understand the need for such a room until they had children of their own.

Until we begin to mature spiritually, we don't understand what it means to have that room that's off limits. That place where there is no clutter, where we usher in Our Lord and spend time alone with Him. If the room remains ready, we can go there when the weight of life becomes heavy. The burdens can be carried there; it's a place of refuge. The more we lavish ourselves with this luxury, the more we long to be there with Him, alone and secluded from the world and its intrusion.

Our knowledge of Him depends entirely on the time we are willing to spend with Him each day.

If you have a desire to know Him, set aside that special place and go there every day. Be selfish and don't let anyone else in.

Prepare a room in which to commune with Him. Retreat. Be still with Him.

Thank You, Lord Jesus, for meeting me daily in the room.

APRIL 11

SOMETIMES

Sometimes when we don't have the words or heart for prayer, we can turn to Psalms. There we find scripture that fills our wordless spirit.

Here in Psalm 62:5-8 (NASB) we need only read the psalmists words and make them ours.

Dear Father,
   I wait here quietly before You, knowing my hope
is in You.
   You only are my rock and my salvation,
   My stronghold; I shall not be shaken.
   On You my salvation and my glory rest;
   The rock of my strength, my refuge is in You.
   I will trust in You at all times.
   I will pour out my heart before You.
   You are my refuge.

APRIL 12

ALLELUIA

But go, tell His disciples and Peter, "He is going ahead of you to Galilee; there you will see Him, just as He told you."

Mark 16:7 (NASB)

The Son of God rose from the dead and no one witnessed it. The evidence was there—an empty tomb, discarded linen wrappings. The most powerfully divine event in history took place in a secluded garden. Angels quietly announced the news. Those who believed He had risen experienced Him. To one, He simply said her name, "Mary!" That day, He walked beside two of them, and in the evening they dined.

When we accept Christ as our Savior, it takes place in the seclusion of our hearts. The evidence is there. We are made new; our old ways discarded. The Good News is proclaimed in heaven by hosts of angels. And we experience Him. He calls us by name, walks with us, and dines with us. And one day, we, too, will be resurrected by the same divine power that raised Jesus from the dead (Revelation 3:20).

It is a glorious Easter morning sunrise at the beach. I am awed by the fathomless power behind an ocean larger than the total land area of the world. God's almighty power that is at work in the universe is working in us. To Him be the power and the glory. Alleluia!

Jesus, I accept You as my Lord and Savior. Alleluia!

APRIL 13

UNDERSTAND

> Therefore many of His disciples, when they heard this said, "This is a difficult statement; who can listen to it?"
>
> John 6:60 (NASB)

In His ministry Jesus spent much of His time answering questions. Scholars and religious leaders were always trying to trip Him up, giving them cause to say He blasphemed.

Some of Jesus's answers were difficult for even His followers to accept.

"Many of His disciples withdrew and were not walking with Him anymore" (v. 66). The chosen twelve found it difficult to understand much of their Master's teaching.

When others had deserted Him, He asked His disciples, "You do not want to go away also, do you?" (v. 67) Peter loved Jesus, and he answered, "Lord, to whom shall we go?" (v. 68) Jesus was their answer.

Following Jesus isn't always easy. There are some answers to our questions we don't like to hear. Some we don't understand. It isn't necessary for us to understand everything in order to receive eternal life. But we must believe in Jesus Christ as the Son of God.

After His resurrection, Jesus appeared to the disciples and opened their minds to understand the scriptures.

He will help us to understand His Word. Read the scriptures. Seek and ask. He will answer.

Lord, help me to understand. I will listen.

APRIL 14

LIP SERVICE

If you confess with your mouth the Lord Jesus and believe in your heart that God has raised Him from the dead, you will be saved. For with the heart one believes unto righteousness, and with the mouth confession is made unto salvation.

Romans 10:9-10 (NKJV)

Believing that God exists is only the beginning. Even demons believed that Jesus was the Son of God. When He met a man possessed with demons, they cried out, calling Jesus the Son of the Most High God. And "Whenever the unclean spirits saw Him, they would fall down before Him and shout, 'You are the Son of God!'" (Mark 3:11). Were the demons saved because they knew Jesus to be God? No.

Mere acknowledgment of His existence does not save us. Mark 3:11

Today's reading says we are not only to confess with our mouth that Jesus is Lord, but we have to believe it in our hearts. If we give lip service to God's existence, it doesn't mean we believe in Him.

What is faith? Hebrews says that it is the assurance of things hoped for, the conviction of things not seen. If we can see something, we know it exists. We don't need faith. Jesus, after proving to Thomas that He was the risen Lord, said to him, "Because you have seen Me, have you believed? Blessed are they who did not see, and yet believed" (John 20:29 NIV).

Do you know about God, or do you know God?

Increase my faith, Lord.

APRIL 15

MY TEACHER

O God, You have taught me from my youth,
   And I still declare Your wondrous deeds.
   And even when I am old and gray, O God, do not forsake me,
   Until I declare Your strength to this generation,
   Your power to all who are to come.
   For Your righteousness, O God, reaches to the heavens,

You who have done great things;

O God, who is like You?

You who have shown me many troubles and distresses

Will revive me again,

And will bring me up again from the depths of the earth.

May You increase my greatness

And turn to comfort me.

Psalm 71:17-23 (NASB)

APRIL 16

DEPENDENT

Joash was seven years old when he became king, and he reigned forty years in Jerusalem; and his mother's name was Zibiah from Beersheba. Joash did what was right in the sight of the Lord all the days of Jehoiada the priest.

2 Chronicles 24:1-2 (NASB)

Johoiada was a great influence on his nephew, King Joash. The two of them were instrumental in rebuilding the temple of God according to its original design. As long as Jehoiada lived, burnt offerings were presented continually in the temple of the Lord.

But when Johoiada died, Joash began to listen to ill advice, and the positive influence of his mentor faded. He allowed idolatry, leading the people away from following God. He used the temple treasuries as a bribe to the King of Aram. He even had Jehoiada's son, Zechariah, stoned to death. Ultimately, Joash's own servants murdered him. Joash became totally dependent on Jehoida but not on God.

What happens when children are never permitted to make their own mistakes? From our birth we are dependent on someone for care, guidance, love, and even our livelihood. But dependence on man alone can lead to independence of God. We must help our children to establish a relationship with God, instructing them in the ways of God. Then when crucial decisions are to be made, they will depend on Him as the ultimate Counselor.

Father, I dedicate my children to You. May their lives reflect total dependence on You and not on man.

APRIL 17

WEIGHED DOWN

Remember my affliction and my wandering...surely my soul remembers and is bowed down within me.

Lamentations 3:19-20 (NASB)

There are days I step onto the sand with a heavy heart. I feel weighed down by the disappointments and concerns that most of us face each day. I hurt for those I love who are sick, troubled, or grieving.

After a brisk walk and absorbing nature's nourishments, I head home, invigorated. Those concerns I carried onto the beach haven't changed. But I meet them with renewed determination.

Sometimes we greet the day feeling bruised, broken, and burned out before we've even begun. God's Word can offer us the comfort and encouragement we need. "He heals the brokenhearted and binds up their wounds" (Psalm 147:3 NASB). God knows our burdened hearts. He looks with tender compassion on our love and concern for others. But when we choose to carry these burdens, we are saying, "No, thank you. I'd rather do it myself."

We don't need to be weighed down by any disturbance. Instead, pray. Remember the words of our loving Savior: "For My yoke is easy, and My burden is light" (Matthew 11:30 NASB).

We can give all of our concerns to Him. He cares for those we love more than we can ourselves.

I need You, Lord. Heal and bind my wounds.

APRIL 18

THE SMALL THINGS

Whatever you do in word or deed, do all in the name of the Lord Jesus, giving thanks through Him to God the Father.

Colossians 3:17 (NASB)

I don't always do it, but I want to be faithful in the little things. When we do everything in the name of the Lord Jesus, we bring honor to Him. We express our love for Him in word and deed. Others know we can be depended on. We keep a promise, guard a confidence. We endeavor to make payments on time and be prompt for appointments—even doctor's appointments, which always seem to run behind.

We make every effort not to neglect our duty or responsibilities. These disciplines may have been taught to us early in life. But spiritual maturity brings the desire to be faithful in the least of things so that our life will be served to His honor and glory.

Whatever I do in word or deed, Father God, may it honor You.

APRIL 19

SPEAKING DIRECTLY

God called to him from the midst of the bush and said, "Moses, Moses!" And he said, "Here I am."

Exodus 3:4 (NKJV)

Moses was the most humble man on earth, and one to whom God spoke directly. He appeared in dreams to other prophets, but "…spoke to Moses face to face, as a man speaks to his friend" (Exodus 33:11).

Moses literally heard the voice of God. When the people had a question, Moses said, "I'll go ask God." He went to God in prayer and expected an answer. It was that simple for Moses. He had come to rely totally on God for his every need. His relationship with God was that of a father and son. He had been led, spent time with God, and was so close to Him that he could ask anything and expect God to answer. Moses didn't always want to hear what God said, but he always wanted to do God's will.

We probably won't have a verbal conversation with God. But we can have a relationship so intimate that we can know His will and feel His Spirit move within us.

Go to Him in prayer and expect Him to hear and answer. O Father, God.

APRIL 20

HOLLOW WITHIN

Woe to you, scribes and Pharisees, hypocrites! For you are like whitewashed tombs which on the outside appear beautiful, but inside they are full of dead men's bones and all uncleanness. So you, too, outwardly appear righteous to men, but inwardly you are full of hypocrisy and lawlessness.

Matthew 23:27-28 (NASB)

I couldn't have been very old when I abandoned any childhood belief that some big Easter bunny hopped around leaving baskets of candy for each of us. But I went along with the notion; I loved searching for my basket, and I loved the candy. That is, all but the chocolate Easter bunnies, tempting on the outside but hollow on the inside. They should have been filled with rich brownie fudge for this chocolate lover.

The hollow Easter Bunny reminds me of being a Christian looking good on the outside but empty within. When we follow our own desires and not those of the Spirit, we are living as our human nature tells us to live. In the past I have lived as a Christian yet conformed to the world. I struggle still. But I rely on Ephesians 3:14-19 (NASB).

For this reason I bow my knees before the Father, from whom every family in heaven and on earth derives its name, that He would grant you, according to the riches of His glory, to be strengthened with power through His Spirit in the inner man, so that Christ may dwell in your hearts through faith; and that you, being rooted and grounded in love, may be able to comprehend with all the saints what is the breadth and length and height and depth, and to know the love of Christ which surpasses knowledge, that you may be filled up to all the fullness of God.

Yes, I want to be rich brownie fudge on the inside.

Examine me, Lord Jesus. May You not find me hollow.

APRIL 21

DEVOTED TO PRAYER

And after He had said these things, He was lifted up while they were looking on, and a cloud received Him out of their sight.

Acts 1:9 NASB

The disciples had just been talking with Jesus, asking Him if He was now going to set up a kingdom. It seemed logical; He had risen from the dead. But then a huge cloud came, and He disappeared out of their sight. They gazed upward for the longest time. When two men appeared telling them that Jesus had been taken up to heaven and He would come back the same way, they were stunned. They might have asked each other, "Did you just see what I saw?" Still wavering between disbelief and reality, the disciples returned to Jerusalem in silence and went to the upstairs room where they were staying.

These were simple men leading simple lives. When Jesus called them, He gradually transformed them. And now they gathered in this room, about 120 of them. "Well, what do we do now," they might have said. They may have been numb as many of us have been after the funeral of a loved one.

And then we are told in Acts 1:14: "These all with one mind were continually devoting themselves to prayer, along with the women, and Mary the mother of Jesus, and with His brothers" (NASB). Yes they knew what to do; they would pray. After all, they had learned from the Master Himself about the power of prayer.

O Father, help me to be devoted to prayer.

APRIL 22

NEEDS NOT WANTS

My God will supply all your needs according to His riches in glory in Jesus Christ.

Philippians 4:19 (NASB)

Dear Father,

I know it is not for You just to make me feel good.

It is not for You to see that I achieve success or avoid pain.

It is more than that.

I must learn to place my trust in You.

Asking for what I want is different than asking for what I need.

Your supply for my needs is overflowing with promise when I just ask.

It is then that my attitude changes from wanting everything to trusting You

for everything.

You know my needs, O Lord.

I only want what You desire for my life.

APRIL 23

KEEP THE SEASON ALIVE

Hope does not disappoint, because the love of God has been poured out in our hearts by the Holy Spirit who was given to us.

Romans 5:5 (NKJV)

Springtime is a joyous season of nature's awakening. Daffodils dressed in yellow splendor, along with daisies, azaleas, irises and others, usher in a new beginning. Their intoxicating fragrances lift our spirits. We drag out the gardening tools, eager to dig in the dirt once again.

My earliest memories of spring are associated with Easter—new hats, pastel colored dresses, and polished white shoes, replacing the winter black. On Easter Sunday the scent of Easter lilies, symbolizing the Resurrection, filled the church.

This Easter holiday is gone, but I have a lingering desire to keep the joy of the season alive. The winter has brought unusually frigid temperatures and a struggling economy. I know family and friends who are fearful and worried. Women have taken on a more stressful role, juggling a leaner budget while trying to meet financial obligations.

But Easter has brought renewed hope for many. I want to keep the season alive. We can keep the joy of the season alive, for Jesus is our joy, no matter the circumstances. He heralds in a glorious hope through His resurrection.

Spring is here—a season of growth, renewal, and hope.

Lord, help us to keep the season alive.

APRIL 24

THE RETURN

For the Lord Himself will descend from heaven with a shout, with the voice of an archangel, and with the trumpet of God. And the dead in Christ will rise first. Then we who are alive and remain shall be caught up together with them in the clouds to meet the Lord in the air. And thus we shall always be with the Lord.

1 Thessalonians 4:16-18 (NKJV)

And so it will be that Jesus Himself in all His majesty will descend, even as He had ascended, from heaven. A shout will be given ordering the dead to rise. An archangel summoning all of God's elect with the sound of a trumpet will repeat the order.

When all the dead in Christ are raised and their bodies made glorious, those who are still alive will be caught up together with them in the clouds to meet Our Lord God in the air.

Yes, those of us who are in Christ, having been cleansed by the blood of the Lamb, will be caught up with our loved ones who have died and taken to our eternal glory to be forever with the Lord.

What a glorious promise! Although death has separated us from our loved ones, we will meet again. We and all God's people will be with Him forever more.

I look with hope and anticipation for Your return, my Lord and my God.

APRIL 25

MY PROMISE: RICHES

Do not be overawed when a man grows rich, when the splendor of his house increases; for he will take nothing with him when he dies, his splendor will not descend with him. Though while he lived, he counted himself blessed—and men praise you when you prosper— he will join the generation of his fathers, who will never see the light [of life].

Psalm 49:16-19 (NIV)

Dear child,

One day, riches will be gone.

I provide you with what you need.

You must decide what you want.

If you are anxious and discontent with what you have and you want more,

then that will be your choice.

But this I promise: you have brought nothing into the world,

so you cannot take anything out of it.

What will become of all you have acquired in this life?

What will become of your soul?

Think on this.

Your Father

APRIL 26

FOOTPRINTS

And I saw the dead, the great and the small standing before the throne, and books were opened; and another book was opened which is the book of life; and the dead were judged from the things which were written in the books, according to their deeds.

Revelation 21:12 (NASB)

It's interesting to take a walk down the beach and on the return trek see my original footprints washed away.

The things we do may seem to disappear, just as those footprints are erased by the advancing tide. But the Bible assures us that every deed is recorded in the book. No matter how minute our acts of kindness may seem, God sees them.

Good deeds don't save us but are the evidence of our commitment to God. Giving the choice seat to another, gently closing a door, or performing disagreeable chores without complaint are some ways that testify to our love for Him. Because they are for Him, it's not necessary that others take notice—but when they do, such acts are a witness of that love.

Each of us will come before the great white throne and be held accountable for our every deed. Those we do for God will have eternal value.

Footprints in the sand are swept away, but God remembers every single thing we do. Practice acts of kindness.

Father God, I want my name in the book of life!

APRIL 27

USEFULNESS

They will still yield fruit in old age; they shall be full of sap and very green.

Psalm 92:14 (NASB)

The grandfather clock that my husband built over forty years ago had quit running. It had traveled with us from the dry climate of Colorado to the moisture of the California coast. The climate change has affected the old gentleman's appearance. The humidity has caused the black walnut case to crack in several spots. He's worn out and doesn't look too good. What are we to do with him?

We sometimes feel like that clock—worn out and want to quit, no longer able to serve as we once had. But our usefulness is not dependent on our years, young or old. In fact, God uses the experiences of His children to further His kingdom.

Moses was one hundred-twenty years old when he died on Mt. Pisgah. Abraham was one hundred when his son Isaac was born, and he died when he was one hundred-seventy five years old. Daniel was over eighty years old when he was thrown into the lion's den.

We are not new, but whatever God calls us to do, we can be useful to carry out His plan for us. Moses, Abraham, and Daniel listened to God. They may have questioned at times, but they obeyed. We must be willing to listen.

We might visit a neighbor that we don't know very well or volunteer to help at schools, teaching children to read. We can visit the shut-ins. The list is endless. God says He will instruct and teach us in the way we should go; He will counsel us with His eye upon us (Psalm 32:8).

If we say yes, He will do the rest.

Father, I want to be useful. Lead me in the way You would have me serve.

APRIL 28

BONDSERVANT

Paul, a bond-servant of God and an apostle of Jesus Christ.

Titus 1:1 (NASB)

Paul humbly calls himself a bondservant of God. A bond-servant is a slave, bound to service without wages.

Paul was a Roman citizen, and for him to choose to be a servant was unthinkable. A Hebrew slave could go free after six years. But if the servant, for love of his master, preferred not to accept freedom in the seventh year, he was brought before the elders and had his ear bored against a door or post with an awl in token of lifelong servitude. This wasn't shameful because the allegiance of love was prized more highly than loveless personal freedom.

Paul says that he bears the brand marks of Jesus. Yes, he had been a slave to sin, but Christ purchased him, and he exchanged a loveless freedom in sin for a love-filled service to Christ.

Do we have the mark of a bonded slave? Are we in servitude and bondage to our Master, the Lord Jesus Christ?

Just as in ancient times a slave had to be redeemed or ransomed, so Jesus bought us with the price of His blood that we could be set free from the slavery of sin.

I am Your bondservant, O Lord. You have redeemed me.

APRIL 29

WHAT DO YOU WANT

You do not have because you do not ask. You ask and do not receive, because you ask with wrong motives, so that you may spend it on your pleasures.

James 4: 2-3 (NASB)

Years ago I attended a Reality Therapy workshop. We were asked, "What do you want? What do you really want? And what are you doing to get it?" We were to write down our decision and outline a plan that would help us accomplish our goals.

Years before I had asked Jesus into my life, but now I wanted a closer relationship with Him. I wrote this simple plan. I would say, "I love you, Jesus," first thing each morning, throughout the day, and the last thing at night. I began to discipline myself to direct my thoughts to Him. I took advantage of every opportunity—in the car, in checkout lines, as I folded laundry or washed a dish. "I love you, Jesus" became a part of both my conscience and my unconscious mind. These love thoughts developed a thirst to know Him better. I appointed a time each day that I would sit with Him and be still. My prayer life blossomed.

James points out that we ask God for things with the wrong motive. We desire worldly pleasures while He desires to fill us with the Holy Spirit.

If you want a closer relationship with Jesus, outline a plan that would work for you.

I want a closer relationship with You, Lord.

APRIL 30

ROUGH WATERS

I will turn the darkness into light before them and
make the rough places smooth.

Isaiah 42:16 NASB

Our visit to the Holy Land was a life changing experience for me; I realized how grateful I was to have made the decision those many years ago to seek a closer relationship with Jesus.

Sitting in a boat on the Sea of Galilee, I felt the words "I love you, Jesus" swell within me, and I cried. As I looked out over this calm sea on such a glorious sun-filled morning, I thought of the rough waters of my life and how He has been with me through it all. He has been my anchor in the storms and has given me peace beyond understanding. And I have learned that peace is compatible with grief and loss, serious illness in all the circumstances of my life.

It isn't that I meet disappointments and trying circumstances with peace; I can do nothing on my own. But I go to the throne of God, lay them wordlessly before Him, and He grants me peace. He is the God of peace.

I know so well that I am a work in progress. Everyday I need to nourish my soul and spirit through spiritual disciplines, most especially with prayer and being in His Word.

And I hold to the promise given in Jeremiah 29:13, "Then you will call upon Me, come and pray to Me, and I will listen to you. You will seek Me and find Me when you search for Me with all your heart."

I love You, Jesus.

MAY 1

FEELING HIS PLEASURE

For it is God who is at work in you both to will and work for His good pleasure.

Philippians 2:13 (NASB)

Sometimes I actually feel His pleasure. I am as a child who knows she is pleasing her father.

When I do something for the love of Him—just because I love Him, expecting nothing in return—I feel His pleasure.

When I walk on the beach, absorbed in the wonder of His creation, entertaining no thoughts but those of praise and worship, I feel His pleasure.

When I sit in my prayer corner with the Bible in my lap, immersed in His Word, I feel His pleasure.

When I am alone with Him in thought, when nothing distracts me, I feel His pleasure.

Heavenly Father, I know that You are at work in me that I might do all for Your good pleasure. To You be the glory.

MAY 2

CONQUERORS

I say then: Walk in the Spirit, and you shall not fulfill the lust of the flesh.

Galatians 5:16 (NKJV)

We are being led by the Spirit, our Guide. But it is up to
us to follow. When we follow Him, we are shielded from
the allure of sin, and we don't have to follow the ways
of the flesh, which conflict with what the Spirit wants.
Empowered by the Spirit, we can be conquerors; not by
ignoring the deeds of the flesh, but by recognizing them
and dealing decisively with them.

We can face those weaknesses in our life, taking control
by the power of the Spirit not to be led by temptation but
to overcome it! Jesus said, "Get behind me, Satan! You are a
stumbling block to Me"(Matthew 16:23, NASB). Satan will
flee if we say that when we are being drawn to follow. The
Spirit comes between us and the enemy.

We need not follow but be guided by the Spirit, which
leads to a transformed life.

Get behind me, Satan.

MAY 3

APPLY

We give thanks to God, the Father of our Lord Jesus Christ, praying always for you.

Colossians 1:3 (NASB)

It is difficult to know how to pray for someone who is ill or experiencing difficult times. I am inspired by the prayer Paul wrote to the Colossians. It helps me to pray for others even though I don't know them. From the Good News Bible, I have memorized the prayer, applying the words to myself and those for whom I pray. I've pluralized and personalized it.

> Fill us with the knowledge of Your Will and all the wisdom and understanding that Your Spirit gives. Then we will be able to live as You want, and always do what pleases You. Our lives will produce all kinds of good deeds and we will grow in our knowledge of You. May we be made strong with all the strength, which comes from Your glorious power, so that we may be able to endure everything with patience. And with joy we give thanks to You, Father, who has made us fit to have our share of what You have reserved for Your people in the kingdom of light. You rescued us from the power of darkness and

brought us safe into the kingdom of Your dear Son,
by whom we are set free, that is our sins are forgiven.

Notice that the prayer does not contain one earthly request for ourselves and those for whom we pray. We ask that we be given an abundant supply of all we need to live as God would have us. We ask for strength and patience for the challenges and heartbreaks of life. And we end with thanksgiving for the gift of His dear Son, Jesus Christ.

Teach me how to pray for others, Lord.

MAY 4

DOUBTING

> So when it was evening on that day, the first day of the week, and when the doors were shut where the disciples were, for fear of the Jews, Jesus came and stood in their midst and said to them, "Peace be with you."

> John 20:19-20 (NASB)

Thomas is best known as the "doubting Thomas." He wasn't with the other disciples when Jesus appeared to them the day of His resurrection. When they told Thomas about seeing the Master and that He had shown them His hands and His side, he didn't believe them.

To be fair, when the women who had been told by the angel to go tell the others that Jesus had risen, the disciples didn't believe it either. It was only when they ran to the tomb to see for themselves that they believed.

Thomas also wanted proof. "Unless I see in His hands the imprint of the nails, and put my finger into the place of the nails, and put my hand into His side, I will not believe" (v. 25).

Eight days later, when He was with them again, Thomas was present.

> Then Jesus said to Thomas, "Reach here with your finger, and see My hands; and reach here your hand and put it into My side; and do not be unbelieving, but believing." Thomas answered and said to Him, "My Lord and my God!" Jesus replied, "Because you have seen Me, have you believed? Blessed are they who did not see, and yet believed.
>
> (v. 27-29)

St. Augustine writes, "He doubted that we might believe."

Yes! You are the Risen Lord. You are my Lord and my God! Of this I have no doubt.

MAY 5

PARTAKERS

Seeing that His divine power has granted to us everything pertaining to life and godliness, through the true knowledge of Him who called us by His own glory and excellence. For by these He has granted to us His precious and magnificent promises, so that by them you may become partakers of the divine nature, having escaped the corruption that is in the world by lust.

2 Peter 1:3-4 NASB

Partakers of divine nature? What a remarkable thought!

We are promised everything we need pertaining to life and godliness; not by our power, but by His. We need only partake. We cannot think of ourselves as being worthy, or that we have earned godliness. We cannot believe that we have accomplished this on our own. We haven't.

For it is only by His grace and His precious and magnificent promises. He allows us to partake of His divine nature, so while the world lives in sin and temptation, we are able to resist. Yes! We can be holy by His divine power. Partake! He has invited you.

Father, You have asked that I partake of Your divine nature. How can I refuse? Thank You.

MAY 6

IN STAGES

And the Lord your God will drive out those nations before you little by little; you will be unable to destroy them at once.

Deuteronomy 7:22 NKJV

When the Israelites entered the Promised Land, they would encounter resistance from enemy nations who possessed the land. God would help them defeat those nations. He could have wiped out the enemy in an instant. But He did it in stages. God knew the Israelites would learn valuable lessons as they waited on His timing.

Before His death, Jesus's disciples were certain that He would free them from the powerful Roman rule and establish an earthly kingdom. He would be King! Would they reign with Him, they wondered? When would He do this? After His resurrection, they asked Him if it was now time. He told them, "It is not for you to know times or epochs which the Father has fixed by His own authority" (Acts 1:7 NASB).

We can't know how God will bring us along. If we think about our spiritual growth, we will see how God's plan for our lives has slowly unfolded. He could instantly bring us to a full knowledge of Himself, but He brings us along little by little.

Yes, God reveals Himself to us in stages. If we trust in Him, we will be patient.

Father, teach me as I learn to wait on You.

MAY 7

BODY AND SOUL

Beloved, I pray that in all respects you may prosper
and be in good health, just as your soul prospers.

3 John 2 (NASB)

I have been in atrial fibrillation, also known as Afib, for a week. It means the upper chambers of the heart, the atria, quiver instead of beating regularly. The fibrillation causes the atria to move around 300-600 times a minute instead of 60-80 times a minute.

In the short letter that John wrote to his friend, Gauis, he was concerned about Gauis's physical and spiritual well-being. He knew of the important connection between being physically fit and spiritually fit. Likewise, God is concerned about our bodies and our souls. Our body is a temple of the Holy Spirit, and we work to keep it physically healthy; we nourish our soul by staying in His Word.

Having Afib for an extended period of time leaves me in a weakened condition. My heart regulates my body, and when it is not functioning properly, my body responds negatively. And so it is when my soul is unnourished, it is not healthy, and my spiritual life suffers.

Lord, help me to remember that I need to care for my body and soul and that they both will prosper.

MAY 8

DEW

Blessed of the Lord be his land, with the choice things of heaven, with the dew—

Deuteronomy 33:13 (NASB)

Dew is sometimes used in the Scriptures as a symbol of the benevolent power of God to revive the objects of nature that have been scorched by the burning heat of the sun. Dew slips in silently and works mightily.

Sheep can go for months, especially if the weather isn't too hot, without actually drinking water if there is heavy dew on the grass each morning. A sheep's habit is to rise just before dawn and start to feed. The stillness of the morning can find them knee deep in dew-drenched grass.

Those Christians who are the most serene and able to cope with the complexities of life are most likely those who feed on God's Word in the quiet early morning hours.

W. Mallis wrote:

The dew falls in the still night when all nature is hushed to rest. What is true in nature holds true in spiritual things; in this we have the key reason why so many of God's people are living dewless lives. They are restless, anxious, impatient, fussy, and busy, with not time at all to be still before the Lord.8

Sit with Him in the stillness of the dew.
Lord, drench me with Your Spirit.

MAY 9

IF GOD SAYS NO

When your days are complete and you lie down with your fathers, I will raise up your descendant after you, who will come forth from you, and I will establish his kingdom. He shall build a house for My name, and I will establish the throne of his kingdom forever.

2 Samuel 7:12-13 (NASB)

King David lived in a luxurious palace. God had been good to him, and he wanted to build God a temple in which He would dwell. But God told him no. Why? God had chosen David to lead Israel and destroy her enemies. He was a warring king, and God did not want His temple built by a warrior. God promised David an heir who would build the temple.

What was David's attitude when God revealed His plan? He went in and sat before the Lord. His humble prayer expresses his acceptance of God's will. David knew God's plan was bigger than just himself. He and his descendants were chosen so that God's purpose for His people would be fulfilled. David's attitude was complete submission to God's will.

We don't know precisely what is best for us. We ask God for things, certain that they will make us truly happy. We believe that our desires align with God's will. Yet when He might say no, how do we react?

If we are grounded in God's Word and are confronted with "No," we can be assured it is because He has a plan for our lives. We can readily say, "According to Your will, O Lord."

Seek God's plan for your life. Give up your will for His!

MAY 10

THE LIGHT

Then your light will break out like the dawn.

Isaiah 58:8 (NASB)

At night, floodlights along our bluffs span the beach. The ocean lies enveloped in darkness. The only evidence that it does indeed exist is the lighted, roaring surf crashing toward shore. Phosphorous in the water gives the lighted waves a luminescence at night. It's mesmerizing to watch the spectacular water works.

There are times when our lives seem pitched in darkness. We can't see beyond the pain and disappointments. Financial concerns, a broken marriage, or troubled teenagers are some of the conflicts that fracture our world. Sorrow can give way to doubt and fear.

It seemed as though my life plunged into darkness when my three-year-old granddaughter, Jessica, died of leukemia. I recall that God was my light through the grief. His assurance during that time helped expel the fear.

The incandescent waves remind me of God's goodness and grace. When we focus on the light, we can't see the dark. God makes Himself visible to us. He is light and dispels the darkness. He calls us to come to Him that He might lighten our burdens.

We must stay focused on God, not on the circumstance.

Lord, You are my light. I have nothing to fear.

MAY 11

AT HOME

And leaving Nazareth, He came and settled in Capernaum, which is by the sea, in the region of Zebulun and Naphtali.

Matthew 4:13 (NASB)

Capernaum was home to Jesus when He began His ministry. Located on the shore of the Sea of Galilee, it appeared to be home also to Peter, Andrew, Matthew, and maybe James and John.

My husband and I visited Capernaum when in the Holy Land. I have a photo of myself standing at the gate that reads, "Capernaum: Home of Jesus." As was the case so often on that trip, just the privilege of being in places where Jesus had walked and ministered left open wonder with no words to fill it. Here I was at the earthly home of Jesus.

When He left this earth, He told His disciples that He was going to His "Father's house" and there He would prepare a place for them—a place for me. He is at home with His Father. I will be there, but not as a visitor. I will dwell there with Him. I will be at home with Jesus.

I long to be at home with You, Lord Jesus.

MAY 12

MOURNING

> Remember the word to Your servant, in which You
> have made me hope. This is my comfort in my
> affliction, that Your word has revived me.
>
> Psalm 119: 49-50 (NASB)

Dear Father,

There is mourning so deep in my heart that it is not visible to even those who know me most intimately. It can be heard only by You.

I don't seek answers but just the will to endure, the determination to trust, and know that You, O God, control the universe, and You will control my helplessness.

I am a wretched sinner, unworthy of even a glance from You.

But I do love You, Lord.

And no matter the outcome, I will continue to trust that all of this is Your will.

And I ask for Your mercy and grace.

MAY 13

SUPPLICATION

Simon, Simon, behold Satan has demanded to sift you like wheat; but I have prayed for you.

Luke 22:32A (NASB)

Here we read that Jesus prayed for Peter, a perfect example of intercessory prayer. How do we pray for others—families and friends?

I have a daily prayer journal. The first of each month, I list all those for whom I will pray, my family and friends, along with special requests I have been given. I put post-it notes on my computer monitor for those who have an immediate need.

And I say arrow prayers—they are short, quick, but sincere. I use arrow prayers when I wear something given to me, jewelry, or clothing. When I read or use something that I've received from a friend or loved one, I remember the giver. Our homes are full of gifts from loved ones—books, jewelry, knickknacks. They are all reminders to pray for that person.

I put the greeting cards I receive in a basket and each day pull out one and say an arrow prayer for the sender.

Disciplining ourselves to pray for the giver will keep us in prayer, and those who are remembered will be blessed.

We may never know the mighty results of our prayer. But that is of no matter to us, because God knows.

Lord, I hold to Your promise in Jeremiah 29:12: "Then you will call upon Me, come and pray to Me, and I will listen to you." (NASB)

MAY 14

LOVE POWER

> Beloved, let us love one another, for love is from God; and everyone who loves is born of God and knows God.
>
> 1 John 4:7 (NASB)

It takes God's supernatural power for us to love others. We know we can't do it on our own. It is hardly a challenge to love those who love us. But consider those you know who aren't loveable.

We feel adequate enough to love our neighbor as ourselves until we realize our harsh criticism of those with whom we disagree; our quickness to judge another's actions gives way to self-righteousness.

We are totally dependent upon God to love. In and of ourselves, it is a miserable attempt doomed to failure. Facing such a daily struggle, we must come humbly before Him, the God of the universe, declare our sinfulness, and complete dependence upon Him. Then, depleted of self, we can love those who are not loveable.

We all have the inability to love unconditionally. Only through God's almighty favor and grace can we love one another.

Help me to depend on You that I may love all Your children.

MAY 15

TURNING POINT

Then Jacob was left alone, and a man wrestled with him until daybreak.

Genesis 32:24 (NASB)

Jacob had been ambitious and deceitful, relying on his own resolves and not on God. Even while in the womb he was willful, taking his brother Esau by the heel. "And in his maturity he contended with God" (Hosea 12:3 NASB).

But this night by the Jordan River was a turning point for Jacob. He grabbed onto God and wouldn't let go. He realized his total dependence on God and hung on for his life. When he surrendered, God took a firm hold. He was changed, and God became essential in his life.

When he saw that he had not prevailed against him, he touched the socket of his thigh; so the socket of

Jacob's thigh was dislocated while he wrestled with him. Then he said, "Let me go, for the dawn is breaking." But he said, "I will not let you go unless you bless me." So he said to him, "What is your name?" And he said, "Jacob." He said, "Your name shall no longer be Jacob, but Israel; for you have striven with God and with men and have prevailed." Then Jacob asked him and said, "Please tell me your name." But he said, "Why is it that you ask my name?" And he blessed him there. So Jacob named the place Peniel, for he said, "I have seen God face to face, yet my life has been preserved."

Genesis 32:25-30 (NASB)

Most of us have come, or will come, to a turning point in our lives. We can pray that at that time we won't let go until God has touched us and blessed us. Hang on as Jacob did!

Change me, O God. I have relied on so many things and not on You. I surrender to You.

MAY 16

HOLD OF YOU

I will also hold you by the hand and watch over you.

Isaiah 42:6 (NASB)

Notice the child whose mother has a firm hold of his hand. He charges fearlessly forward, knowing that if he stumbles, he won't fall because she has hold of him. And although he may be bursting with energy and adventure, he cannot wander from her grip. She has hold of him.

Our day will be easier if we let Him take our hand. Hold on tight, knowing that even though we stumble, we will not fall. We are His children. He will not let go; He has hold of us.

I would rather take His hand than try it on my own. I stumble a lot.

Take hold of me, Lord.

MAY 17

UNAWARE

Your enemy the devil prowls around like a roaring lion looking for someone to devour.

1 Peter 5:8 (NIV)

It is a warm May afternoon here at ocean's edge. I sit in my chair and watch a tern circling an area of water in front of me. Acting very much like the predator, the small white, black-tailed bird flies a short distance away and then circles back.

Suddenly, she is suspended in space, her wings flapping rapidly. She dives like a dart into the shimmering blue water. Yes, she has her prey!

I think about how Satan does that to me. That he doesn't give up but is constantly circling—waiting for the moment when he can dart in and snatch me, his prey. Much like the tern's unsuspecting meal, we go about our lives unaware that he is waiting for us.

But the knowledge of his mission helps us. Being aware of the tenacity with which he seeks the weak, we can resist him. Peter tells us to be alert and to stand firm in faith. He says the God of all grace who called us by His eternal glory in Christ will Himself perfect, confirm, strengthen, and establish us (v.10).

I want to be mindful that this predator is hungry for souls. It is by God's grace that I will escape; I will not be snatched up.

Keep me under Your watchful eye, O Lord.

MAY 18

ASK

Jesus reached out His hand and touched the man. "I am willing," He said. "Be clean!" Immediately he was cured.

Matthew 8:3 (NIV)

"Lord," the leper said, "if You are willing, You can make me clean." He had been banished from his home and was living in caves, exiled from society. He was dirty, with grit-filled ringlets of long hair, and his tattered clothing reeked of foul odors. The disease had marred his skin. Only his eyes pierced through the filthy rags that failed to cover all of his face. He was repulsive.

It was an offense to the Jews to touch a leprous person; it would make those who did ceremonially impure.

Yet in spite of this, Jesus touched him. It says that he was immediately cleansed; he had new skin. Perhaps it was like that of a baby's, soft and pink. New! Life was instantly changed for this leper. Jesus touched him, and he was cleansed of his impurity. Imagine how he must have rejoiced.

Sin, like leprosy, scars us. The deadly results of sin exile us from God. But Christ's healing touch can cleanse us. We have only to ask Jesus to touch us and cleanse us from the sin that mars our souls. We can be like new.

But we need to come to Jesus, just as the leper did. We need to come with faith, bow before Him, and recognize Him as Lord. He will make us clean. No matter how serious the sin may be, if we ask for forgiveness, He will cleanse us of all sin. Pure, clean, whole!

Lord, make me clean.

MAY 19

IN YOUR PRESENCE

David wrote this psalm, thanking God for victory in the battle. We can adapt it as our prayer for the many battles He has brought us through.

> O Lord,
> In Your strength I will be glad,
> And in Your salvation how greatly I will rejoice!
> You have given me my heart's desire,
> And You have not withheld the request of my lips.
> For You meet me with the blessings of good things;
> You set a crown of fine gold on my head.
> I asked life of You;
> You gave it to me
> Length of days forever and ever.
> My glory is great through Your salvation.
> Splendor and majesty You place upon me,
> For You make me most blessed forever;
> You make me joyful with gladness in Your presence.

Psalm 21:1-6

MAY 20

LAVISH BANQUET

The Lord of hosts will prepare a lavish banquet for all peoples on this mountain; a banquet of aged wine, choice pieces with marrow, and refined, aged wine. And on this mountain He will swallow up the covering which is over all peoples, even the veil which is stretched over all nations.

Isaiah 25:6-7 (NASB)

Yes, we will be at this lavish banquet when Christ returns. Having lived by faith, we wait in expectation. God "will swallow up death for all time" (v. 8). The God for whom we have waited will save us. We will rejoice and be glad in His salvation.

Revelation 21:4 promises that

He will wipe away every tear from their eyes; and there will no longer be any death; there will no longer be any mourning, or crying, or pain; the first things have passed away.

The Creator says He will make all things new. Then, He will declare it done—the Alpha and the Omega, the beginning and the end. We will join Him at the banquet. Every time I have read this, I've thought that I want to be there, serving or cleaning up, no matter what the position.

But He promises much more than that! He says we will drink from the spring of water; He will be our God, and we will be His children. We are His, and will be dressed in robes of royalty as the children of the King.

I await Your return, My Lord and My God.

MAY 21

TIME TO LISTEN

> You shall love the Lord your God with all your heart and with all your soul and with all your might. These words, which I am commanding you today, shall be on your heart. You shall teach them diligently to your sons and shall talk of them when you sit in your house and when you walk by the way and when you lie down and when you rise up.
>
> Deuteronomy 6:5-7 (NASB)

Three of our grandchildren—ages thirteen, ten, and seven—were visiting us while on their summer vacation. One evening during dinner, my husband and I were relating stories of "When I was your age."

They listened politely for a brief time and then one asked, "What's for dessert?"

My inclination was to say, "Wait! Aren't you interested? This is information you can pass on to your children." But instead, I told them they could have ice cream.

Moses told the Israelites that they must teach God's statues and commandments to their children and grandchildren. These laws were to be taught diligently and were to become an integral part of everyday life.

Today many grandparents are making audio or videotapes of their life stories. Free classes are offered to help us write our biographies. We can weave God's truths into our stories. It is a way to express our faith, allowing future generations to see our hope and trust in the Lord. They will be a lasting treasure for our grandchildren when they are older.

Lord, show me a way to leave a legacy for future generations.

MAY 22

THOUGHTS OF PRAISE

For behold, He who forms mountains and creates the wind and declares to man what are His thoughts, He who makes dawn into darkness and treads on the high places of the earth, the Lord God of hosts is His name.

Amos 4:13 (NASB)

Can we imagine that God announces to us His very thoughts? He speaks directly to us through His Word.

I turn to Psalm 146:1-4 and praise Him.

I will praise the Lord.

Yes, praise the Lord O my soul.

I will praise the Lord while I live.

I will sing praises to my God while I have my being.

I will not trust in princes or mortal man, in whom there is no salvation.

For his spirit departs and returns to the earth.

In that very day his thoughts perish.

Lord, my thoughts will perish but I am grateful to know Your thoughts are eternal.

MAY 23

PEACE

When day came, Jesus left and went to a secluded place; and the crowds were searching for Him, and came to Him and tried to keep Him from going away from them.

Luke 4:42 (NASB)

It's at the ocean I find peace. Before the world stirs at dawn, I love to be at the shore. A sense of private ownership takes over. Sometimes I see a runner or a surfer, but we don't disturb each other. They seem to respect the solitude of the sea gazer.

As a train passes in the distance, the mighty ocean tempers its clattering intrusion. Even the morning chorus of gulls and terns finds it impossible to drown out the competition of the persistent sea. What a privilege to be here as nature awakens.

It is good to have a place where we can occasionally escape the noise. For some it's a mountain stream or a still lake. Others find tranquility in a pine-scented forest or the soundless desert.

For the most part, it is the daily hardships and experiences that get us down. There are bills to be paid, endless tasks to get done. Our lives are hurried and noisy.

The demands on Jesus's time and energy were exhausting. He often sought peace and quiet in nature's setting to commune with the Father.

Seek a place where you can feel the caressing peace of nature.

I long for Your peace, O Lord.

MAY 24

LIVE FOR HIM

Whatever is true, whatever is honorable, whatever is right, whatever is pure, whatever is lovely, whatever is of good repute, if there is any excellence and if anything worthy of praise, dwell on these things.

Philippians 4:8 (NASB)

I want to live for God, but human nature is opposed to that. What I do, I don't want to do. Paul said it first. "For what I am doing, I do not understand; for I am not practicing what I would like to do, but I am doing the very thing I hate" (Romans 7:15). I relate to what he says. I know I shouldn't waste time on the things of this world; they have no lasting value. The day my spirit departs this life, my body returns to the earth and my thoughts are no more.

You may face the same conflict as I: opposing desires. But I know that the more I give in to how my human nature tells me to live, the more my mind will be controlled by what human nature wants. The more I give in to how the Spirit wants me to live, the more my mind will be controlled by what the Spirit wants.

If we truly want to live for Him, it is imperative to yield our time, thoughts, and energies to God. What we feed our mind is as important as what we feed our body. In our scripture verse today, Paul tells us that if there is any excellence and anything worthy of praise, we are to dwell on it. Every day we make choices as to what book we will read, the music we listen to, and the TV shows we watch. Will any of them help us to live for God? We are what we dwell on.

James says our lives are a "vapor that appears for a little while and then vanishes away" (James 4:14). What will be of lasting value is the result of what we dwell on now. And that will empower us to live for Him.

Help me to live for You, Lord.

MAY 25

JUST

Let the words of my mouth and the meditation of my heart be acceptable in Your sight, O Lord, my Rock and my Redeemer.

Psalm 19:14 (NASB)

Just writing it down helps. We can be free with expressions of love, stress, anger, jealousy, indifference, joy, expectation, and desires. No matter what they are, they will not be judged, applauded, or dismissed. They just are.

At times, writing is the pressure release we can use to express what is going on inside. The more we write, the easier the words take shape. Our thoughts are thrown down to no one in particular. They just are.

Journaling is therapeutic. It is healing. It becomes a place where we can go—free to express, free to just be.

The more I journal, the more important it becomes. I find communion with My Creator. I feel His love and acceptance. I know He loves me just the way I am.

Lord, may my words and the meditation of my heart find favor with You.

MAY 26

PERFECT TIMING

For the Lord your God dried up the waters of the
Jordan before you until you had crossed, just as the
Lord your God had done to the Red Sea, which He
dried up before us until we had crossed; that all the
peoples of the earth may know that the hand of the
Lord is mighty, so that you may fear the Lord your
God forever.

Joshua 4:23-24 (NASB)

Moses had died, and Joshua was appointed by God to lead
the Israelites into the Promised Land. He said to Joshua,
"This day I will begin to exalt you in the sight of all Israel,
that they may know that just as I have been with Moses, I
will be with you" (Joshua 3:7). And with that, God parted
the Jordan and the entire nation crossed on dry land with
Joshua as their leader.

God will do whatever it takes to fulfill His promises.
Sometimes it may be a natural occurrence and sometimes
an unexplained miracle. Whatever He chooses, His great
power is demonstrated with perfect timing.

At times I ask God for things and wonder about His
answer. It's not that I doubt His power, nor do I doubt His
willingness to answer. But I get impatient. I need to learn
to wait on Him. Joshua left Egypt with Moses and waited

forty years to enter the Promised Land. He couldn't see the future. He couldn't have known that he would lead the people across a dry Jordan River bed, let alone in the spring when waters overflow its banks.

If we wait for His perfect timing in our life, we will see His extraordinary demonstration of power.

I look for Your perfect timing in all that concerns me.

MAY 27

THE INNER MAN

When He saw their faith, He said to him, "Man, your sins are forgiven you."

Luke 5:20 (NKJV)

I remember this story as a youngster. The friends of a paralytic lowered him through the roof to meet Jesus and be healed. I thought they were great friends and could not imagine how they got him through the roof. But now I know that in those days, roofs were flat and made of mud and straw. There were outside stairways that led to the roof, so they most likely carried him up the stairs.

Yes, I was more fascinated by that than Jesus facing accusations of the Jewish leaders. When Jesus told the man that his sins were forgiven, the scribes and Pharisees were outraged. "Who is this who speaks blasphemies? Who can forgive sins but God alone?" (v.21). I imagine his friends were disappointed also. It's not exactly why they were there.

Jesus said, "Which is easier, to say, "Your sins are forgiven you," or to say, "Rise up and walk?" (v. 23). To prove He was God, He healed the man. What was the crowd most impressed with—physical healing, or the forgiveness of his sins?

When suffering physically, we pray for healing of our bodies. Although Jesus is concerned about our physical wellbeing, He knows that sin is the deadly disease. How often do we pray that He forgive our sins and relieve us of the bondage that it has on our souls? Do we view the inner man as needing healed?

Jesus is available to us at every moment. We don't have to cut through barriers to get to Him. We have only to approach Him and ask our request.

Jesus, I ask that You lay Your loving, healing hands on me.

MAY 28

DEPEND

This is what Hezekiah did throughout Judah, doing what was good and right and faithful before the Lord his God. In everything that he undertook in the service of God's temple and in obedience to the law and the commands, he sought his God and worked wholeheartedly.

2 Chronicles 31:20-21 (NIV)

Hezekiah is faced with an Assyrian invasion in Judah. I like the fact that he takes charge, making preparations to deal with the situation. And then he assures his troops, "Be strong and courageous. Do not be afraid or discouraged because of the king of Assyria and the vast army with him, for there is a greater power with us than with him" (2 Chronicles 32:7).

He actively involved himself in the war, but he knew God was with them. His preparation came long before the challenge. We know that Hezekiah sought God with all his heart. He served Him. His relationship with God was such that he knew he could depend on Him. Hezekiah didn't fear the Assyrian king or his army. He knew beyond a shadow of a doubt that God could take care of everything.

Fear can cripple us emotionally. If we consider the task ahead as impossible, we won't be disappointed. We need to establish a relationship with God and trust Him in times of need. Commit everything to God in prayer.

It has been said, "We are all faced with a series of great opportunities brilliantly disguised as impossible situations."

Make your plans. Then rely totally on God for the outcome.

When I think I can't, then I can't. Only with You, O God, can I accomplish the task ahead.

MAY 29

THE TREADMILL

The Lord will accomplish what concerns me.

Psalm 138: 8 (NASB)

This morning was one of those bad weather days when it was necessary to walk on the treadmill rather than outside.

As I was trudging along, I began to compare it to trying to achieve goals on my own—a walk for only one. On the treadmill I walk and walk but am still in the same place. I try distractions like listening to music or watching TV. Those things help to make it tolerable, but I still don't look forward to the exercise. I have put on miles, exerted myself, and yet remain in the same place.

That exercise is much like trying to do things without God. There is nothing wrong with attaining goals, but they need to include Him. I must seek His will and what His plans are for me.

When He isn't a part of our walk, it is easy to get distracted by the world, which can make the struggle tolerable. But we tire of it, and as the walk becomes more tedious, we want to get off.

So why would we walk alone? He promises that He will accomplish what concerns us. Wouldn't it be better to walk with Him, the One who cares and loves us? It is so much better than just trying to make our life tolerable.

Lord, help me overcome the burden of walking alone. Come along side of me that we may walk together.

MAY 30

ALL THE DAYS OF MY LIFE

My soul will bless You, O Lord. Yes! All that is within me will bless You.

You heal me and redeem me.

You crown me with loving kindness and compassion.

Oh how You satisfy my years, renewing me each day that I might soar like an eagle.

I know Oh Lord, that my days are like grass, and as a flower flourishes and then is no more, I too shall be gone from this earth.

But I know You are from everlasting to everlasting and You show righteousness to me, because I tell my children's children about You, and I keep Your precepts.

I know, O Lord, that You have established Your throne in heaven and You rule over all.

Angels, mighty in strength, perform Your Word and obey Your voice.

All of creation—everything and everywhere—serves You and praises You!

My soul will bless You, O Lord, all the days of
my life.

Amen.

Psalm 103:1-5

MAY 31

OBSTRUCTED VIEW

He had seven hundred wives of royal birth and three
hundred concubines, and his wives led him astray.
As Solomon grew old, his wives turned his heart
after other gods, and his heart was not devoted to
the Lord his God"

1 Kings 11: 3-4 (NIV)

My husband and I were fascinated as we watched the eclipse
of the moon on a clear May evening. The moon gradually
moved behind the palm tree outside our window. The tree
obstructed the perfect view we had enjoyed. It was in the
way of something I wanted to see, and I needed to move.

Solomon was the wisest man who ever lived. He was
king, and God favored him. Yet he allowed his desire for
women to obstruct his relationship with God. He married
many foreign women even though God told him not to
even associate with them. Eventually he ended up with
seven hundred wives and princesses and three hundred

concubines. He even began to worship their gods! Solomon didn't turn from God all at once. It was gradual. He probably didn't even realize what was happening. When the full view of God was gone, then Solomon realized what he had done.

If we have allowed something or someone to obstruct our relationship with God, we need to remove it or remove ourselves. The obstacle may seem harmless, yet it takes all of our attention and energy. We lose sight of Him.

I want nothing or no one to keep me from You, Lord.

JUNE 1

HOW DO YOU LOVE ME?

But You, O Lord, know me; You have seen me, and You have tested my heart toward You.

Jeremiah 12:3 (NKJV)

"How do you love me?" It is a question we might have been asked. How do we love someone? We can tell why we love them. We love them for the qualities that make them the person they are. We love them for the things they do, how they treat us, and that they love us in return. But how we love them is more difficult to explain. Love is visible, but not tangible. We can't gather it up, spread it out on a table, and examine the intricacies that make it love.

I know my siblings love my mother just as I do. We constantly express our love by the things we do for her, our respect and consideration of her. But none of us can say "Yes, I love her exactly like that!" Exactly like what?

And so it is true of our love for God. Although we share our belief in Him with others, how we love Him is different for everyone. We talk of why we love Him, and how much we love Him, and show by our actions that we do love Him. But we can't express how we love Him.

The only one who knows how we love Him is God Himself. He knows our heart.

The how of love is difficult; the why of love is easy.

God, I am grateful that You know my heart and don't need to ask, "How do you love Me?"

JUNE 2

DISCOURAGED

When my anxious thoughts multiply within me,
Your consolations delight my soul!

Psalm 94:19 (NASB)

Sometimes I get discouraged. I think of the work for which He has called me, and I feel overwhelmed. I feel inadequate and unworthy, certain there is someone who can do it much better than I.

These thoughts are not from God. I discipline myself to put them aside and come with trust and confidence before Him, the One who loves me most. He renews my mind and gives me peace in place of doubt.

There are times when we all experience feelings of discouragement and unworthiness. Discouragement is one of Satan's most useful tools. We must remember that it isn't the work of God. No, we can never be worthy of God, but we find our worth in Him. We can trust Him to strengthen us, resisting such anxious thoughts when they seem to multiply within.

Lord, I want to serve You.

JUNE 3

SURFING

> For the word of God is living and active and sharper than any two-edged sword, and piercing as far as the division of soul and spirit, of both joints and marrow, and able to judge the thoughts and intentions of the heart.

> Hebrews 4:12 (NASB)

I have to admit, I'd rather look at the ocean than be in it. Although I relish its beauty, I dislike the cold temperature and salty taste. I like to walk barefoot along its edge, the water gently wrapping itself around my ankles.

The surfer, however, participates in a life of the sea I can only imagine. The ocean is described in surfer language as the "liquid stage." Here the performer dances across curling tons of water, riding them with exacting movements to the finish. His partner, the board, responds to the energy of both surfer and ocean. They have mastered the wave.

I am neither a surfer in the water nor in God's Word. But I want to know Him more intimately. To do so, I need to spend time reading His Word, which is living, active, and vibrant.

Imagine how much time it takes to develop the skill of surfing. Likewise, studying the Bible takes diligence and effort. It's necessary to have a planned time each day to read and study the Bible. Then as the surfer, we too can experience the joy of riding the wave of God's love.

Lord, help me to be willing to set aside the time for studying.

JUNE 4

FOLLOW

At the command of the Lord they camped, and at the command of the Lord they set out; they kept the Lord's charge, according to the command of the Lord through Moses.

Numbers 9:23 (NASB)

Following God's directions through the wilderness was not complicated. When the cloud moved, the Israelites were to move. When it stopped, they were to stop. And at night the appearance of fire hovered over the tabernacle. God loved His people so much that He went ahead of them all the way. All they had to do was follow.

But it wasn't an easy trek for them. The wilderness was vast and barren. They faced shortages of food and water. Without God's provisions they would have perished.

However they constantly complained, accusing Moses of leading them into the wilderness to die. Life became difficult because they took their eyes off God.

We tend to do the same when faced with trials. We ask, "Why me?"

To follow takes faith especially when we can't see what lies ahead. When we follow God's guidance we know we are where He wants us. Life is unstable and oftentimes not easy. Peter reminds us that we are protected by the power of God through faith.

The journey for the Israelites would have been easier had they followed God's directions, and by faith relied on Him for protection.

Would our journey be easier if we did the same?

Lord, help me to follow You with faith.

JUNE 5

MAJESTIC

O Lord, our Lord, how majestic is Your name in all
the earth, who have displayed Your splendor above
the heavens!

Psalm 8:1 (NASB)

Dear Father,

Your name is majestic in all the earth,

Displaying Your splendor above the heavens!

I marvel at the moon and stars, at the heavens; the work
of Your fingers.

And I wonder why You consider me.

Why do You care for me?

You have made me a little lower than You

And You crown me with glory and majesty.

How can that be?

You give me rule over the works of Your hands.

Rule over the earth, the animals, birds of heaven, and
fish of the sea.

O Father,

How majestic is Your name in all the earth!

JUNE 6

CLINGING

For You are my rock and my fortress.

Psalm 31:3 (NASB)

It was midmorning as I took my daily walk along the Solana Beach shores. The fog had lifted and given way to the warm rays of June sunshine. My attention was fixed on the bluffs that lined the shore. Nature was having its way. More and more sand drifted to the beach, and the houses perched atop the cliffs were losing their battle to the sea.

I was lost in thought when I noticed a clump of brilliant yellow ice plant protruding from the eroding sandstone. Ice plant is drought proof (the reason why there is so much of it here in southern California) and comes in an array of bright colors. There on the desolate and doomed cliff, this resilient succulent bloomed all alone without consideration of its future. I wondered how long it could hang on before it too became part of the seashore.

Sometimes I feel like I'm clinging just like that pathetic patch of ice plant. I'm clinging to the Rock as the slope slides down around me. Jesus is the Rock to which we can cling as the world and all of its trappings slip away.

Lord, as my world slides and crumbles around me, I will cling to You, my Rock. I pray that my joy be as the bright and brilliant yellow bloom of the ice plant.

JUNE 7

HIS NAME

Therefore God also has highly exalted Him and given Him the name which is above every name, that at the name of Jesus every knee should bow, of those in heaven, and of those on earth, and of those under the earth, and that every tongue should confess that Jesus Christ is Lord, to the glory of God the Father.

Philippians 2:9-11 (NKJV)

I cringe when I hear His name used irreverently. Often it is done without thought.

I love Him so much, that when I think of Jesus or hear His name, a soft and tender feeling sweeps through me. I use His name often throughout the day. "Jesus." Just to say it out loud or within brings a peace, joy, and tranquility to my spirit.

These verses are a promise of hope for us in that at the name of Jesus, every knee will bow; every tongue will call Him Jesus, Lord! We will be among them.

I love to call Your name.

JUNE 8

EMPTY PROMISES

He has granted to us His precious and magnificent promises.

2 Peter 1:4 (NASB)

I was bored with the cereal I'd eaten for years and decided to try a new one. So there I stood in the cereal aisle, reading labels on at least ten boxes of cereal, each one promising to be healthy, lower cholesterol, be good for my heart, include more fiber; one bowl of this equals ten bowls of that. I gave the sugar-coated ones a glance. The one with chunks of chocolate was a huge temptation, certainly better than bran flakes. How long must I have looked at the multitude of choices?

We have so many choices that it leads to confusion. Manufacturers dress up their products, advertising them as though our lives will be empty without them. Often times we buy the pretty package, only to find it tasteless or useless.

I think of the times I've succumbed to the lure of what the world offers, only to find my choice empty of the promise. I chose what looked good, not what was good for me.

Spiritual maturity brings us to the book of promises. God's Word is full of rich and soul-satisfying promises. Those of us with faith are promised that His divine power has granted us everything pertaining to life and godliness. This is not an empty promise!

I rely on Your promises, Father, not the empty promises of the world.

JUNE 9

BLESSED ASSURANCE

> When Haman saw that Mordecai neither bowed down nor paid homage to him, Haman was filled with rage. But he disdained to lay hands on Mordecai alone, for they had told him who the people of Mordecai were; therefore Haman sought to destroy all the Jews, the people of Mordecai, who were throughout the whole kingdom of Ahasuerus.
>
> Esther 3:5-6 (NASB)

How could Esther and her uncle Mordecai ever know that God would use them to save His people, the Jews? As events unfold in this book, we read that the Jews, exiles in Persia, were to be annihilated; carried out in a day.

Haman, second in command in the empire, used his power to convince the king that it was not in his best interest to let the Jews live. But God worked through Esther and Mordecai to foil such plans.

This book is a powerful example of God's divine plan for our lives. His sovereignty assures us that He is in control even when the situation looks dismal or hopeless.

Do you need blessed assurance that God will watch out for you no matter what? Find your hope in His Word. Read Esther.

I trust in You, God, for the plans You have for me.

JUNE 10

JUNE GLOOM

Why are you in despair, O my soul? And why have you become disturbed within me? Hope in God, for I shall yet praise Him, the help of my countenance and my God.

Psalm 42:11 (NASB)

Summer's threshold is here. Spring! But while most of the country ushers in the welcomed colorful season, our area sinks into a period known as June Gloom. Fog possessively hugs the coast. Known as advection fog, it occurs when warm land air travels out over cool ocean waters, producing moist marine layers. Some days the coastal clouds remain all day.

It reminds me of the times when gloom settles into our lives. We feel depressed and/or a deep sense of sadness. We are so overwhelmed with trying to cope, we just give up.

As much as I can, I try to practice surrendering those dark, gloomy times to Jesus. My prayer of the heart, "I love You, Jesus," helps me slip into His presence, and for a while gives me relief from the clouds that engulf me. When I cast the discouragement and sadness at His feet, it allows Him to nourish my soul.

The June gloom eventually disappears and glorious sunshine spills across summer days. So it can be in our life. Depression and discouragement will give way to better days. Don't give way to gloom. Instead praise and pray.

I love You, Jesus.

JUNE 11

DAILY HAPPENINGS

You do not know what a day may bring forth.

Proverbs 27:1 (NASB)

Dear Father,
I will take each moment of this day knowing
You are in charge of all its happenings.
I can't know what today will bring
And so I yield everything to You.
If something is not of my liking,
I will say with a submissive spirit,
Your will be done, Abba, Father.

You are the Lord of the Day!
I will fill this day and all of its happenings
with You.

JUNE 12

ALL IS VANITY

Vanity of vanities! All is vanity.

Ecclesiastes 1:2 (NASB)

King Solomon had everything from wisdom and riches to God's favor. Yet near the end of his life he looked back over all he had acquired and accomplished and found most of it meaningless. In Ecclesiastes he asks what advantage we have in all our work. A generation comes and goes; the sun rises and sets only to hasten to its place to do it again. The wind blows, swirling along on its circular course and it returns again. All the rivers flow into the sea, but the sea is not full.

Solomon had tried it all, yet nothing apart from God made him happy. Success and prosperity don't last long. He said all things are wearisome, and there is nothing new under the sun. He was skeptical and pessimistic.

We hurry through life, thinking that all we do has meaning and purpose. But in the scheme of things, does it? What is important in life? Solomon says, "I have seen all the works which have been done under the sun, and behold, all is vanity and striving after wind" (v. 13).

Father, guide me as I rethink my purpose and direction in life. What is lasting, what is fleeting?

JUNE 13

MARRIAGE

Then the Lord God said, "It is not good for man to be alone; I will make him a helper suitable for him."

Genesis 2:18 (NASB)

The Bible says that marriage is like the relationship between Christ and the Church. The wife is to honor her husband, and the husband is to love his wife as Christ loves the church. In fact, husbands are to love their wives as their own bodies.

This scripture is an endorsement for a strong marriage:

Two are better than one because they have a good return for their labor. For if either of them falls, the one will lift up his companion...

Ecclesiastes 4:9-10

Even if one can be overpowered by circumstance, trials, and everyday challenges, two can resist.

Taking it a step further, this scripture writes the formula for a strong Christian marriage. "a cord of three strands is not quickly torn apart" (Ecclesiastes 4:12). It includes God.

A couple can be strong together. But if Christ is part of their marriage, it will be a triple-braided cord and is not easily broken. Untwist the cord, and the individual threads are easily broken.

Is your marriage strong in Christ?

Lord, may You be such an intricate part of our marriage that we might be a cord of three strands.

JUNE 14

MUCH IS EXPECTED

From everyone who has been given much, much will be demanded; and from the one who has been entrusted with much, much more will be asked.

Luke 12:48 (NASB)

Wasted talent; wasted time. We fill our days with idleness or a flurry of unnecessary activities.

What one thing will I do today to express my love for God? What one act of commitment will be for my soul and eternity?

This day is a blank page. I can fill it with those things that might count for earthly gain or credit. Or I can store up treasures in heaven. (Matthew 6:20)

I choose to use what You have given me, Lord. I want to set my eyes on heaven, to use any time or talent with which You have blessed me. I will store my treasures in heaven.

JUNE 15

APPROACH HIS THRONE

Let us have confidence, then, and approach God's throne where there is grace. There we will receive mercy and find grace to help us just when we need it.

Hebrews 4:16 (NASB)

We all pray differently. God hears and honors each prayer. Since we have grown up reciting prayers with others, our prayers can become a litany of recitations that are so common that there is little or no sincerity in talking with God. When we talk to God in prayer, we should talk to God from the heart.

Imagine approaching His throne, bowing before Him in adoration, acknowledging our sinfulness, giving thanks for our blessings, and interceding for others. This simple example has become known as A-C-T-S. Beginning our quiet time with this model of prayer brings our heart and our mind into communion with Him.

ADORATION

Come before His divine majesty exalting Him for who He is. For instance: "I praise you God because You are: Holy, Almighty, King of kings, and Lord of lords."

CONTRITION

The Bible says we are all sinners, and it is necessary each day to confess our sins to God. And when we do, we can be confident that He will forgive us our sins and "purify us from all wrongdoing" (1 John 1:19). He will wash us clean, whiter than snow!

THANKSGIVING

We thank God, not just for material possessions, or families whom we love and who love us, but also for His spiritual gifts. "Thank You God for sending Jesus to die for my sins, for the Holy Spirit, for Your Word, for the privilege of prayer."

SUPPLICATION

Supplication means to implore favor, to plea. The Bible tells us we are to pray for others. Paul told Timothy "I constantly remember you in my prayers night and day" (2 Timothy 1:3).

Yes, "Come, let us worship and bow down. Let us kneel before the Lord our Maker" (Psalm 89:6).

JUNE 16

MOSQUITO BITE

Be anxious for nothing, but in everything by prayer and supplication with thanksgiving let your requests be made known to God. And the peace of God, which surpasses all comprehension, shall guard your hearts and your minds in Christ Jesus.

Philippians 4:6-7 (NASB)

I have a mosquito bite, and no matter how I try to ignore it, I can't. It itches. I scratch it, and the welt only gets bigger.

The worries and concerns we face each day can be like that. Getting to work on time, picking up children after school, scheduled appointments, can all cause stress and take our attention away from God. And like the mosquito bite, sometimes no matter how we try to not let them get to us, how we try to ignore the anxiety, we can't. And the more we concentrate on them, the bigger they seem to become.

Hydrocortisone cream helps reduce the itch of the mosquito bite. The welt may remain for a while, but we're not concentrating on it anymore.

But what can we use to help reduce stress? We must apply God's promise to those situations that cause worry and concern. The Bible tells us to be anxious for nothing, but with a thankful heart we are to tell God about everything through prayer and supplication. If we do this, we are promised peace. The stressful situations may still remain, but we deal with them differently. We can ask ourselves as Jesus asks, "And who of you by being worried can add a single hour to his life?" (Matthew 6:27 NASB).

We can give our concerns to God with simple acts of prayer and receive His peace to deal with everything.

It seems I'm always in a hurry, Lord. Give me peace in the midst of a hectic schedule.

JUNE 17

I KNOW

That you may know that you have eternal life.

1 John 5:13 (NASB)

As I begin my day today, I am aware that I cannot know for certain anything about it. From moment to moment, change is inevitable. My list of "things to do" can come to a halt with just a phone call, a car that won't start, a clumsy accident—so many things. I know I cannot depend on anything to go as planned.

But as I read these words in my quiet corner of prayer, before the start of my day's activities, I am in agreement with what John writes. The one thing I know for certain is I have the promise of eternal life. It is not based on my feelings but on fact. The Bible says, "He who believes in the Son has eternal life" (John 3:36).

I believe in Him, the Son of God. I know I have eternal life. And this morning, that is all I need to know.

I know I will spend eternity with You!

JUNE 18

PRAISE

For the Lord is great and greatly to be praised; He is also to be feared above all gods.

I Chronicles 16:25 (NASB)

There is power in praise. If we say, "I praise You, Lord," the devil runs.

Most of us know someone who has truly suffered and endured great trials. Yet through it all they have experienced God's comfort and strength. For them great praise pours forth effortlessly. They stand firm on God's promise that offers "a garland instead of ashes, the oil of gladness instead of mourning, the mantle of praise instead of a spirit of fainting" (Isaiah 61:3).

Praise is recognizing and expressing God's greatness. Jesus often spoke to His Father with praise. In Matthew 11:25, He begins His conversation with the Father by saying, "I praise You, Father, Lord of heaven and earth..."

Whatever our circumstances, if we praise God we find strength for the battle. Praise can drive out fear, depression, and despair. When we praise, we no longer have a sense of failure but victory. We must not give in to feelings that drag us down. Instead, we must rise above every negative thought as it creeps in. Stare it down, cast it out. Say "I praise You, Lord" until we rest in the peace and joy that only He can supply.

I praise You, Lord.

JUNE 19

IN THE EMPLOY OF THE KING

The Lord is King forever and ever.

Psalm 10:16 (NASB)

My sister was the executive secretary to a powerful man. Presidents and governors call him by his first name. Working for a billionaire was challenging and required her undivided attention. The plush executive suite of offices where she worked has a panoramic view of the Pacific Ocean. Her wardrobe was tailored and fashionable.

In contrast, my office is on the bottom floor of our home. I look out French doors at the cream-colored tile patio dotted with potted plants and flowers and a fountain, which lends a peaceful sound. The window over my desk frames a scene of palm trees, blue sky, and shrubbery. My usual work attire is sweats and socks.

I am in the employ of the King. It is written that He is King of Nations, mighty and powerful. The government rests on His shoulders. Many call Him Wonderful Counselor and Prince of Peace. His net worth? It cannot be estimated.

I am in ministry and part of a team which trains a group of others who speak at organized functions. We tell them of how our King laid down His life for them that they may have eternal life. And although He died, He rose again and is seated on a throne.

It doesn't matter who our employer may be or what our office surroundings are like. We can serve Him.

I adore You, O King, and will serve You.

JUNE 20

PATIENT

Meditate in your heart upon your bed, and be still.

Psalm 4:4 (NASB)

Dear Father,

You know that I've always been impatient when it comes to recovering from accident or illness. The inactivity is difficult.

But as my spiritual life has matured, I find the sweetest communion having to come aside to be still with You.

Extra time in the scriptures is healing.

I don't welcome accident or illness,

but I cherish the time of recovery in Your Almighty care.

My spirit is healed, and I am a willing patient.

JUNE 21

HUMBLE SERVANTS

> Hezekiah answered, "They have seen all that is in my house; there is nothing among my treasures that I have not shown them."
>
> 2 Kings 20:15 (NASB)

Hezekiah was one of the few kings of Judah who honored God. But he fell victim to pride. When men from Babylon visited the king, he gave them the grand tour, rashly showing them all the treasures. He took credit. Isaiah told him how foolish that was and that one day the Babylonians would carry everything away. And they did.

While we honor those in powerful positions who serve our county, like Hezekiah they can become proud, taking credit for their gift of leadership.

But we are all guilty of pride. It is a tenacious enemy and an abomination to the Lord.

If we become proud, considering our material and spiritual gifts as something we deserve, we give Satan the opportunity to sneak in. "A man's pride will bring him low, but a humble spirit will obtain honor" (Proverbs 29:23).

Who of us can be proud when everything we've been given comes from God? Paul says in Romans 11:36, "For from Him and through Him and to Him are all things. To Him be the glory forever. Amen."

Pray for our president and all those in authority that they be humble servants.

Expose the pride in my life, Lord. Teach me to be humble.

JUNE 22

RESCUED

Now the time that the sons of Israel lived in Egypt was four hundred and thirty years. And at the end of four hundred and thirty years, to the very day, all the hosts of the Lord went out from the land of Egypt.

Exodus 12:40-41 (NASB)

I haven't actually seen a lifeguard rescue, but I've read about them. Sometimes a rip tide—a narrow, intense current that moves seaward through the surf zone—becomes a danger to ocean swimmers. The force of the tide grasps its victims, drawing them out to sea. They need rescued.

God's people needed rescued. It had been more than four hundred years since Joseph had moved his family to Egypt. Numbering over two million, the Hebrews were in the grasp of cruel slavery. The time had come for God to fulfill His promise. He would rescue His people and lead them to the Promised Land.

There are times God needs to rescue us. Like the rip tide, the force of the world's lure grasps us as victims and draws us away from God. But we must submit, allowing Him to bring us in. If a drowning victim fights his rescuer, saving him will be more difficult, sometimes impossible.

Surrendering our lives to Him frees us from the grip of sin and death. We don't have to be victims in Satan's grasp. "For He rescued us from the domain of darkness, and transferred us to the kingdom of His beloved Son, in whom we have redemption, the forgiveness of sin" (Colossians 1:13-14). He is our Rescuer.

What a glorious promise. Just as God led His people "to a land flowing with milk and honey, He will bring us into His kingdom" (Exodus 3:17).

Read of God's rescue in Exodus 12:1-51.

God, I willingly submit. Thank You for rescuing me from the power of sin.

JUNE 23

RAIN

He will come to us like the rain, like the spring rain
watering the earth.

Hosea 6:3 (NASB)

I like rainy days; there are few of them here in San Diego.
When we get even a drizzle we are happy. A spring or summer shower brings childhood memories of playing in the
rain with no concern about getting wet.

Occasionally our spiritual life can be like ground that is
parched and dry. It is an effort to pray or read His Word.
We don't think of Him much. Maybe we have been caught
up in our busy world spending less time with Him. We
need refreshed with the likes of a spring rain.

When we open up to God, He can refresh us. Our spirit
drinks the rain He sends. It brings forth springs of new life.

Hebrews 6:7 (NASB) says the ground that drinks the
rain which falls on it and brings forth vegetation receives a
blessing from God.

After the rain, everything is fresh. And so it is with us
when we soak up God's renewing rain. We will be show-
ered with blessings.

Father, when my soul feels like a desert, parched and
dry, You revive me as with spring rain; a soft drizzle, gently
washing over me, bringing sprouts of praise and worship.

I feel it, welcoming it as its freshness renews and replenishes me.

Thank You for this gift "raining" in my soul.

JUNE 24

SUNSEEKERS

Finally, be strong in the Lord and in the strength of His might. Put on the full armor of God, so that you will be able to stand firm against the schemes of the devil.

Ephesians 6:10-11 (NASB)

Basal cell carcinoma is the most common form of skin cancer and accounts for more than ninety percent of all skin cancer in the United States. Chronic exposure to sunlight is the main cause of most all this form of cancer. Still, with a backdrop of summer beaches, there stretches a canvas of bikini-clad bodies, absorbing the ultra violet rays. Warnings of the deadly killer go unheeded.

I'm of the Coppertone Generation. Thinking a tan was enviable, we spent hours lying in the sun inviting its powerful rays. I love the sunshine and spend a great deal of time outdoors, but I protect myself with sunscreen.

In these verses, Paul warns us about the schemes of the devil. Without God's strength, we are helpless against such forces. Only by putting on the armor of God can we resist and stand firm. Paul draws a clear picture of what we need for the battle.

We can't escape from the sun, but we can use sunscreen. We can't isolate ourselves from the world, but we can lather our minds with God's Word. It will strengthen us and protect us from the wickedness of Satan.

When you feel the tug of the world, pray. Paul urges us to pray in the Spirit at all times.

Father, help me to resist the powers of Satan.

JUNE 25

THE INNER ROOM

> But you, when you pray, go into your inner room, close your door and pray to your Father who is in secret, and your Father who sees what is done in secret will reward you.
>
> Matthew 6:6 (NASB)

Several windows in our home display incredible views of the Pacific Ocean. Sometimes while lost in daily chores, I glance out my kitchen window. Rooster tail waves sweep toward the beach. The sea seems to beckon. I drop what I'm doing and head for a brisk walk along the shore. Other times, however, there's too much to be done. I pass up the opportunity.

Jesus calls us into an intimate relationship with Himself. He beckons us to stop what we're doing and just be with Him. Few of us today can find time alone or a secluded spot away from family demands and responsibilities. For many, a shut door is a luxury. Still, He tells us to pray.

Perhaps the inner room is not a physical place but the deepest sanctuary of our being. We can meet Him there, no matter what we're doing at the moment. A long wait in the doctor's office or another red traffic light offer opportunities to pray.

As the world rushes around us, we can be alone with Him. In peaceful communion, we become aware of His abiding presence.

When He beckons, respond and head for the inner room.

Lord, I long to leave the cares of this world and be alone with You.

JUNE 26

WATCH EXPECTANTLY

Dear Father,
As for me, I will watch expectantly for You;
I will wait for You, the God of my salvation.
You will hear me.
I can tell my enemies not to rejoice over me,
for even when I fall I will rise; and though I might
dwell in darkness at times, You are a light for me.

I know that I will bear Your indignation because I have sinned against You,

until You plead my case and execute justice for me.

You will bring me out to the light, and I will see Your righteousness.

Micah 7:7-9 (NASB)

JUNE 27

STORE UP

But God said to him, "You fool! This very night your soul is required of you; and now who will own what you have prepared?"

Luke 12:20 (NASB)

Cherry picking time! When growing up, my sisters and I sat around the kitchen table and spent hours pitting cherries. We used bobby pins to dig out the stubborn pits while messy red juice ran down our arms. It was a tiring and seemingly endless job. But it was necessary for us to make provisions for the winter to fill the root cellar that would feed our large family.

It is necessary to make provisions. We are obligated to provide for our families and ourselves. But in this reading, Jesus refers to excess as greed.

In the parable Jesus tells of a man of wealth who didn't know what to do with all his possessions. He reasoned that he would tear down his barns and build bigger ones. He was proud of all he had achieved and certain that he had many years left to enjoy all he had acquired. He would take it easy; eat, drink, and be merry. Jesus called him a fool, storing up riches for himself, but not rich toward God.

There is a big difference between filling a dirt cellar with winter provisions, and the barns referred to in today's reading. If the man had too much, why didn't he share a portion with those in need? Greed?

Jesus tells us, "Beware, and be on your guard against every form of greed; for not even when one has an abundance does his life consist of his possessions" (v. 15).

Lord, make me a frugal, not a possessive, servant.

JUNE 28

WHO AM I?

Who do you say that I am?

Matthew 16:15 (NASB)

Jesus was nearing the end of His earthly ministry. He had been with the disciples for nearly three years, teaching them, performing miracles, showing and telling them who He was.

This day He asked them "Who do people say that the Son of Man is?" And they said, "Some say John the Baptist; and others, Elijah; but still others, Jeremiah, or one of the prophets." He said to them, "But who do you say that I am?" Simon Peter answered, "You are the Christ, the Son of the living God" (v 13-16).

Today many still believe that Jesus was a prophet, a good man.

But He asks of us, "Who do you say that I am?"

Jesus, Son of the living God, You are the Messiah!

JUNE 29

THOUGHTS

For You formed my inward parts; You wove me in my mother's womb. I will give thanks to You, for I am fearfully and wonderfully made; wonderful are Your works, and my soul knows it very well. My frame was not hidden from You, when I was made in secret, and skillfully wrought in the depths of the earth; Your eyes have seen my unformed substance; and in Your book were all written the days that were ordained for me, when as yet there was not one of them. How precious also are Your thoughts to me, O God! How vast is the sum of them! If I should count them, they would outnumber the sand. When I awake, I am still with You.

Psalm 139:13-18 (NASB)

Studies have shown that the average person has approximately 65,000 thoughts per day. How many of those are thoughts of God? How much time do we spend just thinking about Him? His thoughts of us are so numerous that they can't be counted!

Sand is often used in the Bible to symbolize amounts impossible to measure. Sitting in my beach chair, I burrow my toes through the soft layer of sun-soaked sand. As they snuggle into the cool, wet dampness beneath, I consider that I will never be able to comprehend God's intimate love or precious thoughts of me. I want to think of God, to be in constant communion with Him. I want to send love thoughts to Him as often as I can.

There are few things over which we actually have control. But our thoughts are ours alone. We can dismiss those we consider frivolous yet cling to those that draw us nearer to God. No other relationship we share is so intimate. All we have to do is think of Him, and He knows it. Nothing is hidden from Him.

As often as possible, think of God. Dwell on His holiness, His majesty. Take every thought into captivity and give it to Christ.

You are a wondrous Father. I want to be Your thoughtfull child.

JUNE 30

THE SUN

In them [the heavens] He has placed a tent for the sun.

Psalm 19:4 (NASB)

Dear Father,

This morning the sun is streaming in the window, touching my back and spilling over the pages of Your Word. It creates a shadow of my pen as it glides across the paper.

I love the sun.

In David's psalm he compares the sun to a bridegroom coming out of his chamber. I try to imagine the joy he feels as he anticipates his bride-their wedding day!

David tells of the sun rejoicing as a strong man to run his course. I imagine him anxious and ready.

"Its rising is from one end of the heavens and its circuit to the other end of them. And nothing is hidden from its heat" (v. 6).

Yes, Father. I am happy in Your sunshine; I am happy in You.

I will bask in the joy and warmth of Your sun and Your love.

JULY 1

PURITY

How can a young man keep his way pure? By keeping it according to Your Word.

Psalm 119:9 (NASB)

Because of its white winter coloring, the ermine is a symbol of moral purity and innocence.

Legend has it that hunters easily caught ermine by smearing mud on the entrance of the creature's home, usually tree roots, hollow logs, or stonewalls. When the hounds were turned loose, the carnivore naturally turned to his place of refuge. But when reaching it, rather than sully his coat by running through the dirty entranceway, the exhausted animal turned and faced the yelping dogs.

The phrase "Death before Dishonor" is associated with the ermine. He appears on coats of arms as the emblem of knights who would perform any unpleasant deed and suffer any hardship, including death, rather than stain their reputation or conscience.

David asked God to wash him whiter than snow and to purify him. To purify means to keep free from the corruption of sin. To what lengths will we go to remain pure?

Purify me, O God, that I might be whiter than snow.

JULY 2

EXAMINE

Now there went forth a wind from the Lord and it brought quail from the sea, and let them fall beside the camp, about a day's journey on this side and a day's journey on the other side, all around the camp and about two cubits deep on the surface of the ground. The people spent all day and all night and all the next day, and gathered the quail (he who gathered least gathered ten homers) and they spread them out for themselves all around the camp. While the meat was still between their teeth, before it was chewed, the anger of the Lord was kindled against the people, and the Lord struck the people with a very severe plague.

Numbers 11:31-33 (NASB)

God's people wanted meat and He gave them more quail that than they could even use. A homer is ten bushels. So the least that each one gathered was one hundred bushels. They were full of greed and lust.

God was so sickened by what He observed, He sent a plague. There were many who died while eating with such unbridled lust. The place where this happened was called Kibroth-hattaavah, which means "the graves of lust." King Solomon, greater than all the kings of the earth, was blessed with wealth and wisdom. Yet Solomon's desires and appetites eventually distanced him from God. He had seven hundred wives, princesses, along with three hundred concubines. Soon he began to worship other idols.

Excessive desires can lead us to the same greed and lust that destroyed the Israelites. Like Solomon, we can turn from God. When we can no longer be satisfied, we need to examine what is important.

I examine my life, Lord. May I know what is needed and what is excessive.

JULY 3

APPROACH

With what shall I come to the Lord and bow down before the exalted God?

Micah 6:6 (NIV)

Some people seem unapproachable, while others, when you first meet them, can make you feel as though you were life-long friends.

God is approachable. In the Old Testament, only the high priest was allowed once a year to enter the innermost room of the temple, the Holy of Holies, to perform a ceremony that would atone for the sins of the nation.

In His time, God sent His Son to make atonement for sin. God became accessible for all those who believed in

Jesus, for He is our only High Priest. There is no room designated to which we must go; we can go right to Him.

But how do we approach him? We approach Him with humility, bowing before Him. What is required? We are to love Him with all our heart, body, and soul, and our neighbor as ourselves. We are to do what justice requires and treat others with mercy and kindness. And we must not deprive our souls of what God has provided, avoiding excess in everything. We are to humble ourselves, to walk with Him, and to confess our sins.

O Lord, I must examine my life regularly. I humbly approach You, knowing You are waiting.

JULY 4

JUST ONE

It is not the will of your Father who is in heaven
that one of these little ones perish.

Matthew 18:14 (NASB)

How important is one to God? In Acts we read that Phillip had a successful preaching ministry in Samaria. But God ordered him to travel to Ethiopia, where he was to preach the gospel to just one, an Ethiopian eunuch, a court official of the queen. Phillip found the eunuch reading the scriptures without understanding. When he asked Phillip to help him, Phillip "preached Jesus to him" (v.35). He confessed his belief in Jesus as the Son of God, and Phillip baptized him. (Acts 8:26-40)

Jesus tells of a man who left ninety-nine of his sheep to search for one who was lost. Just one! When he found it, his friends and neighbors gathered to rejoice with him. (Luke 15:4)

The Bible continually affirms the value of each individual. You are just one, but you are one for whom Jesus died. You are just one, but you can make a difference in your circle of influence. Will you be one that He can depend upon, to pray, to care, to share the good news with other "ones" who need to know Him? Just one—plus God—can help change the world.

What a caring, loving Father You are, O God. I am just one, but am so important to You that You died for me. Just one!

JULY 5

EXPECT

Where can I get meat for all these people? The burden is too heavy for me.

Numbers 11:13-14 (NIV)

God's people were tired of manna. They wanted meat. When they complained to Moses, he took their request to God, and He told him He would give them meat. But Moses questioned God, asking how He was going to do such a thing. After all, there were at least 600,000 of His people who needed to eat.

God asked Moses if he thought the Lord's power was limited. Time and again God had proven Himself to Moses. Still, Moses doubted what God could and would do.

Moses was God's obedient servant, but he was human. And when something loomed ahead that seemed impossible, he couldn't help but wonder how God was going to accomplish it.

We limit God. We ask without expecting. He tells us that He will give exceedingly abundantly more than we can even think or ask. He has a plan for our lives and will cause all things to work together for good because we love Him and are called according to His purpose. Don't question God. Stand on His promises. Just as He led His people through the wilderness, so He will lead us to the promise of eternal life shared with Him in His kingdom.

Ask and then watch eagerly with expectation for His answer. His power is unlimited.

"In the morning, O Lord, You will hear my voice; in the morning I will order my prayer to You and eagerly watch" (Psalm 5:3).

JULY 6

LOOK UP

I will lift my eyes to the mountains.

Psalm 121:1 (NASB)

Dear Father,
I look up!
I lift up my eyes to the mountains,
And I know my help comes from You.
I look up!
Creator of heaven and earth.
And I know You will not allow me to fall nor my foot to slip.
You are my keeper; I trust in You.
I look up!
And I know You protect me from all evil,
You keep my soul,
And guard my comings and goings,
Today and forever.
I look up!

JULY 7

LEAVE IT ALL TO HIM

For You have tried us, O God; You have refined us as silver is refined.

Psalm 66:10 (NASB)

Sometimes we feel we are tried beyond our strength, but do we really know our strength to endure? Only God knows. Without testing we might not know what we are capable of, nor would we grow. Suffering is not a consequence but God's way of purifying us.

We must leave it all to Him.

The Bible tells us to consider it a joy to encounter various trials. Maybe we don't dance up and down, telling everyone how thrilled we are to face yet another endurance test, but a positive outlook in the face of trial brings a quiet peace and acceptance. When we have experienced great trials, we have the potential for great praise.

We must leave it all to Him.

Think back on the trials you've endured. What can you see as the result of the suffering? Might you say with certainty that you realize life is a gift to be cherished and not a right to be taken for granted? Can you say with Paul that no matter how severe the test, nothing has kept you from the love of God? Do you know with certainty that there is nothing so high, nothing so deep, nothing now or ever that you cannot overwhelmingly conquer through Him who loves you?

We must leave it all to Him.

If we feel as though we have been burdened with trials, there are some we have not been called to bear. We can thank God for those that have been withheld from us and then, leave it all to Him.

Father, help me to let go and leave it all to You.

JULY 8

DISCARDED

For all of us have become like one who is unclean,
and all our righteous deeds are like a filthy garment.

Isaiah 64:6 (NASB)

The rag was worn out and had just been used for a major task. It was too soiled to launder. I threw it away.

Our sinful souls are like filthy rags. They are used and soiled. But we can be grateful for God's mercy; He doesn't throw us away. No, He launders us again and again.

I rely on Your promise, Lord, that "If we confess our sins, You are faithful and just to forgive us and cleanse us from all unrighteousness" (1 John 1:9). Yes, You are faithful. I confess I am a sinner and seek Your mercy and grace.

JULY 9

PRUNING

Your hands made me and fashioned me.

Psalm 119:73 (NASB)

I clipped unmercifully at the evergreen plants in the pot that sat on the patio. They were overgrown and needed a major pruning. They resented it. For weeks they continued to drop brown needles onto the tile floor. They looked as though they were dead and didn't intend to flourish again. It was weeks before I began to see new budding. Still sparsely clad in the brown of mourning color, they offered me hope with the sign of green. I was relieved. I thought they may not live and now they were attempting to bring forth new life. Yeah! The pruning worked.

I've been pruned before to the point that I didn't think or even want to revive my life. But I realize now that I was overgrown with the desires and wants of this life. The brown, dead needles that stunted any spiritual growth were embedded into the branches of my life, sapping all nourishment necessary for growth. There was no alternative but to do a major pruning. God did that. I didn't like it, and I looked as though dead for a long time. I felt stripped and barren of all I had known in my life.

Eventually, without even realizing it, signs of new life began to sprout. My life was taking on a green color; the

Word of God was becoming my nourishment. I was watered and fed by His promises. I didn't prune, and I didn't water. I didn't want it, and I wouldn't have done it. The Pruner saw the need to rid me of the dead life that existed. What a joyous event when the branches sprung forth with exuberant life, the budding became full foliage and the beauty of my soul belonged to Him. How could I have possibly survived had I not been pruned?

Thank You for caring enough to prune, Lord.

JULY 10

A TIME FOR EVERYTHING

"There is a time for everything, and a season for every activity under heaven:

A time to be born and a time to die,

A time to plant and a time to uproot,

A time to kill and a time to heal,

A time to tear down and a time to build,

A time to weep and a time to laugh,

A time to mourn and a time to dance,

A time to scatter stones and a time to gather them,

A time to embrace and a time to refrain,

A time to search and a time to give up,

A time to keep and a time to throw away,

A time to tear and a time to mend,

A time to be silent and a time to speak,

A time to love and a time to hate,

A time for war and a time for peace."

Ecclesiastics 3:1-8 (NIV)

In this list, two things are to be done by God of which we have little or no influence—when we are born, and when we die. The others are left to us.

There is a time for everything, Lord. May my times be in Your hands.

JULY 11

PRIDE

Pride goes before destruction, and a haughty spirit before stumbling.

Proverbs 16:18 (NASB)

Pride! What a killer. It is a grievous sin, and we are all filled with it. Constantly rearing its ugly head, pride prevents us from a close, personal relationship with God.

Think of Pharaoh. He saw Moses's staff become a serpent, the Nile turn to blood, Egypt covered with frogs, every man and beast covered with gnats, swarms of insects blacken the air, and all Egyptian livestock die, along with plagues of hail, boils, and locusts. Total darkness enveloped his country for three days. When the final blow brought the death of all the Egyptian firstborn, he let God's people go. Pharaoh had a hardened heart, crusted with pride. But God got his attention.

The attention getters in our lives may not be as severe, but God uses circumstances to help us depend on Him and not ourselves. We can be as stubborn as Pharaoh.

Being aware of our pride will help us to weed it out of our lives. Slay your pride, take it captive, and put it away forever.

Lord, help me to recognize the pride in my life and to abandon it all for You.

JULY 12

FED BY THE WORD

I, the Lord, am your God, who brought you up from the land of Egypt; open your mouth wide and I will fill it.

Psalm 81:10 (NASB)

The finch's nest in the hanging asparagus plant outside our bedroom door is host to a new family. At mealtime the featherless little creatures have nothing on their minds but eating. In their frenzied state, they scramble to be first as the mother drops food into each wide-open mouth.

Are we so hungry for God's Word that we just can't get enough? God tells us He will fill us with His Word. And it is more than filling. It is sweet. "How sweet are your words to my taste! Yes sweeter than honey to my mouth!" (Psalm 119:103).

God promises that if we will listen to Him and walk with Him, He will feed us with the finest wheat, and with honey He will satisfy us. We need to be fed spiritually by reading the Bible, digesting His Word as regularly as we would feed ourselves physically.

If a mother bird is faithful to feed her young, how much more Our Heavenly Father longs to feed us through His Word. It will be sweet, will make us strong in our faith, and we will grow in the knowledge of our Father.

Let God feed you with His Word.

Lord, I want to be nourished by Your sweet Word.

JULY 13

CONTROL

Who enclosed the sea with doors when, bursting forth, it went out from the womb; when I made a cloud its garment and thick darkness its swaddling band, and I placed boundaries on it and set a bolt and doors, and I said, "Thus far you shall come, but no farther; and here shall your proud waves stop?"

Job 38:8-11 (NASB)

Sometimes when the turbulent tide slams against the cliffs, it looks as though no one is in charge. The sea is out of control, answering to nothing or no one.

There are times when circumstances seem to slam us into the cliff. We're dealt severe blows with the news of illness, death of a loved one, a rebellious child, or an unfaithful spouse. It seems all is out of control. Is no one in charge?

How do we escape feelings of despondency when our world crashes around us? We rely on God's promises. Today's reading gives a powerful assurance of the Creator's control. When we trust in Him we know for certain that, "The Lord will accomplish what concerns me…" (Psalm 138:8).

Our lives are not playthings of chance. God is in charge. Just as He controls the earth speeding around the sun at 67,000 miles per hour, He monitors the ocean. He tells the waves where to stop! He secures us in His sovereign care.

Is God so personal to us that we know whatever happens in our lives, He is in control? Give God charge of your life. Have no concern.

Lord, I know You control the heavens and the earth. I surrender my life to Your care.

JULY 14

SERVE

God said to Moses, "I AM WHO I AM"; and He said, "Thus you shall say to the sons of Israel," I AM has sent me to you.

Exodus 3:14 (NASB)

God spoke to Moses from a burning bush. Imagine Moses trying to comprehend what God was telling him to do. He was to go to the Israelites enslaved in Egypt for four hundred years and tell them that he was going to lead them to freedom, to a land flowing with milk and honey.

Moses was skeptical, to say the least. "What if they will not believe me?" he asked (Exodus 4:1). God assured him that He would be with him every step of the way. His people would listen.

We most likely won't be called to the level Moses was called, but God does use the obedient servant. Do we question? "I'm not capable of what I've been asked to do." That may be true. God doesn't always call the equipped. But He will equip us and help us. He didn't abandon Moses, but was with him all the way to the Promised Land.

I have read about that bush used to get Moses's attention: "Any old bush will do if God sets it alight with His fire."

Has He laid it on your heart to serve Him in a special way?

If God tells us to do it, He will help us do it.
I want to serve You, Lord. Tell me what to do.

JULY 15

MY PROMISE: I FORGIVE

If we confess our sins, He is faithful and just to forgive us our sins and to cleanse us from all unrighteousness.

1 John 1:9 (NKJV)

Dear child,

You know the sin you have committed.

Your conscious and your heart know.

I want you to tell Me about it; to confess.

Do that, and I promise I will forgive you.

I will wash you whiter than snow.

There will be no mention of it again, and you will be purified.

All I ask of you is that you confess, are heartily sorry, and that you resolve never to do it again.

You are cleansed from all unrighteousness.

I love you.

Your Father

JULY 16

CHANGED

For the Son of Man came to seek and to save what was lost.

Luke 19:10 (NIV)

Tax collectors were Jews by birth and worked for the Romans. They became rich by gouging fellow Jews. Zaccheus, a chief tax collector, had heard about Jesus and wanted to get a look at Him. He didn't use his position as tax collector to make his way to the front. He didn't call out to Him. Since he was too little to see over the crowds, he climbed a sycamore tree. Jesus singled him out, telling him to come down immediately and that He would be staying at his house that day. Zaccheus must have scrambled down that tree. But the crowd grumbled. Why would Jesus stay with such a sinner? He is nothing but a crooked tax collector!

What must that visit have been like? We do know Zaccheus's heart was changed. He said, "Look, Lord! Here and now I give half of my possessions to the poor, and if I have cheated anybody out of anything, I will pay back four times the amount" (v. 8). That was a major change of the heart, proven by outward actions.

Zaccheus was changed first because he was interested in Jesus. Secondly, he welcomed Jesus when He told him He would stay with him. Jesus stands at the door and knocks, asking us to welcome Him. When we invite Him in He changes us, much like the major change we see in Zaccheus. It is so simple.

I am willing to be changed, Lord. Change me.

JULY 17

FAMILY PRAYER

> Therefore, confess your sins to one another, and pray for one another so that you may be healed. The effective prayer of a righteous man can accomplish much.
>
> James 5:16 (NASB)

Each month I send out a family prayer calendar. Since I have nine siblings all of whom have children and grand-children, the calendar is full. If it's your birthday, it's your prayer day. A simple prayer is included on the calendar for those who may not know how to pray for one another. Everyone gets it by email.

Praying for our families is a way to truly love them. It narrows the distance that might separate us. The calendar has brought our family closer. Prayer unites families, and can accomplish much.

Consider a way that your family may draw closer through prayer. Would a calendar work for you?

I pray for guidance and protection for my family today, Lord.

JULY 18

OPEN TO CHANGE

That you would walk in a manner worthy of the
God who calls you into His own kingdom and glory.

1 Thessalonians 2:12 (NASB)

I have served in ministry, believing it to be God's will for
my life. There was a time when routine of duty had left
me with a routine prayer life. Dullness settled in; the joy
and enthusiasm which had driven me to the position were
gone. My effectiveness was jeopardized.

I began seeking new opportunities in which God might
use me. I sought to remain open to God's leading, not my
own idea of what I might do. I look back on that time
and believe that God was beckoning me to a form of
higher service.

There will be times when routine may become only
repetition, when serving in church and ministry loses its
meaning or significance.

It is important for us to open ourselves to the need for
change. We can trust in His timing as we wait for guidance.
And when given the go-ahead, follow. When enthusiasm
for serving Him is dulled, be open to change.

I am open to change, Lord. I will wait for Your timing.

JULY 19

SPEECH

Day to day pours forth speech

Psalm 19:2-3 (NASB)

There is a summer storm thousands of miles from here, resulting in waves from seven to ten feet at our beach. To the north of us, they are reaching twenty to twenty-five feet—a very rare occurrence.

For me and many others, it was an "ooh, ah" mid-July morning. I watched in wonder as surfers sailed exultantly across the thunderous, towering waves. What a joy to watch such a powerful demonstration of man interacting with nature.

"The heavens are telling of the glory of God; and their expanse is declaring the work of His hands" (Psalm 19:1). Oh yes, today pours forth speech and declares the work of His hands as its boisterous voice shouts of the extraordinary display of God's creation.

God speaks to us every day in the diversity and wonder of life around us. Some days are more amazing than others, but all are miraculous.

Thank You, Father, for every day—ordinary and extraordinary. Each one speaks of Your wonder.

JULY 20

SURRENDER

Joseph said to them, "Do not be afraid, for am I in God's place? As for you, you meant evil against me, but God meant it for good in order to bring about this present result"

Genesis 50:19-20 (NASB)

Joseph had been sold into slavery. For twenty shekels his brothers let him be carted off to Egypt. He served in the house of Potiphar, an Egyptian officer of Pharaoh. Unjustly accused by Potiphar's wife, Joseph found himself in jail.

But God's plan for Joseph could not be altered by man's plans for the young slave. The chief jailer gave Joseph charge of all the prisoners. Even in prison God was with him. The humble sheepherder went on to be second in command in all of Egypt.

Maybe the prison in your life is fear, loneliness, or poverty. Whatever the situation, we need not be victims of our circumstances if we surrender them to Christ. He has a plan for our life. We must trust Him.

Joseph endured many hardships. But He knew God controlled the circumstances. He goes so far as to assure his brothers that no harm would come to them because of their betrayal of him. He knew that God meant it for good that His plans would bring this result. That is ultimately trusting God. Can we say we trust no matter what?

Can we totally surrender control of our life to God? Can we do so knowing that whatever happens, it is His plan for us?

I surrender control to You, Lord, and trust You for the outcome.

JULY 21

V.I.P.

> Do nothing from selfishness or empty conceit, but with humility of mind regard one another as more important than yourselves; do not merely look out for your own personal interests, but also for the interests of others. Have this attitude in yourselves which was also in Christ Jesus.
>
> Philippians 2:3-5 (NASB)

Most of us have felt important at one time or another. Someone or something made us feel like a Very Important Person. What makes one person seem more important than another? Is it fame, athletic ability, beauty, wealth? These verses tell us we should not feel more important than the next person.

I stand on this tiny parcel of earth, viewing the largest and deepest body of water on the planet. Huge waves tumble over one another, rushing toward me. The massive scope of power and energy is so overwhelming that it's difficult to feel too important.

Then I realize each of us is only important because God sees us as such. After all, He died for us. We may not be important to the world outside of those who love us, but our importance finds its worth in God, Our Father. The God Who created the heavens and the earth created us in His image and likeness. We are important to Him; we are His precious children. That is V.I.P. status.

Lord, help me always remember it's only Your love that makes me a V.I.P.

JULY 22

STONES

Set a guard O Lord, over my mouth; keep watch over the door of my lips.

Psalm 141:3 (NASB)

On a sunny afternoon, I sat in my beach chair watching a flock of seagulls that lined the water's edge. A young man, his wife, and young son came across the sand. The father picked up a rock and threw it at an unsuspecting seagull standing in the water.

The gull went down instantly, flapping and struggling. The woman looked shocked, while the man laughed nervously, glancing around to see if anyone was watching. He took the little boy's hand, and the family moved down the beach. The gull was helpless and unable to move.

I don't believe this man really meant to hurt the bird. I think he threw the rock to show his son how the gull would fly if startled. But his thoughtless action caused pain and injury.

Gossip is like that. We throw stones and hurt people. We may not mean to do harm, but our words can leave someone helpless and hurt. When I was a young mother, an acquaintance of mine became the talk of the town. I joined in the gossip, condemning her lifestyle. Words cannot describe the devastation I felt when I learned that she had taken her own life. I was ashamed of the role I had played in judging her instead of reaching out to help her.

Some try to justify gossip by stating that they are just being truthful and honest. But the Apostle Paul admonishes us, "Do not let any unwholesome talk come out of your mouths, but only what is helpful for building others up according to their needs, that it may benefit those who listen" (Ephesians 4:29). Consider this: stones can be used as weapons or as building blocks. How will you use the "stones" of your words?

May every word that comes from my mouth be pleasing to You, O Lord.

JULY 23

RESTORE

Bear with each other and forgive whatever griev-
ances you may have against one another. Forgive as
the Lord forgave you. And over all these virtues put
on love, which binds them all together in perfect
unity.

Colossians 3:13-14 (NIV)

Most people aren't familiar with a GFIC. It's a ground fault circuit interrupter. Many homeowners when loosing power in an outlet don't know that simply pushing the red reset button restores the power.

It makes me think of broken relationships. Words or actions hurt and damage, sometimes severing all communication. It would be nice if we could simply push the button and restore relationships.

I also know of relationships that simply fade away. It can happen without our knowing it. We gradually begin to realize we're just not close to that person anymore. We have little in common. Perhaps different interests and lifestyles have distanced us from each other. It is particularly sad when it happens between parents and adult children or between adult siblings.

Is it time for you to restore communication? Push the reset button by maybe writing a note or making a phone call. Distance does not have to separate us.

Lord, help me to restore broken relationships.

JULY 24

TERMITES

When an unclean spirit goes out of a man, he goes through dry places, seeking rest, and finds none. Then he says, "I will return to my house from which I came." And when he comes, he finds it empty, swept, and put in order. Then he goes and takes with him seven other spirits more wicked than himself, and they enter and dwell there; and the last state of that man is worse than the first. So shall it also be with this wicked generation.

Matthew 12:43-45 (NKJV)

We had no choice. The termites had come back for the third time and insisted on taking up residence in our home. We had to tent. Every living plant had to be removed, food stored in plastic bags, and we had to be gone for 24 hours. We had been driven from our home by the wood-destroying organisms.

The first signs of their existence were wood droppings that appeared in the kitchen walls and eventually in the fireplace wall. They were eating through our house, and the evidence of their invasion was not evident until they had fully established residency.

In today's reading, Jesus is talking to the Israelites about the evil kings they had allowed to rule. They would have a good king who would help rid themselves of idolatry. But they had not replaced it with a love for God, and an evil king found it easy to bring back idol worship.

However, the message is for all of us. It is not enough to rid ourselves of the sin in our lives, but we must be filled with the Holy Spirit. If we are empty and not praying, reading God's Word, and communing with Him, Satan will be back finding us to be an easy target.

The termites remind me of how necessary it is for us to purge the sinful nature and return to God, being so full of Him, absolutely nothing can take His place in our souls.

Fill me with the Holy Spirit so that nothing will take up residence in my heart but You, Lord God.

JULY 25

TO THE BRIM

Dear Father,
I will be glad in Your strength and rejoice in Your salvation.

You have given me my heart's desires, and not withheld anything I have asked of You. You bless me with good, and crown me with Your goodness, which is as precious as gold to me.

I asked life of You and You have given it to me, extending my length of days.

Through Your salvation, I have known abundant blessings, for You have blessed me.

I am joyful, filled to the brim with gladness in Your presence.

Psalm 21:1-6

JULY 26

WAIT

Now he waited seven days, according to the appointed time set by Samuel, but Samuel did not come to Gilgal; and the people were scattering from him. So Saul said, "Bring to me the burnt offering and the peace offerings." And he offered the burnt offering.

1 Samuel 13:8-9 (NASB)

The Israelites were ready to fight the Philistines. But before doing battle, the prophet Samuel was to offer a burnt offering, asking for God's favor. Saul waited seven days, and when Samuel didn't show, Saul became anxious and offered the sacrifice. He couldn't wait on God and took matters into his own hands.

What was the big deal for Saul to offer the sacrifice? After all, he was king, Samuel was late, and something needed to be done about the situation. His men were fearful, hiding themselves from the Philistines who were great in number. But God didn't accept Saul's excuses. God had told him to wait, and he didn't. He lost his kingdom. "But now your kingdom shall not endure" (v. 14).

Andrew Murray says,

> The whole duty and blessedness of waiting on God has its root in this, that He is such a blessed Being, full to overflowing, of goodness and power and life and joy, that we, however wretched, cannot for any time come into contact with Him, without that life and power secretly, silently, beginning to enter into us and blessing us.9

Wait.

No matter how I feel, help me to wait in Your Presence.

JULY 27

JEALOUSY

His brothers were jealous of him.

Genesis 37:11 (NASB)

Jealousy is destructive and unproductive. As the story of Joseph's brothers' jealousy and hatred unfolds, we find them plotting to kill him.

We think we aren't jealous enough of anyone to want to kill them. Oh, we may admit being a little jealous, but we can justify the reasons for it. It can disguise itself as self-righteousness or constructive criticism. Therefore, it is just not all that serious.

But left unchecked, it grows. We may find ourselves wishing that bad times or even harm might come to those who are the object of our jealousy.

We are capable of jealousy. We must rein it in! How? The source of all our resolve, Our Father. He can heal us of it; He can wipe it away.

Deliver me from the snares of jealousy, Father. Replace the restless uneasy feeling with peace and contentment. Help me love the one who is the object of my jealousy. Help me to be triumphant in this battle.

JULY 28

ASSURANCE

The time of my departure has come. I have fought the good fight, I have finished the course, I have kept the faith; in the future there is laid up for me a crown of righteousness.

2 Timothy 4:7-8 (NASB)

The dungeon was damp and chilly when Paul sat in a Roman prison awaiting execution. He had his writing materials, an occasional visitor or two, and his trusted friend, Luke. In these circumstances the apostle wrote his last letter to Timothy.

Paul knew that he would soon die, and he was ready. He told Timothy there was a "crown of righteousness" waiting for him. He looked forward to the eternal glory that would be his. Imagine how comforted Timothy was by this touching letter. He knew he would not see his beloved friend and mentor again in this life but was confident he would see him in heaven.

In the weeks preceding my husband's heart surgery, we talked at length about the peace he had in knowing that if he didn't survive the surgery, he would be with Our Lord. This assurance from him afforded me peace of mind knowing he was able to confidently put his faith and fate into the hands of his Lord.

Are you at peace when thinking about death? Can you say, as Paul, that you have fought a good fight, that you have kept the faith and are ready to receive your crown of righteousness?

Father, give me peace and confidence in You to face death.

JULY 29

ACTIONS

In everything set them an example by doing what is good.

Titus 2:7 (NIV)

"Bev, I'd like you to meet my husband," she said, introducing him to her ministry coworker. "I recognize you," he told Bev. "It was at the grocery store, and I watched you return your cart to the pick-up area." Unknowingly, Bev was observed in her courtesy and consideration for others.

"Actions speak louder than words" is an overused cliché. But our actions, especially when we think no one is watching, speak volumes about who we really are. As we become more like Christ, we act more like Christ. Godly people are thoughtful people.

Examine your actions. Are you setting a good example?

Help me, Lord, that in everything I do it may bear a reflection of my love for You.

JULY 30

DWELLS

> Do you not know that you are the temple of God
> and that the Spirit of God dwells in you?
>
> 1 Corinthians 3:16 (NKJV)

It is an awesome thought: Christ dwells in us!

Yes, He lives in us.

I don't always feel Him; sometimes when I want to hear Him, I don't.

But that is okay, because I know He is here, dwelling in me.

I need only to wait quietly, patiently.

And I need to continue to be here with Him, here in our place of hushed communion.

I don't need to talk.

He doesn't need to talk.

That is okay, because I know He dwells in me.

I am here, Lord.

JULY 31

HE IS IN YOUR HANDS

Now I know that the Lord saves His anointed; He will answer him from His holy heaven with the saving strength of His right hand.

Psalm 20:6 (NASB)

Dear Father,

I sit here in this early morning hour, reading Your Word. Yesterday's news that gripped my heart lies at peace within me. I faced the disturbing facts, brought my prayer to You, and settle in the firm belief that all is in Your hands.

He is in Your hands, O Father.

To those of us who love him, his future looks bleak. But I know "The Lord has established His throne in the heavens, and His sovereignty rules over all" (Psalm 103:19).

I know "The Lord will accomplish what concerns me" (Psalm 138:8).

Yes, Father, Your Word brings truth and assurance that he is in Your hands. I hold on to the hope. I commit him to You and will face this day doing those things that are expected of me.

He is in Your hands.

AUGUST 1

FASTING

So we fasted and sought our God concerning this matter, and He listened to our entreaty.

Ezra 8:23 (NASB)

Fasting humbles us because it reminds us of our complete dependence upon God. When Nehemiah heard that the walls of Jerusalem had not been rebuilt, he sat down and wept and mourned for days. He says "I was fasting and praying before the God of heaven" (Nehemiah 1:4).

There are different societal uses for fasting, but for the Christian, fasting is a voluntary abstinence from food for spiritual purposes. When going without food for a designated time, we can devote time to God by not following the daily routine of preparing and eating food. When we fast, we discover that much of the food we normally eat is unnecessary. Hunger can remind us of our dependence on God. Fasting can honor God by expressing that He is more important to us than food.

Some schedules make it difficult to fast all day; try fasting from midnight to noon.

Jesus teaches us about fasting in Matthew 6:16-18, cautioning us not to put on a gloomy face so that everyone will know we are going without food. Our Father knows the sacrifice we are making.

May my fasting remind me of my complete dependence on You, Lord God.

AUGUST 2

CARELESSNESS

The wisdom of the prudent is to give thought to their ways.

Proverbs 14:8 (NIV)

It wasn't with criminal intent, but carelessness. Still nineteen hundred acres burned, two hundred homes destroyed, and two dozen people were injured. Aided by strong Santa Ana winds, fire swept across southern California, leaving destruction and grief in its path. Failure to make sure a campfire was completely put out left embers that roared to life as the winds swept in.

Sometimes we act without prudence, not making the effort to assure no one will get hurt by our actions. We may not list carelessness as our most grievous act. But it seemed so simple to make sure the campfire was out. Carelessness led to disaster.

Lord, help me to be careful in all my actions. Sometimes I charge carelessly into situations and forget to consider the consequences. I want to be care-full.

AUGUST 3

NEGATIVE FEELINGS

For what I am doing, I do not understand; for I am not practicing what I would like to do, but I am doing the very thing I hate.

Romans 7:15 (NASB)

I relate to Paul when he talks of the conflict. I find it difficult to reign in negative feelings. I want to always be joyful, to be so in tune with God that nothing disturbs me. But my best intentions don't change me. Most often it is the smallest things that drag me away from the peace and contentment I seek.

For instance: when my internet goes down or I'm kept waiting; when the car in front of me is going too slow and I can't pass, or I get an automated answer when I want a knowledgeable person. The list can go on.

Like Paul, I abhor the sin in me, knowing that I am doing the very thing I don't want to do. I want to be patient and understanding; yet in some circumstances, I'm not. He called himself a wretched man. Yes, I too know that nothing good dwells in my flesh, and if it were not for Christ setting me free from this grip of sin, I would be doomed to hopelessness. Sin dwells in me, and if I try to deal with it apart from God's saving grace, I lose.

I have learned to say my heart prayer, "I love You, Jesus," when I am confronted with impatience and negative feelings. Annoyances don't bother me when I depend on Him.

Father, draw me close, that I am able to reign in any negative feelings.

AUGUST 4

MY ROCK

Psalm 31:1-5

Where do we turn when in distress? King David prays that God would deliver him from the snares of his enemies. But if God chose not to act immediately, David asks that He would protect him, be his rock and house of defense. We too can pray with the psalmist that by God's grace we may be safe in Him.

Dear Father,

I have taken refuge in You. Let me not be ashamed.

In Your righteousness deliver me.

Oh please listen to me and rescue me quickly.

Be my Rock of strength, and

a Stronghold that will save me.

Yes Lord! You are my Rock and my Fortress.

For Your names sake, You will lead and guide me.

The world lays in wait to snare me,

but You will pull me out of its net,

for You are my strength.
I submit all to You.
You are the Lord God of truth.
Amen!

AUGUST 5

A TURN OF THE HEAD

Set your mind on the things above, not on the things that are on the earth.

Colossians 3:2 (NASB)

The beach was nearly deserted as I walked briskly on my regular route along the cliffs of the shoreline. The breaking dawn cast its shades of soft pink on the rolling waves. Godwits, plovers, and sanderlings ignored my presence as they busily moved about, jabbing their bills in the wet sand.

I was absorbed in the wonder of God's creation, praising and thanking Him for the sweet communion we shared, when a house under construction along the cliffs caught my attention. As I walked, I became engrossed in the residences that were perched stately upon the shore, capturing pristine views from La Jolla to San Clemente. "Oh, Lord," I prayed, "how I would love to live on Pacific Avenue right at the water's edge. You know how much I love the water."

I walked for several blocks, gazing up and imagining what it would be like to live in one of those houses.

Some time passed before I looked back toward the sea. Wow! What had I done? I had abandoned all thoughts of praising God for what I had to be caught up in thoughts of what I wanted. And all it had taken was a simple turn of the head.

When I focused on God's creation, I centered my thoughts on Him and all that He had given me. My heart was filled with peace. But when I turned my head and looked away from Him, I found an urgent, restless longing for the things I wanted.

We do this often every day. We allow ourselves to get caught up in the world and in the things we want. Through prayer, we can turn toward God and His abiding presence in our lives and away from that longing for empty things.

Today I will turn my head toward You.

AUGUST 6

BE CAREFUL

We do not know what we ought to pray for.

Romans 8:26 (NIV)

Be careful what you pray for. I was certain that I wanted to live on Pacific Avenue, right at the ocean's edge with its panoramic white water views. But I didn't know what the future held for those houses perched on the cliffs. Decks and patios hang perilously over the edge as the earth beneath them shifts and the sandstone cliffs erode.

Homeowners want to shore up the cliffs with man made methods, but others believe in planned retreat. This means that as nature decides, so go the cliffs, and the houses would fall into the sea. Countless hours and millions of dollars have been invested by those fighting to save their homes.

We often pray, asking God for things; not what we need, but what we want, only to find that if we had gotten what we asked for, it would not have been good for us. Indeed, it may have been harmful. I am grateful that I didn't get what I wanted.

God could give us anything we wanted whether it's good for us or not. But He knows what's best and what we need. Leave all in His hands, knowing that He will give you those gifts of lasting value—the eternal rewards.

We don't live on the cliff, but the spectacular white water views we enjoy from our home make us grateful for what we have.

I pray for Your will in my life, Lord. Not mine, but Yours.

AUGUST 7

SWIFT PUNISHMENT

Then Moses lifted up his hand and struck the rock
twice with his rod; and water came forth abundantly, and the congregation and their beasts drank.

Numbers 20:11 (NASB)

Time was near for Moses and the Israelites to enter the
Promised Land; it had been almost forty years. They were
camped at Kadesh in the wilderness, and there was not
enough water. Harsh complaints by the people against
Moses and Aaron brought the brothers to God begging for
His help. He told them that with all the people watching,
Moses was to take a rod and speak to the rock, telling it to
yield water.

They called the congregation together, and Moses said,
"Listen now, you rebels, shall we bring forth water for you
out of this rock?" (v. 10). He lifted the rod and struck the
rock twice; water gushed forth. What was he thinking? He
was told to speak to the rock, not strike it!

He was obviously very upset with his people, calling
them rebels. And he asks, shall we bring forth water? So
when he raised the rod and struck the rock, not once but
twice, it was an act of show, demonstrating his power, not
God's. He was terribly provoked and tired of their complaints. But he did not acknowledge God in the miracle.

God's punishment for disobedience was swift and final. Moses and Aaron would not enter the Promised Land.

The Bible has numerous accounts of the consequences of disobedience, but we think it doesn't apply to us. He gave us His commandments. When we disobey, why do we think our punishment would be any less than that of His servant, Moses? He was denied entrance into the Promised Land. Will we be denied heaven?

I know of Your commandments, Lord. I will obey.

AUGUST 8

BLOOM

> But Jonah ran away from the Lord…and sailed for Tarshish to flee from the Lord.
>
> Jonah 1:3 (NIV)

We've all heard it: "Bloom where you are planted." But for me, God has planted me where I can bloom. He uprooted me from familiar earth and transplanted me into rich, fertile soil.

I resisted and fought to stay where I was, even though the weeds were beginning to choke the life out of my soul. My roots were deep, and I hung on tenaciously with the belief that I would overcome the threatening enemy; I could do it on my own. When I couldn't, God thrust me out of my comfort zone and transplanted me. With His tender care for me, I have bloomed.

I think of Jonah's resistance to God's plan for him. Nineveh was a wicked city, and Jonah had always hated and feared the Assyrians. He tried to run, but God got his attention in the belly of a whale (v. 12). Then Jonah obeyed.

God may not take such drastic measures with us as He did with Jonah, to plant us where He wants us. But He does what it takes. Has God uprooted and transplanted you? Maybe like me, you can you look back at the process and see positive results. Don't resist when God moves you to other ground; the Gardener knows what you need. Read His Word, and seek His guidance. He will care for you; you can blossom.

Help me to be open to Your will for my life, O Lord. I want to bloom for You.

AUGUST 9

THE FAMILIAR

Dawn is breaking.

I hear the plaintive cooing of a mourning dove outside the window as the grandfather clock chimes in on the hour.

Coffee is brewing.

The house is still except for the familiar.

My Bible is opened to Psalm 5:11-12 (NASB):

But let all who take refuge in You be glad, let them ever sing for joy; and may You shelter them, that those who love Your name may exult in You. For it is You who blesses the righteous man, O Lord, You surround him with favor as with a shield.

He alone is our Refuge. And the sights, sounds, and smells of all that is familiar bring feelings of comfort for those of us who love His name and exult in Him. He blesses us, and surrounds us with favor. We enjoy the familiar surroundings.

Yes, Lord, all is futile today unless You are in it. I take pleasure in the familiar. But without You, all would be nothing. Only You.

AUGUST 10

ENDURE

My soul, wait in silence for God only, for my hope is from Him.

Psalm 62:5 (NASB)

I wonder if I would be able to endure the physical suffering and pain I've seen friends and loved ones go through.

When I learned of my friend's stroke, I begged God to take her quickly home. I petitioned Him unceasingly that she would not linger but enter her heavenly reward immediately. After a time I realized that God's plans for her, or anyone for whom I pray, are above my plans for them.

Then I prayed: "In Your time, Lord, not in my time. I ask that You fill her with supernatural peace and tranquility in the battle her body is raging with nature. May she have complete trust in Your promise that no matter what happens, You will never leave her nor forsake her."

When our bodies struggle with disease, Satan looks for the opportunity to prescribe discouragement. But we can endure, because God promises His grace, which is sufficient for anything.

Expect that God will provide. Trust Him to give the supply you will need—strength and endurance for the battle.

Lord, help me remember that You will uphold me and those I love in times of need.

AUGUST 11

TREASURES

O how I love Your law! It is my meditation all the day. Your commandments make me wiser than my enemies, for they are ever mine.

Psalm 119: 97- 98 (NASB)

There are days when the beach is strewn with ocean treasures; seashells more numerous than I can gather. My favorite is the sand dollar. When I find one, I'm thrilled and scoop it right up.

A sand dollar is thin with a circular body about two to four inches wide. It looks like a large, white coin. The top surface has an arrangement in the shape of a five-pointed star. Each one looks as though it has been personally etched by nature's hand.

God's word is filled with spiritual treasures, each one irresistible. We don't have to be theologians to understand the Bible. We can begin with simple steps, reading a little each day. "Then He opened their minds to understand the Scriptures" (Luke 24:45). Jesus is the author. He can teach us. What joy to sit at His feet and be able to learn.

I think what I would miss if I didn't walk on the beach. But more so, I think what I would miss if I didn't read God's Word daily. There I find jeweled treasures that make my life rich, full of peace and joy.

Search for God's treasures in His Word. They have been personally etched for you.

Thank You, Father, for the wonder of Your Word.

AUGUST 12

OUR ENVIRONMENT

Do not be yoked together with unbelievers. For what do righteousness and wickedness have in common? Or what fellowship can light have with darkness?

2 Corinthians 6:14 (NIV)

We had lived here at the water's edge for only a month or two. I was on my early-morning beach walk when I spotted a starfish on the sand. I wasn't well acquainted with the sea life that existed here, but I knew a starfish when I saw it. I was thrilled, scooped it up, and brought it home.

Starfish are usually fairly sluggish, have five or six arms and get pretty stiff when you try to pick them up. I learned that only later. I didn't realize it was alive. It soon died. I felt terrible that I had removed the creature from its environment and it couldn't survive.

Today's reading cautions us about seeking companionship outside of our Christian environment. Of course we associate with others who are not believers, but to marry one who is not of our belief or to spend a lot of time with someone who doesn't believe can test our faith. Faith can die if not in an environment that nourishes the soul.

Is our faith strong enough not to be scooped up from the vitality of life that it feeds on through hearing God's Word, studying the Bible with others, praying with others? Our faith can die slowly when removed from those things that make it alive!

Father, I want my faith to be alive. I will seek out others who help contribute to a healthy, active, believing environment.

AUGUST 13

GUIDANCE

Lead me in Your truth and teach me, for You are the God of my salvation; for You I wait all the day. Remember, O Lord, Your compassion and Your loving kindnesses, for they have been from of old. Do not remember the sins of my youth or my transgressions; according to Your loving kindness remember me, for Your goodness' sake, O Lord.

Psalm 25:4-7 (NASB)

Dear Father,

David's psalm expresses the desire of my heart.

I long for Your guidance, knowing it is here in Your Word.

I don't demand answers as to the direction I should go, but I ask.

Help me to learn from Your Word, that I might obey Your commands.

The sins of my youth are many, as I followed my own stubborn will.

Even now I slip occasionally into that mind-set.

But I seek Your great mercy and love.

I know that You love me and want only my good.

Father, I lift up my soul to You!

AUGUST 14

BASKING IN THE MOMENT

Oh give thanks to the Lord, call upon His name...

1 Chronicles 16:8 (NASB)

I sit here in the warm afternoon August sun, grateful for the time to relax and absorb the beauty of the day. I close my eyes, thankful for these rare, precious moments, hosting a tranquil heart, and praising God for each second. I call it basking in the moment.

It is no wonder I cherish these moments. When I went shopping the other day, music was blaring in the huge outlet store. Every aisle was jam packed with Halloween, Thanksgiving, and Christmas items. It is difficult to look at Christmas trees in August! I refused to be drawn into the commercialism, parked the empty cart, and left.

I do love Thanksgiving and Christmas. I look forward to both holidays with great anticipation. Families and friends, even our nation, come together at Thanksgiving to give thanks for God's blessings. And think of Christmas—a season alive with carols filling the air, praising the newborn King.

Each holiday brings a bountiful spirit of giving. Countless boxes of food are given away. Volunteers donate time to facilities where generous dinners with all the trimmings are available to those who otherwise can't afford such a feast. Yes, we know that although Thanksgiving and Christmas besiege us with materialism, the spirit of generosity and kindness exist.

And those of us who belong to Christ Jesus can resist the worldly allure of a material holiday. We can look past the commercialism. "Thank You Jesus," should always be in our hearts and on our lips. Every day is a holiday of Thanksgiving. Every day is a holiday of praising our King. Every day we can bask in the moment of His presence.

I am here, Lord, basking in the moment.

AUGUST 15

RICH OR POOR

> Blessed are you who are poor, for yours is the kingdom of God.
>
> Luke 6:20 (NASB)

I grew up poor, so as a youngster I felt these words meant God intended me to be poor so I could go to heaven, and there I would live in God's kingdom. It was simple.

But growing in God's Word has taught me the true meaning of Christ's words. Poor in spirit is my awareness of spiritual bankruptcy. Not so simple. My desire for the riches of the earth is at odds with my spiritual desires for

God. I can be wealthy or poor, but I am blessed if I know the poverty of my soul without God.

If on the outside my appearance is one of means, but my soul is worn and tattered, I need to recognize that state and adorn it with God's Word. I need to dress my soul in robes of godliness and righteousness.

Rich or poor, the things of this world don't last. I must seek the kingdom of God and all things will come to me. I'm grateful that I'm growing up.

I am rich in Your Spirit, O Lord.

AUGUST 16

DISAPPOINTED

To You they cried out and were delivered; In You they trusted and were not disappointed.

Psalm 22:5 (NASB)

It's been a tumultuous week, Lord, and I'm exhausted. I am continually disappointed by the actions of others, and I get weary from struggling to overcome my reaction.

I realize that my anger toward those who disappoint me is a defense mechanism. I've used it often, because I'm not equipped to deal with it any other way. There are those I love and want so much for, and yet I can't help.

You know how I feel, don't You, Lord? You love me with an even greater love. Yet I continue to turn from You, follow my own stubborn will, and repeatedly disappoint You.

Yes, You know this disappointed heart.

Lord, help me to stay focused on You through all the disappointments.

AUGUST 17

RISE ABOVE IT

"Rise above it," I tell myself. But it can be so difficult at times to rise above it—the pain, disappointment, illness. But for this moment, I have done it. I have come here discouraged and tired, opened the Word, and read Psalm 95:1-7 (NASB):

> Dear Father,
> I come and sing for joy to You.
> I shout joyfully to You, the rock of my salvation.
> I come into Your presence with thanksgiving and shout joyfully to You with song.
> Oh, You are a great God; a great King.
> The depths of the earth and the highest mountain peaks are in Your hands.
> The sea is also Yours; You made it; You formed all the dry land.
> I come and worship; bowing down before You.
> I kneel before You, my Lord and Maker!

You are my God, and I am Yours, a sheep of Your pasture; a sheep of Your hand.

Yes! It works.

By reading the words and feeling it in my soul, I am lifted up, ready to face what comes.

Only in the joy of You, O Lord am I able to rise above it. Thank You!

AUGUST 18

A LOVING RELATIONSHIP

"And just as He called and they would not listen, so they called and I would not listen," says the Lord of hosts.

Zechariah 7:13 (NASB)

God's people no longer desired a loving relationship with Him. They were much too involved in their lives, which were devoid of God. Even their fasting became a ritual, lacking repentance, or reverence for Him. They paid no attention to His commands but "turned a stubborn shoulder" (v. 11).

Zechariah warned them that just as they would not listen to Him, there would come a day when they would call to Him, and He would not listen.

Our lives unfold each day with little thought of Him. Most of what we do is for earthly provisions and possessions. We seek unlimited pleasure, doing what it takes to get what we want. We have hardened our heart toward Him, ignoring and refusing Him. When difficulty, tragedy, or illnesses strike, we turn to Him, desperate for help.

Our Father desires a relationship with us. Imagine living in our home, having no communication with our loved ones. Is it any more possible to be in a relationship with God, only talking to Him when calling on Him in time of need?

His warning—and it is indeed a warning—if you don't listen to Him, He won't listen to you.

Father, I long for a loving relationship with You. My heart is softened toward You. Help me to draw ever closer to You.

AUGUST 19

CALLED

But Peter put them all out, and knelt down and prayed. And turning to the body he said, "Tabitha, arise." And she opened her eyes, and when she saw Peter she sat up. Then he gave her his hand and lifted her up; and when he had called the saints and widows, he presented her alive.

Acts 9:40-41 (NKJV)

From Abraham to the disciples, God called people to serve Him. When they responded, He didn't give them new and different abilities but instead molded and used the personalities for His purpose.

There are many examples in the Bible of God's continual use for His servants. Think of Peter who was a fisherman on the Sea of Galilee when Jesus called him. And here we read that this same fisherman raised Dorcas from the dead. That is powerful!

God has found us imperfect, just as He did Peter. We are impatient, selfish, self-centered, and full of pride. But even though God sees our imperfections, He longs to use us for His good. Sometimes He prepares hearts to respond to His call the moment we are needed. When God calls us, there is such a burden on our hearts, that we really have no choice but to respond. We will know when this happens.

When He is ready for the use of His vessel, we don't need to ask, "How must I change to serve Him?" But we can ask,

How will You use me, Lord?

AUGUST 20

PRAYER

It was at this time that He went off to the mountain
to pray, and He spent the whole night in prayer to
God.

Luke 6:12-13 (NASB)

It wasn't unusual for Jesus to spend much time in prayer.
This verse in Luke says He spent all night. In Mark 1:35
it says, " In the early morning, while it was still dark, Jesus
got up, left the house, and went away to a secluded place,
and was praying there."

I've wondered how Jesus prayed to His Father. What
did He say? Whom did He pray for? He told us how to
pray when He said, "Pray then in this way, 'Our Father who
is in heaven, hallowed be Your name'" (Matthew 6:9).

We know He prayed for Peter. He said, "Simon, Simon,
behold, Satan has demanded permission to sift you like
wheat; but I have prayed for you, that your faith may not
fail" (Luke 22:31).

Jesus was God, so why in His divinity did He pray?
Because He was also man, subject to the same suffering as
we; He needed His Father's direction and blessing.

And here is a Son's prayer to His Father. The hour is
drawing near when He will die; He prays,

Father, the hour has come; glorify Your Son, that the Son may glorify You, even as You gave Him authority over all flesh, that to all whom You have given Him, He may give eternal life. This is eternal life, that they may know You, the only true God, and Jesus Christ whom You have sent. I glorified You on the earth, having accomplished the work which You have given Me to do. Now, Father, glorify Me together with Yourself, with the glory which I had with You before the world was.

John 17:1-5 (NASB)

Jesus, You have taught me how to pray. May I glorify Your Name before the Father.

AUGUST 21

BEYOND UNDERSTANDING

And the peace of God, which surpasses all understanding, will guard your hearts and minds through Christ Jesus.

Philippians 4:7 (NKJV)

God promises peace in all circumstances. Times of my life have been stormy, tossing me about in tumultuously rough waters. I longed for the peace promised me in Gods'

Word—peace beyond understanding, not peace because of understanding.

I wondered if peace because of understanding might come if I tried to live a good life. It might come if I thought positive thoughts, attended support groups where I could share my difficulties with those who were experiencing the same trials. Maybe if I tried a life change. I could move, find new friends, begin an exercise program, or go back to school. I wanted peace.

But I've learned peace only comes from knowing that God is in control. And that I must be anxious for nothing, and in everything by prayer and supplication, always with thanksgiving, I am to let my request be made known to God. I can make all the changes that I deem necessary to find peace. But I need only to stand firm right where I am and trust in Him. That is something I must practice daily.

Though the storm rages around us, we find peace and serenity in Him, intimacy with Him who is the Prince of Peace.

Lord God, I long for peace. Help me to draw close to You in every situation, resting on Your promise that I can know peace beyond understanding.

AUGUST 22

RESTORING

Have mercy on me, O God, according to Your unfailing love; according to Your great compassion blot out my transgressions. Wash away all my iniquity and cleanse me from my sin.

Psalm 51:1-2 (NIV)

One of my favorite beach times is just after high tide. The sand appears to be in its purest state. The debris that cluttered the shore is swept away. The surging waves have restored it to a pristine condition. The ocean and the beach interact with each other moving and cleansing. Likewise, the debris that clutters our lives can be swept clean. When we interact with a forgiving God, we welcome His love and forgiveness that wash over us like the surging waves, purifying us and literally sweeping our lives clean from sin.

God calls us to live a life wholly pleasing to Him. He desires us to examine our true attitudes and motives. He knows our sinful natures, but He tells us to come before Him and acknowledge our sins. "For I know my transgressions and my sin is ever before me" (v.3). Then as promised, He renews a steadfast spirit within, sustaining us to know and do His will.

We ask Him to restore us that we might say, "I am cleansed, renewed, and forgiven!" God's mercies are new every morning. Just as the rushing tide restores the littered beach, so His grace and mercy wash over us restoring joy and gladness to our lives.

Acknowledge your transgressions before Almighty God today.

Father, cleanse me. Wash me clean.

AUGUST 23

TRUST

> Go to the sea and throw in a hook, and take the first fish that comes up; and when you open its mouth, you will find a shekel. Take that and give it to them for you and Me.
>
> Matthew 17:27 (NASB)

I've read this scripture many times, but have brushed over it, never meditating on the depth of its lesson. Jesus provides everything! He meets all my needs, right down to the smallest detail. A fish was the means Jesus used to pay taxes. How simple.

One day I suffered a disappointment. It rocked me. After a few hours of battling injured feelings, I turned it over to God.

Waking tired from a restless night, the words from Proverbs 3:5,6 came to mind. "Trust in the Lord with all your heart and do not lean on your own understanding.

In all your ways acknowledge Him, and He will make your paths straight." Yes! Trust Him. He would handle my situation.

With a lightened heart, I entered the daily time of peaceful communion with Him, the One who loves me most! The situation didn't change, but I was changed. I was grateful for the peace I found in the turmoil.

Does having a personal relationship with Him take us through the storm? Yes!

Jesus does see to every detail. Peter didn't question; he trusted the Lord and then went fishing!

Trust Him with everything. There is nothing He can't handle.

Thank You, Jesus, for the peace.

AUGUST 24

CONTENT

> I have learned to be content in whatever circumstances I am.
>
> Philippians 4:11 (NASB)

I am grateful that this is an example (not a command) of how Paul was content, no matter what the circumstances were. This same disciple tells us to rejoice always and to be anxious about nothing. How can we live as Paul tells us? Is he saying that in trials and grief that we are to be content, rejoice, and not to be anxious? It seems that is out of the realm of nature. It is. It is a super nature that lives in us. The Holy Spirit lives in us as He lived in Paul.

> But you are not in the flesh but in the Spirit, if indeed the Spirit of God dwells in you. Now if anyone does not have the Spirit of Christ, he is not His. And if Christ is in you, the body is dead because of sin, but the Spirit is life because of righteousness. But if the Spirit of Him who raised Jesus from the dead dwells in you, He who raised Christ from the dead will also give life to your mortal bodies through His Spirit who dwells in you.

> Romans 8:9-11 (NASB)

I admit that I would like to face adversity—indeed, even the irritating challenges of everyday life—without stress and anxiety. The only way I can is to remember that it is not my struggle alone, for I could never accomplish that on my own. I've tried and failed miserably. But I rely on the Holy Spirit to help me, because He lives in me. It is supernatural, not natural.

Remind me, most Holy Spirit, it is not by my power but by Yours that I can be content in every circumstance.

AUGUST 25

FALLING IN LOVE

For God so loved the world that He gave His only begotten Son, that whoever believes in Him shall not perish, but have eternal life.

John 3:16 (NASB)

When we fall in love, the initial state is brimming with excitement and joy. Consideration of self is so wrapped up in another that it is difficult to identify ourselves. We have a persistent longing to be together. No matter in what stage of life we are, we can think back and recall our first love. The feelings and thrills can be remembered.

But there is no short road to lasting love. We learn that love is oftentimes sacrifice, compromise, patience and at times, repressing our feelings in lieu of conflict.

Today's verse speaks of such perfect love that we can't comprehend it. It is God's love for us. It is a love so deep that He gave His only Son to die for us on the cross. Would we actually sacrifice our lives for the one we love?

Have we ever loved God with such intensity that our identity is wrapped in Him? Do we feel joy and excitement in such pure love? Do we long to be with Him? These are questions we might ask ourselves when we know He loves us so much that He gave His Son for us.

God, such love I cannot comprehend!

AUGUST 26
WHAT YOU WANT

Now the God of peace…equip you in every good
thing to do His will, working in us that which is
pleasing in His sight, through Jesus Christ, to
whom be the glory forever and ever.

Hebrews 13:20-21 (NASB)

They were in the checkout line at a small market. The two-year-old was persistent. "Please, Daddy, can I have these?
Please? Please?"

"We have some at home, son," his father patiently
responded. But it was time to check the item, and the
father finally gave in. I smiled as I watched him carry the
child through the parking lot.

"But why can't I open them now," the boy whined as he
clung to his box of fish crackers.

The scene reminds me of how often I have persistently
asked my heavenly Father for things. I have been like that
child, insisting upon having my way and wanting it now. But
I like to think that I have grown, giving way to spiritual maturity. "When I was a child, I spoke as a child, I understood as
a child, I thought as a child; but when I became a man, I put
away childish things" (1 Corinthians 13:11-12 NKJV).

I have learned to say, "I want what You want," and I
often say it out loud. Saying those words brings tranquility

of spirit, thanksgiving, and complete rest of heart. Someone wrote, "God's will on earth is always joy, always tranquility."

Father, I want what You want.

AUGUST 27

EVIDENCE

Even before there is a word on my tongue, behold ,
O Lord, You know it all.

Psalm 139:4 (NASB)

Dear Father,

A difficult truth for me to comprehend is that You, the God of the universe

Are a personal God to me.

You care for me, concerned about every feeling and emotion,

Every move that I make.

You know my heart, read my mind.

You know what I'm going to say and do before I do.

No, I don't understand, and I cannot fathom such a God.

But by faith I know it to be so.

I know because of the evidence of Your presence in my life.

You and I have an intimate relationship.

I cherish our relationship, My Lord and My God.

AUGUST 28

YESTERDAY

This is the day the Lord has made; let us rejoice and
be glad in it.

Psalm 118:24 (NIV)

Yesterday was another stinging day. For me a stinging day
is one that at the end is full of emotion and regret—things
I shouldn't have said or done and things I could have said
or done.

I can usually trace the end of such a day to the beginning of it. It's a day when I had too much to do and couldn't
afford the time to be alone with God. It's a day when I
failed to remember what the psalmist expresses; God has
made the day, and I can rejoice and be glad in it.

It is tempting to rehash events of yesterday. And yet,
why would I choose to spend today concentrating on yesterday? Instead I can resolve that no matter how busy I
think I am, I must take time to be with Him.

Lord, thank You for this new day; I will rejoice in it, be
glad in it, and include You in it.

AUGUST 29

TURN

The Lord is my shepherd, I shall not want. He makes me lie down in green pastures; He leads me beside quiet waters. He restores my soul.

Psalm 23:1-3 (NASB)

The sparrow had built a nest in the shrubbery outside our guest bedroom window. At a certain time of day when the sun reflected off the glass, the new mother slammed repeatedly into the window. She probably saw her reflection and considered it to be the enemy. The bird felt threatened.

She could have sat contentedly on the nest, providing warmth to her unborn babies. Instead, she was nervous and agitated. I wanted to tell the feathered creature that there was no danger to her or to her little family. But I sat helplessly by.

Constantly battling what we consider an enemy takes our focus off God. We worry. We live in a fear-filled world. But we don't need to fear. Because the Lord is with us, we can be content as in green pastures and beside quiet waters.

It has been said, "When God alone can win the victory, faith lets God do it all. It is better to trust than to try."

If the bird had turned the opposite direction, she wouldn't have seen herself in the window.

Don't give in to fear and worry. Turn toward God and find peace and contentment.

Lord, help me to stay focused only on You.

AUGUST 30

SEEK

> When he was in distress, he entreated the Lord his God and humbled himself greatly before the God of his fathers. When he prayed to Him, He was moved by his entreaty and heard his supplication, and brought him again to Jerusalem to his kingdom. Then Manasseh knew that the Lord was God.
>
> 2 Chronicles 33:12-13 (NASB)

The life of Manasseh is fascinating. He was as evil a king as there had been. Manasseh reigned for fifty-five years, longer than any king of Judah. He worshiped idols, practiced witchcraft, even sacrificed his own children to the pagan gods. He provoked God's anger so much that God had him hauled out of his country bound in hooks and chains to Babylon.

But there Manasseh humbled himself before God, begging Him for forgiveness. God heard him and not only forgave him but restored his reign as king. Then Manasseh knew that the Lord was God.

Whatever we have done, God will forgive us. The Bible says that God treasures a broken and contrite heart. If we confess our sin, are truly sorry, and repent, we will be forgiven.

Think about Judas. He betrayed the Son of God, knowing that He would be crucified. When he realized what he had done, Judas hung himself. What if instead, he had gone to the foot of the cross to seek mercy and forgiveness from the Savior?

When we think of what Manasseh did, we can realize that no matter how grievous the sin, God will forgive. Go to Him with a contrite heart.

Father, I confess that I am a sinner. I am truly sorry and ask You to forgive me.

AUGUST 31

WISDOM

Behold, I have done according to your words. Behold, I have given you a wise and discerning heart, so that there has been no one like you before you, nor shall one like you arise after you.

1 Kings 3:12 (NASB)

Do you ever pray for wisdom? Solomon was a young king following in the footsteps of his father, King David. God appeared to him in a dream and said, "Ask what you wish me to give you" (v. 5). Given the opportunity to ask for anything, he asked for wisdom.

Solomon was the wisest man who ever lived. With the inspiration of the Holy Spirit he writes about wisdom in Proverbs 3:13-18 (NASB):

> How blessed is the man who finds wisdom, and the man who gains understanding.
>
> For her profit is better than the profit of silver, and her gain better than fine gold.
>
> She is more precious than jewels; and nothing you desire compares with her. Long life is in her right hand; in her left hand are riches and honor. Her ways are pleasant ways and all her paths are peace. She is a tree of life to those who take hold of her, and happy are all who hold her fast.

Lord, I pray for wisdom.

SEPTEMBER 1

CHIPPED CUP

You are weak in your natural selves. Just as you used to offer the parts of your body in slavery to impurity and ever increasing wickedness, so now offer them in slavery to righteousness, leading to holiness.

Romans 6:19 (NIV)

I was certain God could not use me. I had rejected Him; my life filled with mistakes and bad choices. I felt unworthy, having turned from following Him. Then I read in the Readers Digest (May 2000), "Usefulness is not impaired by imperfection. You can drink from a chipped cup."

Gideon was threshing wheat when the Lord called him to save Israel from the Midiantes, an enemy who had oppressed His people for seven years. But Gideon protested. "Lord, look at me! Not only is my clan the weakest in Manasseh, but I'm the least in my family. I'm nothing, Lord!" But the Lord called Gideon because He wanted Gideon to accomplish His will for the Israelites. He told him, "I will be with you" (Judges 6:16).

God uses the lowly as well as the mighty to act for Him. And He will use you and me with all of our imperfections and inadequacies. He told Gideon He would be with Him, just as He is with us when we obey Him.

God is allowing me, imperfection personified, to serve Him. Like a cup that was shattered, my life has been pieced back together by His love and grace. Now I want to be useful for His glory.

Thank you, God, for using me, for I am a "chipped cup."

SEPTEMBER 2
WANTING MORE

They assembled together against Moses and Aaron.

Numbers 16:3 (NASB)

Korah and some of his fellow Levites came to Moses and his brother, Aaron. They told Moses, "You are not better than anyone else, we are all God's chosen, and we don't have to obey you" (v. 3). Moses agreed with the first two arguments; he wasn't better than anyone else, and all were chosen to be God's people. However, God had chosen only Moses to lead the Israelites.

Korah was a Levite who assisted in the functions of the tabernacle. But he wanted more; he was hungry for leadership and power. God dealt severely with Korah and the rest. They and their families were swallowed up by the earth.

The desire for what someone else has can lead to restlessness and discontent in all areas of our lives. In a driving ambition to attain what we don't have, we stumble over the valuable things we do possess. The stumble can result in a fall. When that happens, we look up, but it may be too late.

Father, teach me to appreciate what I have, knowing that there is nothing wrong with setting goals and achieving what I want. But show me those areas in my life when striving to attain becomes hunger for what others have.

SEPTEMBER 3

MY PROMISE: I WILL COME IN

Behold, I stand at the door and knock; if anyone hears My voice and opens the door, I will come in to him, and will dine with him, and he with Me. He who overcomes, I will grant to him to sit down with Me on My throne, as I also overcame and sat down with My Father on His throne.

Revelation 3:20-21 (NASB)

Dear child,

Be still; listen.

Do you hear My voice asking that I might come in and abide in you?

Open the door to your heart.

Invite Me in.

Do you understand the unspeakable joy you will know as you sit with

Me on My throne?

Don't shut Me out.

I love you and want to have fellowship with you.

I want you to feel My presence in your life.

Your Father

SEPTEMBER 4

GIVE IT LIGHT

Now in the morning David wrote a letter to Joab and sent it by the hand of Uriah. He had written in the letter, saying, "Place Uriah in the front line of the fiercest battle and withdraw from him, so that he may be struck down and die."

2 Samuel 11:14-15 (NASB)

On his web site gty.org, pastor and author John MacArthur writes, "The conscience functions like a skylight, not a light bulb. It lets light into the soul; it does not produce its own. Its effectiveness is determined by the amount of light we expose it to, and how clean we keep it. Cover it or put it in total darkness, and it ceases to function."

David was a servant of God, a mighty and just king. Yet after Bathsheba told him she was pregnant with his child, he tried to get her husband, Uriah, to sleep with her, that he might be deceived into believing it was his child. David was willing to allow another man to raise his child, the son of a king, as his own. Had David even thought this through? Or had he become so immersed in his own sin that his conscience no longer functioned?

If we don't expose our conscience to God's law, we can lose it. We will have no gauge with which to recognize sin in our lives.

As we grow closer to God, our sensitivity to sin increases. Because we are Christians doesn't mean we don't commit sin. But we are not slaves to it. When we sin, we must confess and repent.

Check your sensitivity to sin.

Father, forgive me, for I am a sinner.

SEPTEMBER 5

KING OF NATIONS

Great and marvelous are Your works, O Lord God, the Almighty;
    Righteous and true are Your ways,
    King of the nations!
    Who will not fear, O Lord, and glorify Your name?
    For You alone are holy;
    For all the nations will come and worship before You,
    For all Your righteous acts have been revealed.

Revelation 15:3-4 (NASB)

Thank You, Lord God Almighty, for Your promise of the time to come when all nations will bow before You in worship and adoration. All nations! You are the King of Nations!

SEPTEMBER 6
VOCAL PRAYER

For I know the plans that I have for you, declares the Lord, plans for welfare and not for calamity to give you a future and a hope. Then you will call upon Me and come and pray to Me, and I will listen to you.

Jeremiah 29:11-12 (NASB)

I've been surprised more than once when in dire need I have voiced my prayer out loud. Alone with Him, I've vocalized my feelings, telling Him that I love Him and that I know He loves me.

Today I asked out loud, "Lord, I know you can do all things, and no purpose of Yours can be thwarted" (Job 42:2 NASB). I have taken this verse to memory and say it often. Because of my anxious need, I added: "Please take this from me." I knew He could, and so I asked. But He didn't.

"I know the plans I have for you." I believe this, and that is good enough for me. I know He has answered.

Call upon Him with voice; He will listen. You won't be talking to an empty room but to God.

I lift my voice in adoration and supplication. I know You hear me, Father.

SEPTEMBER 7
STAND STILL

Do not be afraid. Stand still.

Exodus 14:13 (NKJV)

Pharaoh and his Egyptian army are descending on the Israelites. They have given chase after Pharaoh changed his mind about setting God's people free. Camped by the Red Sea, with no escape, the people panic, fearing for their lives.

Moses tells them, "Do not be afraid. Stand still, and see the salvation of the Lord, which He will accomplish for you today. For the Egyptians whom you see today, you shall see again no more forever. The Lord will fight for you, and you shall hold your peace" (v. 13-14). They are trapped, but God would intervene.

There may not be an army chasing us, but sometimes we might feel trapped. We panic, feeling there is nowhere or no one to whom we can turn to for help. I've felt trapped in a relationship that was not good. I knew that. But I didn't know what to do. These words weren't there for me then, and I wonder if I would have paid attention if they were. To stand still would have seemed like an impossible suggestion. But I have learned I can stand still.

We can be determined to stand still and see what the Lord will accomplish for us. It will be in these circumstances that God longs to reveal Himself to us. But we need to stand still, immovable, until He guides us through the waters. He may even part them for us! Can you stand still?

I am trapped, Lord. Even if it is only in my mind, I am trapped. Fight for me; intervene for me. Lead me through the waters.

SEPTEMBER 8

CONFLICT

> For what I am doing, I do not understand; for I am not practicing what I would like to do, but I am doing the very thing I hate.
>
> Romans 7:15 (NASB)

Paul speaks of the conflict between his human nature and the Spirit. He tells the Galatians that what our human nature wants is opposed to what the Spirit wants, and what the Spirit wants is opposed to what our human nature wants. We are pulled in opposite directions. The Spirit of God inclining us in one direction, the lusts of the flesh in another. These two conflicts will never harmonize.

Our human nature overcomes us, robbing us of peace and distancing us from God. And then we become conscious of our imperfections and sin; we feel terrible about it, and we're drawn into conflict again.

The Bible says that if we live as our human nature tells us to, our minds are controlled by what human nature wants. But if we live as the Spirit tells us to, our minds are controlled by what the Spirit wants. Our goal should be to seek God's desires as our own—to actually be controlled by His desires.

What does that mean for us as Christians? Do we have to abandon all thoughts of earthly happiness and possessions to enjoy a relationship with God? What can we do with conflicting desires of the flesh and our desire for the Spirit of God?

We all have desires, of course. But we can evaluate them; what brings enjoyment and satisfaction? We can ask ourselves, how much influence do my desires have on my life? How much influence do God's desires have on my life?

Holy Spirit, I surrender the control of my mind to You, not the world.

SEPTEMBER 9

TWO MEN

The Pharisee stood and was praying this to himself: "God, I thank You that I am not like other people: swindlers, unjust, adulterers, or even like this tax collector. I fast twice a week; I pay tithes of all that I get. But the tax collector, standing some distance away, was even unwilling to lift up his eyes to heaven, but was beating his breast, saying, 'God, be merciful to me, the sinner!"

Luke 18:11-14 (NASB)

The parable of the two men who went to the temple to pray gives us much to dwell on. We can identify with both, can't we? At times we recognize the ugly sin in our lives and cry to God for mercy. "Against You, You only, I have sinned and done what is evil in Your sight" (Psalm 51:4).

But sometimes we appear as the Pharisee, grateful that we aren't like others, that our degree of sin is less than a murderer, thief, or adulterer.

But we are all sinners, falling short of the glory of God. Sin is missing the mark, turning away from God. Sin is not judged by weights and measures. Even thinking we are better than others is sin, giving way to pride and self-righteousness.

Christ did not die for the few; He died for all. He died for you and me with no distinction of our sin but because we are sinners. We must not be tempted to believe we are less a sinner than our neighbor.

Lord, have mercy on me.

SEPTEMBER 10

NEEDS

Come to me all you who labor and are heavy laden
and I will give you rest.

Matthew 11:28 (NKJV)

"We need our needs," I read. How can that possibly be?
I thought. I long to be free from needs, just one day void
of cares and concerns. A day when those I love would be
free from sorrow and heavy burdens. Give me a day when I
know that our world is free from evil and filled with peace.

But if that would happen, would I fail to come before
God in prayer? Would I think that I have no need for Him
in my life?

He tells us to bring our burdens to Him in prayer.
Bowing humbly before Him, we can abandon every need
at His feet, trusting Him to relieve us of the care. God's
promises are efficient for every area of our life. It is said
of His promises, "Your weakness can't defeat them; your
strength can't fulfill them."

God Himself will make good on His promises. Claim
those for every need. Plant your feet in midair and let go.

I lay my needs at Your feet, Lord, confident of
Your sufficiency.

SEPTEMBER 11

THE BEAT OF MY HEART

I will praise You, for I am fearfully and wonderfully
made; marvelous are Your works, and that my soul
knows very well.

Psalm 139:14 (NKJV)

I had rheumatic fever as a youngster and have lived
with a heart murmur, a condition called mitral steno-
sis. As an adult, it has become necessary for me to have
annual echocardiograms.

I lay on the table in the small, dark room as the echo
technologist applies a colorless gel to what looks something like a microphone—called an echo transducer—then
moves it gently around my chest. I lay on my left side
watching the monitor. She turns up the sound; I can hear
the rhythmic beat of my heart, and the swooshing of the
blood pumping to and from the chambers. The sound fills
the silent room.

Oh my! From my position I take in the image, the
sound, the wonder. My body lies still on the table, but my
being cries out, "Wonderful are Your works. I am wonderfully made!"

Lord God, how can I ever take for granted the beat of
my heart?

SEPTEMBER 12

STEADFAST

The steadfast of mind You will keep in perfect peace because he trusts in You.

Isaiah 26:3 (NASB)

Dear Father,

I want to be strong, to meet my problems with peace.

But it seems that each time I am determined to do so, something arises that leaves me feeling helpless and not knowing what to do. I need once again to learn the lesson of perfect peace.

I can do nothing on my own and so I must discipline my mind to stay fixed on You.

Here I am again, here with a sad heart, grieving at the death of a dear friend.

I come before Your throne and wordlessly lay all this before You.

I know it is here that You grant me peace.

You are the God of Peace.

Yes, Father.

I will steadfastly keep my mind on You and trust in You for all things.

SEPTEMBER 13

THE MINOR THINGS

In God I have put my trust; I shall not be afraid.

Psalm 56:4 (NASB)

For me, God is present in the major events of my life but also keenly evident in the minor things.

After His resurrection, Jesus appeared to the disciples. The third time was while they were fishing. They weren't having much luck. Jesus was on the beach watching them, but they didn't recognize Him. "You don't have any fish yet, do you?" He said. "No," they answered.

He told them to cast the net on the right hand side of the boat, and so they did. The net became so full of fish they weren't able to haul them all in.

Then John recognized Jesus. When the disciples got on shore, Jesus had a fire going to cook the fish. He even had bread for their meal. He said, "Come and have breakfast."

Jesus, the Son of God who healed the sick and the lame and raised the dead, fixed breakfast!

I have read, "God is great in great things, but very great in little things."

Lord, I know You love me and see to all my needs. Teach me to trust You in all things—major and minor.

SEPTEMBER 14

ASSOCIATE

But as He who called you is holy, you also be holy
in all your conduct.

1 Peter 1:15 (NKJV)

When my son was a teenager, he began to associate with
a group of boys who had a negative influence on him. He
plunged from good grades and excelling in sports to behavior that neither society nor our family considered acceptable.
Peer pressure—it is difficult for teenagers not to cave into it.

But as adults we sometimes do what it takes to fit in. We
laugh at the dirty joke. We join in making fun of someone
or criticizing others. There are times we try to blend into
the crowd.

Today's reading reminds us that we have been redeemed
by the blood of Jesus. We have been purified and made
holy. We are to be holy; that is, set apart, different from the
world and its influence.

We can recognize the danger when teenagers choose
the wrong friends. Why can't we realize we are susceptible
to the same trap? If those with whom we associate don't
have a positive influence on our spiritual life, we must walk
away. We must choose wise behavior.

Help me, Lord, to know when to be quiet and when to
speak up.

SEPTEMBER 15

WINGS

Oh, that I had wings like a dove!

Psalm 55:6 (NASB)

David most likely wrote this psalm during his son Absolom's rebellion against him and the betrayal of his friend and counselor, Ahithophel. His anguish is evident by the written words.

Have you felt the desperation of betrayal by family or friend? Have you longed for wings like a dove that you could fly away?

David expresses his sorrow in Psalm 55:1, 2, 12-14 (NASB):

> Give ear to my prayer, O God; and do not hide Yourself from my supplication. Give heed to me and answer me; I am restless in my complaint and am surely distracted. For it is not an enemy who reproaches me; then I could bear it; nor is it one who hates me who has exalted himself against me, then I could hide myself from him. But it is you, a man my equal, my companion and my familiar friend; we who had sweet fellowship together; walked in the house of God in the throng.

There was a time when I wondered where I could escape from accusing tongues that spread lies about me. David said it. He says we are to cast all of our burdens on the Lord. He will sustain us and never allow us to be shaken. Yes, I could only cast those cares upon Him and walk away. I had no defense for minds already steeped in untruth.

The Lord did sustain me. I was battered but not beaten. I found my solace in Him, and in the words of David, "My soul takes refuge in You; and in the shadow of Your wings I will take refuge until destruction passes by. I will cry to God Most High, to God who accomplishes all things for me" (Psalm 57:1-2 NASB).

Oh, that I had wings like a dove! I would fly away and be at rest!

SEPTEMBER 16

FAMILY REUNION

> Then I saw a new heaven and a new earth; for the first heaven and the first earth passed away, and there is no longer any sea. And I saw the holy city, new Jerusalem, coming down out of heaven from God, made ready as a bride adorned for her husband.
>
> Revelation 21:1-2 (NASB)

We had a family reunion on the farm in North Dakota. A canvas tablecloth draped the 20' X 8' flatbed trailer. Fried chicken, corn on the cob, meats, potatoes, salads, casseroles, and desserts covered every inch of the makeshift table-top. The September air was filled with reminiscing, guitar music, and singing. Most of us hadn't seen each other since childhood. Now we proudly carried photo albums of children and grandchildren.

We will have a reunion in heaven with those we love. Jesus said He has gone to prepare a place for us. It is a place of union with Him and the Father and reunion with those who are there.

Who do you want at your reunion? Have they received their invitation to accept the Lord Jesus Christ as their Savior? That's how the invitation reads. "If you confess with your mouth Jesus as Lord and believe in your heart that God raised Him from the dead, you will be saved" (Romans 10:9).

Is there someone you want at the eternal reunion? You should invite them now. It takes a reservation to get in.

Don't leave anyone out. Reunite in heaven with them.

Lead me to invite those I love to our heavenly reunion.

SEPTEMBER 17

TRIALS

For a little while you may have had to suffer grief in all kinds of trials.

1 Peter 1:6 (NIV)

We suffer. We question. We wonder why. St. Peter tells us clearly about trials.

> Praise be to the God and Father of our Lord Jesus Christ!
>
> In his great mercy he has given us new birth into a living hope
>
> through the resurrection of Jesus Christ from the dead,
>
> and into an inheritance that can never perish, spoil or fade-
>
> kept in heaven for you, who through faith are shielded by God's power
>
> until the coming of the salvation that is ready to be revealed in the last time.
>
> In this you greatly rejoice, though now for a little while
>
> you may have had to suffer grief in all kinds of trials.
>
> These have come so that your faith-of greater worth than gold,
>
> which perishes even though refined by fire-may be proved genuine
>
> and may result in praise, glory and honor when Jesus Christ is revealed.
>
> 1 Peter 1:3-8

We can mediate on this, finding hope in the midst of trials.
Father, may I be proved genuine to Your honor and glory.

SEPTEMBER 18

JEWELS TODAY—JUNK TOMORROW

Jesus Christ is the same yesterday and today and forever.

Hebrews 13:8 (NASB)

Have you been a part of the fad the older it looks, the more fashionable it is? Do you remember the item you bought thinking you just had to have it? It was so "in" at the time; everyone had one; so did you. But the fad wore out, and it was stored away in the closet, soon forgotten.

We get caught up in what the media tells us is the latest in fashion, cars, home decorating, and the latest technology gadgets. Today a jewel; tomorrow, junk.

As the world of change surrounds us, we must keep our eyes on Jesus, our unchangeable Lord. We know that to Him a thousand years is like yesterday when it passes by. He is the always the same. We can count on Him. When our priorities are based on jewels, we can be assured that they will become as junk.

Lord Jesus, help me to keep my eyes on You. Thank You for never changing. You are my stability.

SEPTEMBER 19

WINGING IT

> Do you not know? Have you not heard? The Everlasting God, the Lord, the Creator of the ends of the earth does not become weary or tired. His understanding is inscrutable. He gives strength to the weary, and to him who lacks might He increases power. Though youths grow weary and tired, and vigorous young men stumble badly, yet those who wait for the Lord will gain new strength; they will mount up with wings like eagles, they will run and not get tired, they will walk and not become weary.
>
> Isaiah 40:28-31 (NASB)

One chore I particularly disliked while growing up on the farm was pulling milkweeds. My sisters and I would spread out and head down the couple acres of alfalfa pulling the pesky weed. After going a short distance and looking behind me, they seemed to be growing as fast as I could pull them! It was discouraging.

Problems are like that. They keep cropping up. When one is resolved, we know there will be more. We will never be free of problems.

Must we plod wearily along believing there is no escape from the burdens? No! We can mount up with wings like eagles if we wait on the Lord instead of trying to solve the problem by ourselves.

The eagle represents freedom. He lives on lofty mountaintops and in the solitary grandeur of nature. He sweeps into valleys below and upward into boundless spaces. He uses thermals, rising currents of warm air, to help him soar. So he needs very little wing-flapping, enabling him to conserve energy. Oh, that we would soar like the eagle and allow God to take care of the wearisome problems that disturb us.

Test your wings.

Help me to rise above the problems, Lord. I want to soar!

SEPTEMBER 20

YOURS, O LORD

"Yours is the greatness and the power and the glory
And the majesty and the splendor.
For everything in heaven and earth is Yours.
Yours, O Lord, is the kingdom.
You are exalted as head over all.
Wealth and honor come from You.
You are the ruler of all things.
In Your hands are strength and power to exalt and
give strength to all."

1 Chronicles 29:11-12 (NIV)

My Father, I give You thanks. All is Yours. I am Yours! I praise Your glorious name!

SEPTEMBER 21

DILIGENT

Be diligent to present yourself approved to God as a workman who does not need to be ashamed

2 Timothy 2:15 (NASB)

Joseph was sold as a slave by his brothers, taken to Egypt, and thrown into prison for resisting the advances of his owner's wife. When called from prison to interpret a dream for the Pharaoh, he was placed in a position of power, second only to Pharaoh.

From the time he was enslaved to his rise in status, he was tempted and tested. He served with efficiency in the Egyptian officer's home, he tended to criminals in jail, and gave wise advise to the king. He was faithful in little things resulting in a position of power over many things.

We are expected to be conscientious in all we do. God expects us to be faithful in the regular routines of life. Those things that seem insignificant to us give opportunity to present ourselves approved before Him. We may not attain the status Joseph did through his faithfulness to God. But God had a plan for Joseph, and He has a plan for us. We can be thorough and diligent in all we do, knowing the reward is approval by our Master.

I will be diligent in all I do, Lord.

SEPTEMBER 22

HOLINESS

Give unto the Lord the glory due to His name; worship the Lord in the beauty of holiness.

Psalm 29:2 (NKJV)

When I've thought of holiness I picture someone devoutly kneeling, head bowed, eyes closed, and hands folded in prayer. I wanted to be that someone, but I could not imagine myself as a picture of holiness.

Romans 12:1 says, "present your bodies a living sacrifice, holy, acceptable to God." To me, that means that I must give the best of myself as a sacrifice to Him—not what is left over at the end of the day but the freshness of my morning mind, the first of my time and the vigor of my energy when I wake up. Yes, the offering of the best fruits of my day.

I don't have to be sick or old, thinking that would make me holy and acceptable to God. I don't have to be on my knees in exhibition of prayer. I am to be the best I can be, offering my heart and soul to Him, my health and strength, entirely and completely.

I have heard it said that holiness is the Christian's crown and glory. I like that picture of holiness.

May the Lord establish my heart blameless in holiness before Him, at the coming of our Lord Jesus Christ with all His saints.

SEPTEMBER 23

THE ROCK HOUSE

Therefore, everyone who hears these words of Mine and acts on them, may be compared to a wise man who built his house on the rock.

Matthew 7:24 (NASB)

Someone had put a lot of work into the sand pyramids. Two well-defined pyramids, about two feet tall and two feet wide, seemed to tower at the water's edge. *When the high tide sweeps in they will disappear*, I thought. The sand builders know this but are excited to create, paying little attention that the pyramids would soon be gone; washed away.

Jesus spoke often of those who heard His message but didn't obey. Here He tells of the man who built his house on the sand. "The rain fell, and the floods came, and the winds blew and slammed against that house; and it fell—and great was its fall" (v. 25). He calls this man "foolish."

And He describes the house built on the rock. It would not fall when rain fell, floods came, and winds blew. He calls this man "wise."

I was the fool, building my life on sand. I didn't deliberately decide on this inferior foundation, but I wasn't obeying. When the first of a series of storms washed away what I had built, I started over and began to patiently rebuild with Jesus as my Rock.

Building a house takes time, starting from the foundation to the roof. If we are building our life on the Rock, we are daily responding to His call for obedience. The foundation is firm, so that we are able to weather the storms of life.

James tells us to be doers of the Word and not merely hearers who delude themselves (James 1:22).

I want to build my foundation on You, Lord, that I may weather the storms.

SEPTEMBER 24

SING

> When they began singing and praising, the Lord set ambushes against the sons of Ammon, Moab and Mount Seir, who had come against Judah; so they were routed.
>
> 2 Chronicles 20:22 (NASB)

This is a story of tremendous faith. Judah was about to be invaded by a huge army. The Israelites felt powerless and afraid. God, through His prophet Jahaziel, told the people and their king, Jehoshaphat, not to fear. The prophet said the battle was God's not theirs. He told them to go out and face the enemy because the Lord was with them.

Jehoshaphat and all the people of Judah bowed, worshiping God. The king told the people to put their trust in the Lord. Then they began singing and praising God.

God defeated the enemy. Upon returning to Jerusalem with their spoils, the Israelites praised and thanked God with harps, lyres, and trumpets (v. 28).

What battle are you facing? No matter how big or small the enemy may seem, keep your eyes on God and sing. Sing instead of worry. Sing instead of fear. Sing instead of complain. Face the enemy head on and know the battle is the Lords. And then give thanks and praise for His victory.

When little disturbances disrupt your day, sing. When major obstacles block your way, sing.

Lord, help me to trust that the battle is Yours, not mine. Help me to sing in the face of trouble.

SEPTEMBER 25

FEAR OF THE LORD

Listen to me; I will teach you the fear of the Lord.

Psalm 34:11 (NASB)

The fear of the Lord means to respect and stand in awe of Him because of who He is. There is no want for any good thing for those who fear Him.

Some are frightened of God and try to abstain from sin for fear of punishment.

Some have no fear of the Lord and, therefore, no restraints. They plunge into things as though nothing bad will happen to them. They fear only what their neighbors or friends might think of them.

And some comprehend the fear of the Lord, seeking God's pleasure in all they do. They worship His holiness, obey His commandments, and submit to His will.

Proverbs 9:10 tells us the fear of the Lord is the beginning of wisdom. It is produced in the soul by the Holy Spirit, and we are blessed by it.

Fear coexists with love for those who truly desire to please and serve a holy God.

Today, we come reverently before Him and proclaim His majesty. Bow down and adore Him with awesome fear and love.

I come in awe before You. I adore You and worship You as God of my life.

SEPTEMBER 26

WILLING

> For you have need of endurance, so that when you have done the will of God, you may receive what was promised.
>
> Hebrews 10:36 (NASB)

Bad habits can be tenacious. Mine was smoking. I began as a teenager. I had been called "pleasingly plump" for most of my teenage years. To me, the words really meant: "You are fat." Friends convinced me that if I smoked instead of eating, I would lose weight. I worked hard at smoking; it made me so sick I would have to lie down. With each puff, I was dizzy and nursing an uneasy stomach. But I was determined and eventually mastered the habit. I was disappointed that even then, I battled my weight problem.

I inhaled carcinogens, all the while knowing it was not good for my body. After several failed attempts to kick the habit, I began my own stop smoking campaign. I turned to the Lord, beginning with small steps. I prayed fervently and frequently, "Lord, make me willing to be willing." It wasn't easy, but by His grace, I eventually quit.

Most likely we have all been faced with overcoming a bad habit. Some are more challenging than others and seem insurmountable to break. On one hand we don't want to stop, and on the other hand something inside urges us to stop. We try to ignore that. Can we at least be willing to be willing? It is a first step.

Father, thank You for making me willing to be willing.

SEPTEMBER 27

WORDLESS MAJESTY

The heavens are telling of the glory of God; and
their expanse is declaring the work of His hands.

Psalm 19:1 (NASB)

Brilliant shades of rose exploded across a blue sky as the
sun exited for another day. Standing on the condominium
deck, I looked across an unusually still ocean. Facing the
horizon, a lone surfer clad in a black wetsuit sat motionless on his board. Nothing but the vast expanse of water
lay between him and a glorious display of God's sunset.
Suddenly he raised his arms exuberantly toward the heavens as though this event was created just for him.

"There is no speech, nor are there words; their voice
is not heard" (v.3). In The Best of C.H. Spurgeon , the
author writes of this verse, "that is to say, their [the heav-
ens] teaching is not addressed to the ear, and is not uttered
in articulate sounds; it is pictorial, and directed to the eye
and heart." [10]

Yes, God is wordlessly revealed in nature. We find testi-
mony of His love in simple pleasures—the tender touch of
one we love, the fragrance of spring flowers, or a carpet of
freshly fallen snow.

It is in His Word that we hear His voice. When we come before Him and listen, He reveals Himself more intimately to each of us.

Look for God's expressions of love in the smallest and greatest of circumstances.

I am in awe of Your majesty.

SEPTEMBER 28

DRIVE AND STRIVE

> For a man may do his work with wisdom, knowledge and skill, and then he must leave all he owns to someone who has not worked for it. This too is meaningless and a great misfortune. What does a man get for all the toil and anxious striving with which he labors under the sun?
>
> Ecclesiastes 2:21-22 (NIV)

I imagine if we sat down to have a talk with Solomon, he might ask, "What in the world are you thinking? You work, driving yourself to achieve success, acquire possessions, and make more and more money. What will it gain you when today your life might be over? Have you given one minute of thought to your soul? Where will you spend eternity? For tomorrow, those you have left behind will enjoy your possessions and spend your money. Your success will be noted and then forgotten."

I imagine his advice might be: Stop! Take inventory of what is important.

Today's reading was written by Solomon, the wisest man in the world, as he reflects on his journey through life. He had it all, yet realized it was an exercise in futility.

He concludes that we should put God first and keep His commandments.

I commit my life, my work, and all to You, Lord God. Teach me that striving and driving myself to acquire all is futile. Nothing of any value will be found in my human endeavors but only in You.

SEPTEMBER 29

YOU ARE

Dear Father,

You are my light and salvation; whom shall I fear?

You are the defense of my life; whom shall I dread?

One thing I ask from You, Father, that I shall seek;

May I dwell in Your house all the days of my life?

May I behold Your beauty, and mediate upon You?

I know you will hide me in the secret place when I am in trouble,

And You will lift me high on a rock.

My head will be lifted above all that tries to separate me from You

And I will offer myself to You with shouts of joy.

I will sing of Your praise.

Hear me, Father, be gracious to me and answer me,

For I shall seek Your face.

You are my God!

Psalm 27: 1, 4-7 (NASB)

SEPTEMBER 30

WORK

For even when we were with you, we gave you this rule: "If a man will not work, he shall not eat."

2 Thessalonians 3:10 (NIV)

One of my favorite early-morning farm chores while growing up was gathering eggs. Pushing open the creaky wooden door always sent the hens into a cackling uproar. But I ignored their protest. Moving down the row of straw-filled wooden cubbyholes, I wrestled my hand under the warm breast of the chicken to gather her eggs.

I was raised in a family with nine siblings. My sisters and I shared everything from beds to clothes. And we shared the work. We were expected from an early age to participate in daily chores. We learned a good work ethic that has contributed to a productive life for all of us.

Thomas Edison said, "Opportunity is missed by most people because it's dressed in overalls and looks like work."

Paul's letter is clear. If you don't work, you don't eat. He addresses those who are lazy and undisciplined. Instead of working, they spend time being busybodies. Idle time can lead to unhealthy habits. Even if we are no longer in the work force, there are countless opportunities to spend time helping others. Engage in productive activity.

Thank you for the ability to work and contribute, Lord.

OCTOBER 1

LIVING IN THE FOG

> You will make known to me the path of life; in Your presence is fullness of joy; in Your right hand are pleasures forever.
>
> Psalm 16:11 (NASB)

It was just before dawn when I stood on the hill overlooking the small community nestled in the valley of the Greenhorn Mountains. I gazed at the bank of fog stretching low across the town, leaving me a top-level view of the trees dressed in autumn splendor, along with the towering mountain peaks. I thought of those in the midst of the fog who knew nothing of the clear October Colorado sky just above them.

How many do we know who are enveloped in a state of fog, their vision obscured and hazy? They don't know Christ, and their world is diffused by layers of fog, reducing their visibility of Him. They live in it instead of above it.

Those who know Christ are able to rise above the fog, relishing a glorious, clear vision. We have no control over the atmosphere and what it renders the earth. But we do have control over our ability to rise above the conditions that would keep us immersed in fog.

I stood there that morning grateful for where He has put me but with a sad heart for those who are living in the fog.

May I keep my eyes on You, O Lord, rising above the everyday difficulties of life.

OCTOBER 2

ABANDONMENT

Nor do I consider my life of any account as dear to myself.

Acts 20:24 (NASB)

Paul summoned the elders of the church in Ephesus to tell them goodbye. He knew he probably would not see them again. He was anxious to get to Jerusalem to celebrate the day of Pentecost. "And now, bound in spirit, I am on my way to Jerusalem not knowing what will happen to me there except that the Holy Spirit solemnly testifies to me in every city saying that bonds and afflictions await me" (v. 22-23).

Paul's example to these church leaders was that of total abandonment of his own welfare, his future. He didn't know what would happen, but he was submissive, humble, and trusting.

He abandoned self "to testify solemnly of the gospel of the grace of God" (v. 24).

Can we do this? Can we abandon all for Him? We may never accomplish such complete surrender in this life, but we can pursue it.

"There is no stay so strong as an unreserved abandonment of self into God's hand" (H. L. Sidney Lear).

My desire is to abandon all of myself into Your hands, Lord.

OCTOBER 3

OBEY

If you walk in My statutes and keep My commandments so as to carry them out, then I shall give you rains in their season, so that the land will yield its produce and the trees of the field will bear their fruit.

Leviticus 26:3-4 (NASB)

I was talking with my daughter on the phone when her four-year-old came in from the backyard. "You won't be mad. Right, Mom?" I heard him say. He knew he had done something that most likely involved consequence.

Chapter twenty-six of Leviticus is devoted to the benefits of obedience and the consequences of disobedience. God brought the Israelites along much as a parent does His children. He laid down rules and regulations. If they kept His commandments, He promised plentiful crops and peace in their land. They would be fruitful and multiply. He would dwell with them, they would be His people, and He would never reject them.

The next few chapters that deal with the consequences of their disobedience are frightening. They would suffer physical illness, failed crops, and war with their enemies. They would live in constant fear. The results of their willful disobedience seem severe. But God's children were stubborn, and He knew it.

Just as my grandson knew he had done wrong, we know when we have disobeyed God. He is our Father and has given us the commandments. They are found in His Word. Obey them.

Father, I want to be Your obedient child.

OCTOBER 4
RUN THE RACE

Let us lay aside every weight, and the sin which so easily ensnares us, and let us run with endurance the race that is set before us, looking unto Jesus, the author and finisher of our faith, who for the joy that was set before Him endured the cross, despising the shame, and has sat down at the right hand of the throne of God.

Hebrews 12:1-2 (NKJV)

"Get on your mark. Get set. Go!" The runner fixes his eyes ahead and waits for the start. There's only one thing in sight and one thing on his mind—the finish line. At the signal, his body springs into action.

The scriptures are full of words of action. The apostle Paul tells us in Hebrews that we are to lay aside every encumbrance and the sin that so easily entangles us. We are to run the race before us with endurance, fixing our eyes on Jesus. Joy awaits us at the finish line!

As much as we are able, we must look ahead; if we need to look back, make it only a glance. We can't dwell on the past. We shall set our eyes on a goal, engaging all our resources in this race. Then with Jesus in sight, we will "get on our mark, get set, go!"

Help me to run the race, Lord.

OCTOBER 5

WORDLESS ENDURANCE

We count those blessed who endured…the Lord is
full of compassion and is merciful.

James 5:11 (NASB)

At times we are asked to endure, to bear suffering. Such a
calling draws us deep into ourselves, perhaps places we've
not gone before.

Early one morning I tripped and fell in my office. I
landed on a clay planter, breaking two ribs and damaging
my spleen. I lay in shock as the ambulance rushed me to
the hospital trauma unit. I had always imagined that if I
were in an ambulance, I would pray out loud, calling on the
name of Jesus to help me. But this day I had no words. All
my energies were focused on the pain that had seized my
body. Instead, I reached for God's hand and held on. For
the next hours of tests and surgery to remove the spleen, I
endured only by His hand in mine.

We can endure all that comes our way with total trust
that He is there. I think of a father who sits at the bedside
of his gravely ill child, holding her hand and gently rub-
bing her brow. Words aren't necessary. She feels his loving presence. I felt God's loving presence with me. Words
weren't necessary.

"When you pass through the waters, I will be with you" (Isaiah 43:2).

Thank You, Lord Jesus, for Your compassion and mercy.

OCTOBER 6

THE MORNING

They who dwell in the ends of the earth stand in awe of Your signs;

You make the dawn and the sunset shout for joy.

Psalm 65:8 (NASB)

Dear Father,

I believe you created this morning just for me.

In spite of the rough day that I had yesterday, You blessed me with a good night's sleep.

This morning I awoke, eager to be with You in Your Word and then ready to head for the beach as dawn was breaking.

Sometimes the sun rises softly, gradually spreading warmth and light to the newborn day.

But this morning it explodes with majesty, enveloping all of nature with its brilliance, turning white clouds to rose, and brown sand to pink.

The shimmering effect on the crashing waves is almost blinding.

I am in awe of Your wonder. Yes, I do believe You created this morning just for me.

Thank You.

OCTOBER 7

SOLITUDE

Come aside by yourselves to a deserted place and rest a while.

Mark 6:31 (NKJV)

Solitude. We seek it often but rarely find it. Webster says solitude is the state of being alone—to enjoy one's solitude; it is the absence of human activity.

Solitude is a spiritual discipline when we voluntarily withdraw to be alone with God. Jesus sought it. People clamored for His attention, and He longed to find solitude away from the crowds. He often rose early in the morning while it was still dark and found a secluded place to be alone with His Father. If we are quiet outside, we will be quiet inside.

The web site oChristian.com quotes Austin Phelps:

It has been said that no great work in literature or in science was ever wrought by a man who did not love solitude. We may lay it down as an elemental principle of religion, that no large growth in holiness was ever gained by one who did not take time to be often long alone with God.

There is power in solitude. We need to come aside as Jesus did, to find the silence in our soul and fill it with Him.

Lord, I will find You in the solitude.

OCTOBER 8

HARVEST TIME

The harvest is plentiful, but the workers are few.

Matthew 9:37 (NASB)

Autumn slips into southern California with less fanfare than most parts of the country. But it has arrived, bringing chilly mornings and evenings—time again for long pants and sweatshirts.

This time of year I bask in childhood memories of the Colorado mountains, aflame with color as trees displayed their spectacular autumn dress. My family lived on a five-acre farm on the outskirts of town. As the days grew cooler and shorter, everyone was expected to participate in gathering the crops we had tended all summer. The tedious hours of weeding, watering, and hoeing brought an abundant crop. Our garden was lush with tomatoes, corn, beets, green beans, and many more vegetable varieties; enough to feed our large family in the winter. We all knew that when the crops were ready, it was necessary to harvest.

When Jesus looked at the crowds of people around Him, He saw right into their hearts. Matthew 9:36 says, "He felt compassion for them because they were distressed and dispirited like sheep without a shepherd." He viewed those hopeless, hurting people as a field ripe for harvesting (v. 37-38).

We may think that some we know are not ready to believe. But we can't see into people's hearts to know who will respond to the Gospel, but God does. We must be willing to be a harvester, a witness for Christ. When we look around, we may see those ready to hear God's Word. The crops are ready; it is harvest time.

I am willing, Lord.

OCTOBER 9

ADVOCATE

I will ask the Father and He will give you another Helper, that He may be with you forever.

John 14:16 (NASB)

When my husband was to undergo major heart surgery, our daughters said, "One of us will have to be with him all the time. He needs an advocate."

And he did. He was unable to convey his needs to a busy hospital staff, so one of us was there to call for pain medication, give him a drink of water, or just to make him more comfortable. We were mediators and used these simple interventions to bring his needs to the attention of those who could help.

Helper, or advocate, applies well to both Jesus and the Holy Spirit. In his writings, John says that Jesus is our Advocate with God, the Father. Here the word is used as one who speaks on our behalf. Jesus applied this same word, *parakletos* (Greek, meaning "summoned to one's side"), when He told His disciples He would ask the Father to send them another helper, referring to the Holy Spirit. Jesus was trying to prepare them for the difficult times ahead. He knew how lost they would be when He left them and provided a substitute, the Holy Spirit, who would carry on Christ's work in them.

The Holy Spirit lives within every believer and is our Helper on earth. He searches our hearts and intercedes for us according to God's will. Christ is our Advocate in heaven, interceding for us with the Father.

Imagine the peace a patient can have when confined to the hospital and knowing that a loved one is always seeing to his needs. We are confined to this world yet can rest assured that we have an Advocate in heaven and on earth, seeing to our needs.

I praise You, Lord, that You are my Advocate.

OCTOBER 10

CLOUDS

The Lord was going before them in a pillar of cloud by day to lead them on the way.

Exodus 13:21 (NASB)

From 32,000 feet I gazed out the plane window at the Rocky Mountains below. The peaks were dusted with snow. It was mid October, and already winter was evident. Puffs of clouds dotted the sky.

I thought of how throughout the Bible, clouds represent God's majesty and awesome presence. One fascinating story is the pillar of cloud that guided the Israelites from Egypt to Canaan. By day this pillar of cloud led the way, and at night a pillar of fire gave them light. These were visible symbols of God's presence with Israel, guiding them from Egypt to Canaan.

But imagine this! Jesus Christ Himself tells us that one day the sun will go dark, the moon will lose its light, and stars will plummet from the sky. The earth will shake, and then Jesus, the Son of God, will come on the clouds of heaven. Armies of angels will accompany Him and trumpets will sound as He gathers His followers from the ends of the earth.

"Clouds are the dust beneath His feet" (Nahum 1:3 NASB).

Lord, when I look at clouds I think of Your imminent return.

OCTOBER 11

HELPFUL HINTS

> Then you will call on Me, and come and pray to Me
> and I will listen to you. And you will seek Me and
> find Me when you search for Me with all your heart.
>
> Jeremiah 29:12-13 (NASB)

If you don't use fabric softener in your towels, they will be fluffier. It's true! I tried it.

I love hints like that. Here are a few biblical *ifs* we can consider helpful.

If you commit your ways to Him, He will direct you (Proverbs 16:3).

If you ask anything in the name of Jesus, the Father will give it to you (John 16:23).

If you sow bountifully, you will reap bountifully (II Corinthians 9:6).

If you lay aside anxiety and go to the Father in prayer, you will have peace beyond comprehension (Philippians 4:6-7).

If you ask Him, He will open your mind to understand the Scriptures (Luke 24:45).

Only by acting on the promises can you know that they are true. Just reading them doesn't fulfill them. You won't know if your towels will be fluffier without fabric softener if you don't try it.

How are we going to know if these scriptural promises are true unless we give them a try? We can begin by seeking Him with all our heart. The greatest promise of all is we will find Him.

I will search for You with all my heart, Lord.

OCTOBER 12

TIGHT PLACES

Then the Lord opened the eyes of Balaam, and he saw the angel of the Lord standing in the way with his drawn sword in his hand; and he bowed all the way to the ground.

Numbers 22:31 (NASB)

Balaam was a sorcerer and was hired by a pagan king to curse Israel. God told him not to go, and although he listened to God at first, he was eventually lured by his evil desire for money. God was angry with him.

Balaam made the four hundred-mile journey on his donkey to meet the king. At times the roads became narrow with stone or mud fences on either side, making it difficult to travel. God's anger rose against Balaam, and He sent an angel to stand in the narrow way. The angel stood with an arrow in his hand, and the donkey had no escape. When the donkey saw the angel, it ran into a wall and even fell under Balaam, refusing to go on. Balaam began striking the donkey. "What did you do that for?" asked the donkey. "I've been faithful all these years, and what have I done to you that would make you strike me?"

Balaam was in a tight place. At one time I took a road, knowing that God didn't approve, but I followed my own stubborn will. I found myself in a tight place, unable to escape. God didn't use a drawn sword or a talking donkey to get my attention, but He got it.

If you find yourself alone on such a road, take courage and hope. You will find as I did that the Lord Himself is ahead. The more narrow the road, the more He loves to show us His power. And it is here that we experience His omnipotence. Don't turn to the right or to the left, just keep your eyes ahead and He will lead you out.

> When you get into a tight place, and everything goes against you, till it seems as if you could not hold on a minute longer, never give up then, for that is just the place and the time that the tide will turn. 11

Lord, I want to keep my eyes always on You and not on the circumstances.

OCTOBER 13
ASKING

Give me now wisdom and knowledge.

2 Chronicles 1:10 (NASB)

God said to Solomon, "Ask what I should give you." He could have asked God for anything. He said, "Give me now wisdom and knowledge." God was so pleased with Solomon's priorities that He gave him wealth and honor as no other king before him or after him would enjoy.

> Because you had this in mind, and did not ask for riches, wealth or honor, or the life of those who hate you, nor have you even asked for long life, but you have asked for yourself wisdom and knowledge that you may rule My people over whom I have made you king, wisdom and knowledge have been granted to you. And I will give you riches and wealth and honor, such as none of the kings who were before you has possessed nor those who will come after you.
>
> (v. 11-12)

Wow, Solomon got more than he had even imagined!

Jesus taught that we are to seek God first and everything that we need will be given to us.

What are your priorities? What will you ask of God today?

Lord, given anything I ask, I would ask that You reign in my life.

OCTOBER 14
OF LASTING VALUE

What advantage does man have in all his work
which he does under the sun? A generation goes and
a generation comes, but the earth remains forever.

Ecclesiastes 1:3-4 (NASB)

We live across the street from a famous racetrack. Bing
Crosby and Jimmy Durante were on hand at its opening in
1937. They, along with many other Hollywood celebrities,
took up residence here to be near the track. Most of them
have died, but their legacy lives on through film and music.

I walk along the beach they considered home. I contemplate my own mortality. "Let me know how transient I am"
(Psalm 39:4). Long after I'm gone, these same shores will
host other generations of beach lovers.

What legacy will I leave? What of lasting value can I
leave my children and grandchildren? Timothy's mother
and grandmother taught him the Scriptures from his earliest years. "...from childhood you have known the sacred
writings...that leads to salvation through faith..." (2
Timothy 3:15 NASB). Now that's a precious legacy!

We can leave our loved ones knowledge of scriptural
truths. The Word of God implanted in their hearts is worth
more than any material wealth we could bequeath.

Insure that those you love know God's Word.

Lord, I want those I love, to know You. That is of lasting value!

OCTOBER 15

ACT OF FAITH

Now faith is the assurance of things hoped for, the conviction of things not seen.

Hebrews 11:1 (NASB)

Chapter 11 of Hebrews is a litany of the triumphs of faith. In our Bible study we were studying Genesis 3, and a question in the study book was: "What would you call your supreme act of faith?" I recalled several major acts of faith. However, the daily acts of faith that I must practice are those that require attention to the discipline of faith.

For instance, placing trust in a pilot. How do I know he has had a good day? Did he wake up tired, have a disagreement with his wife or a coworker and is in a bad mood? Is he mentally prepared?

There is the act of faith to drive on the freeway. Who are all these hundreds of fellow travelers with potential weapons? Are they distracted by radios or phones, thinking about the next appointment, or maybe they are headed to a family emergency situation. Are their minds on their driving?

I think it a supreme act of faith when placing my life in the surgeon's hands. He is well respected, experienced, and skilled in his profession. But what kind of day is he having? Would he rather be anywhere else than here; is he feeling rushed to get to the next patient?

It is fruitless to place our faith in anyone or anything unless we first place it in God. Every day we practice acts of faith, and we can "fix our eyes on Jesus, the author and perfector of faith…" (Hebrews 12:2).

Jesus, first I place my complete faith in You. The rest will follow.

OCTOBER 16

SOMEDAY

All came from the dust and all return to the dust.

Ecclesiastes 3:20 (NASB)

Dear Father,

I woke earlier than usual and couldn't go back to sleep.

I have so much to do today.

I slipped into our time together, knowing it might be cut short so I could get started on my list of things to do.

And then I read this verse in Ecclesiastes and think of the word *temporary*.

All is temporary here.

I ask myself, "What will I do today that will have lasting value?

What will I say?

What will I acquire that will have the promise of eternal life?"

I am setting aside my list, at least for now.
Someday all will be dust.
Someday I will be before Your throne.
Today I just want to be here with You!

OCTOBER 17

GIVE ALL

One of His disciples, Andrew, Simon Peter's brother, said to Him, "There is a lad here who has five barley loaves and two fish, but what are these for so many people?"

John 6:8-9 (NASB)

The disciples would had to have about two hundred denarii, which was equivalent to about eight months' wages—not near enough to buy bread for five thousand hungry followers.

It was foolish of Andrew to even mention to Jesus that the young lad had five loaves and two fish when he knew that little bit would do no good. He asked the Master, "But what are these for so many people?" Jesus, however, knew there was not a human solution. So he sent Andrew to ask the boy, who could have said, "Hey, I brought these for my family and me. They can't feed all these people anyway." But instead he gave what little he had, and it fed five thousand!

There are many examples in the Bible of those who had little but gave all. Jesus uses the example of the poor widow who gave all she had as her gift to the treasury. She didn't give of her surplus, for she had none.

In another instance, Elijah asked the widow for a drink and piece of bread. She had no bread, only a handful of flour and a little oil, which she intended to use to feed her and her son. But Elijah told her to make it and bring some to him, and that she can have the rest. She did as he asked and found that the bowl of flour was never exhausted and the oil never empty. She gave what she had and received more than she could ever have asked.

It's been said, "Give all He asks, then take all He gives."

"For all things come from You, and from Your hand we have given You" (1 Chronicles 29:14, NASB).

OCTOBER 18

CHOICES

But if serving the Lord is undesirable to you, then choose for yourselves this day who you will serve.

Joshua 24:15 (NIV)

There are areas of my life that are rewarding because I am in control. I take charge, make choices. I am grateful for that.

One choice I made a long time ago is to trust in the Lord. Each day I make a conscience decision to lean on

Him. My depending on Him helps me to act, not react, to situations over which I have no control.

I am inspired by the author Viktor Frankl, who wrote *Man's Search for Meaning*. During World War II, Frankl was imprisoned by the Nazis because he was a Jew. His wife, parents, and children were all killed in the Holocaust. He alone survived.

On the web site ThinkExist.com he is quoted as saying:

> Everything can be taken from a man but one thing; the last of the human freedoms—to choose one's attitude in any given set of circumstances, to choose one's own way.

O Lord, I choose to depend on You in all circumstances. You are my Way.

OCTOBER 19

YIELD

> He said, "Is not this the great Babylon I have built as the royal residence, by my mighty power and for the glory of my majesty?"
>
> Daniel 4:30 (NIV)

King Nebuchadnezzar made a golden image and commanded that all the people worship it. When three young

Jewish captives, Shadrach, Meshach, and Abednego refused, Nebuchadnezzar ordered them into the fiery furnace. When they were untouched by the fire, the king was amazed. He had worshiped many gods, but theirs was impressive.

In spite of God's display of sovereignty, the king was full of pride. He took credit for a powerful Babylonian kingdom that he claimed was built for his majesty. He thought of himself as god.

Because of Nebuchadnezzar's pride, God humiliated him, relegating him to the fields to eat grass like the cattle. His hair was like eagle feathers and his nails like bird's claws. God proved who was King. After about seven years Nebuchadnezzar yielded to God as the Most High and honored Him as King.

Pride is a most grievous sin. We are all filled with it. It prevents us from yielding to God. Is God trying to get your attention? Are you stubborn and refusing to recognize Him as Lord of your life? Let go of your pride and yield to Him.

I praise Your Majesty, O God. You alone are sovereign.

OCTOBER 20

SILENCE

A time to keep silent, and a time to speak.

Ecclesiastes 3:7 (NKJV)

There is immense power in silence. Most of us have yet to learn it. Some people seem to have an addiction to noise. The coffee pot and TV go on simultaneously in the morning. When the engine starts, so does the car radio. And no matter where we shop—from the grocery store to the mall, in doctors and dentists offices—music (and not the one-size-fits-all kind) intrusively invades the air. We're conditioned not to even notice it anymore. But it's there.

Try turning off some of the noise in your life. Make time for silence. We need to be listening to the Spirit that He might control our lives, not the world. God whispers, but the world is loud.

Do you realize that *silent* and *listen* have the same letters?

Heavenly Father, may I be silent, that I might listen to You.

OCTOBER 21

SERVING IN THE BASEMENT

For we are God's workmanship, created in Christ Jesus to do good works, which God prepared in advance for us to do.

Ephesians 2:10 (NIV)

I followed her down the wooden steps that lead to the basement. At ninety-one, she moves cautiously, holding on to the railing as she descends the steep, narrow stairs.

In one small room, mounds of large black plastic bags hold used, donated children's clothing. The other room has a table for sorting and a washer and dryer. Shelves are lined with clear plastic tubs, each labeled with sizes, infants to five years old. Only the unsoiled will be lovingly folded and put in the tubs. When they are ready, they will be taken upstairs to be given away.

My mother volunteers eight hours a week tucked away in the basement of an old brick house converted into the Pregnancy Center. She could sit back and enjoy these last years of her life, having raised ten children, retired from the Women's Correctional Institution, and given most of her life to volunteerism. But it is here she serves, not with fanfare or accolades, but in a quiet setting, away from the public eye.

Is service an option? No. Jesus calls us to lead productive lives, serving others and sharing our faith. In Luke 13, He tells the parable of a man who planted a fig tree and when after three years it had produced absolutely no fruit, he ordered the useless tree cut down, asking why it even used up space. Jesus was warning us that God would not tolerate the lack of productivity forever. Genuine faith means actively sharing in service to others. A tree might look good all dressed in an array of leaves, but what good is it if it bears no fruit?

Am I dressed up looking like a Christian but producing no fruit? Following Jesus means acting on what He says. You may not receive a call asking for your help, but you can make the call. Seek out those who need your time or talent. You have been created in Christ to do good works. Share your faith. It may be in a basement, but you can impact your community with the Gospel of Jesus Christ.

Lead me, and I will serve wherever You would call me.

OCTOBER 22

VICTORY

David is the author of this song, and believed to have been written when he was delivered from his enemies. It is probable that it was used by the Jews in thanksgiving when they were victorious over their enemies. We can make it our prayer.

Psalm 138:1-6 (NASB)

Dear Father,

I will give You thanks with all my heart;

I will sing praises to You before the gods;

I will bow down toward Your holy temple

And give thanks to Your name for Your loving kindness and Your truth;

For You have magnified Your word according to all Your name.

On the day I called, You answered me;

You made me bold with strength in my soul.

All the kings of the earth will give thanks to You

When they have heard the words of Your mouth.

And they will sing of Your ways

For great is Your glory.

For though You are exalted,

You regard us, lowly as we are.

But the haughty You only know from afar.

OCTOBER 23

TENDERHEARTED

Be kind to one another, tender-hearted.

Ephesians 4:32 (NASB)

Deep tenderness of spirit is the very soul and marrow of the Christ-life. What specific gravity is to the planet, what beauty is to the rainbow, what perfume is to the rose, what marrow is to the bone, what rhythm is to poetry, what the pulse is to the heart, what harmony is to music, what heat is to the human body-all this, and much more is tenderness of spirit in religion. It is possible to be very religious, and staunch and persevering in all Christian duties; possible even, to be sanctified, to be a brave defender and preacher of holiness, to be mathematically orthodox, and blameless in outward life, and very zealous in good works, and yet to be greatly lacking in tenderness of spirit-that all subduing, all melting love, which is the very cream and quintessence of Heaven, and which incessantly streamed out from the voice and eyes of the blessed Jesus.12

Are we tenderhearted, moved quickly to compassion and pity for those who suffer and are in distress? Or is it easier to ignore the condition, feeling it doesn't affect us? Tenderness of spirit is not natural; we don't wake up one morning and find ourselves tenderhearted. It is a process, springing forth from our living a Christ-like life.

Father, give me a heart of tenderness, that I might reflect Your love and compassion.

OCTOBER 24

SPIRITUAL DISCIPLINE

> Anyone who lives on milk, being still an infant, is not acquainted with the teaching about righteousness. But solid food is for the mature, who by constant use have trained themselves to distinguish good from evil.
>
> Hebrews 5:13-14 (NIV)

When I first heard of spiritual discipline I had no idea what that meant. I went to church, prayed, and occasionally read the Bible. To me, I was well disciplined in the spiritual realm of my life. But I was drinking only milk. As Paul says, solid food is for the mature, and I was as a child. I needed to grow up!

Infants drink only milk; baby formula or breast milk for about the first four months. But then they are ready for some solid food. It's a process—a gradual transition from milk to solid food. Our spiritual lives develop in the same way. We begin as infants, drinking only milk. But as we grow, we should be eating solid food.

Milk is used as a symbol in the New Testament. In each instance it speaks concerning what is basic to the Christian life but not all that is needed. To be spiritually mature takes spiritual discipline.

We try to exercise each day, a physical discipline that helps us stay fit, keep our weight down, and a variety of other healthy benefits. Healthy habits bring physical health. Spiritual habits bring spiritual health, which address matters of eternal value.

Worshiping with others, praying unceasingly, and daily reading God's Word are spiritual disciplines that lead to maturity. Try some solid food and watch the growth!

I want to be a mature Christian, Lord.

OCTOBER 25

EVERLASTING ARMS

For you shall see the land at a distance, but you shall not go there, into the land which I am giving the sons of Israel.

Deuteronomy 32:52 (NASB)

I can't imagine what went through Moses's mind when God said he would not enter the Promised Land. He had endured so much, putting up with all the complaining and disobedience from the ungrateful Hebrews. Years and years (forty!) spent full of hardship and disappointments. All the while he had one goal in mind—get to the land His God had promised, a land flowing with milk and honey.

Now here he stood on Mount Nebo (as we did when visiting the Holy Land) looking at the land of Canaan. God said, "You can look, and then die here because you disobeyed Me, Moses. You can see the land at a distance, but your feet will never walk on it."

I have things for which I have strived. I believe that my intentions are good and pleasing to God. I spend a great deal of time rooting out pride, searching deep to examine motives. I've met with discouragement and disappointments. So why does God say no?

I don't know why He does. But we must obey, being submissive to His will. And we can say as Moses did, "The eternal God is a dwelling place, and underneath are the everlasting arms" (Deuteronomy 33:27 NASB).

I rest there, Lord, in Your everlasting arms.

OCTOBER 26
THE STREAM

For God is not a God of confusion, but of peace.

1 Corinthians 14:33

It was midmorning when I drug myself out of bed and dressed. I had been depressed for too long. I slipped into the little red Pontiac and headed toward the mountains. Fall was in the air. The trees were draped in brilliant colors of red, yellow, and orange. I parked next to the creek that wound its way through the maze of color and settled on a large rock lodged along the stream. I don't know how long I sat there in the comforting sunshine, listening to the sounds of the rushing water.

I began to pray, asking God to lift the feeling of hopelessness that I had been immersed in for so long. "I surrender all the circumstances that have brought me to this place, Lord. I seek your grace, most Merciful Father, to release these desperate feelings that have taken over." Slowly peace moved quietly through me. I recognized it. It was the peace that had eluded me since I had begun to do things my own way, trying to fix everything I felt was wrong in my life. I'd left God out of the circumstances. Now with complete confidence, I let go, giving it to Him.

As I drove home, I knew that something was different. I was different. Jesus said it is in Him that we have peace.

In the world we will have tribulation, but He has overcome the world. How could I have known it would take giving up (to Jesus) instead of the usual giving in (to the world)?

The future looked as illusive as it had when I drove to the mountains. But I was no longer afraid of it. It is by His grace that my life blossomed into something I could not have imagined.

Thank You for leading me to the stream, Your gift of refreshing water.

OCTOBER 27

ALL KNOWING

> For God is greater than our heart and knows all things.
>
> 1 John 3:21 (NASB)

I sat in a room filled with egos. I couldn't participate, only listen to the intellectual exchange of a broad spectrum of politics, history, music, books, and world travel. I wasn't equipped to participate in such a pool of knowledge, but I was impressed.

This morning I sit here with just one book reading the words of my Omniscient Creator, the One who knows everything—past, present and future. I cannot comprehend such a God. But His Word equips me to participate in the wonder of His omniscience.

I am content to listen to all He has to say to me. I may leave here not knowing more but knowing more about Him, my Omniscient Creator.

You know all things, Lord.

OCTOBER 28

HOLDING MY HAND

The steps of a man are established by the Lord, and He delights in his way. When he falls, he will not be hurled headlong, because the Lord is the One who holds his hand.

Psalm 37:23-24 (NASB)

I was gripped with fear when my son called to tell us that our three-year-old granddaughter Jessica had leukemia.

There was nothing to calm me. It seemed all my trust flew out the window. "Do something!" I begged. Where was the faith on which I had come to rely? Was it so shallow that such a tragedy could wipe it away?

It has been years since that call, but I still remember the moment. And now I know God did do something. He held me so close that I was able to minister to those around me. He gave me the strength to get through.

I praise You, God, that You took control of all things during that time. Your promise is true, for I fell but was not hurled headlong because You held my hand. You called her home, and she waits with You for our reunion.

OCTOBER 29
TAKING CONTROL

Each pursues his own course like a horse charging
into battle.

Jeremiah 8:6 (NIV)

One of the questions posed in a Bible study I was attending
was "Do you have authority problems? Mark the box yes or
no." I made an arrow between the boxes and labeled it "gray
area." I included the gray area in my answer because I am
consciously trying to surrender more to God's authority,
bringing my need to control under check.

Of the nine women in the study, nine of us agreed
that we have control problems. We asked ourselves why.
Perhaps one explanation may be that as mothers it was
necessary to take control in order to discipline. When our
children asked why, the usual reply was, "Because I said so,"
or "Because I'm your mother."

Many of us have a tendency to act as Jeremiah says,
like a horse charging into battle. I've found it necessary to
practice control in many areas of my life. But when control
demands its own way, it is called controlling and can be
a detriment.

I am still working in gray areas. There are occasions
when I need to make a conscious decision to temper my

need to take charge and a conscious decision to yield to God, for He is the ultimate authority.

I relinquish the control to You, O Lord.

OCTOBER 30

LOOK TO JESUS

Peace I leave with you; My peace I give to you; not as the world gives do I give to you. Do not let your heart be troubled, nor let it be fearful.

John 14:27 (NASB)

Between God's promise of the gift of peace and the realization of peace, there may come a sense of failure, hopelessness, disappointment, and turmoil.

But peace is not something to be grasped or achieved. It is a gift, real to us only when we focus on Jesus and not on the circumstance.

Keep your eyes on Him. If you long for peace right now in a situation that seems hopeless, turn your heart and thought to Him. Let go, look at Jesus, and feel His peace!

Lord Jesus, I long for Your gift of peace. I will remain focused on You, not on the circumstance.

OCTOBER 31

MY PROMISE: I WILL TEACH YOU

I will instruct you and teach you in the way which you should go; I will counsel you with My eye upon you.

Psalm 32:8 (NASB)

Dear Child,

To whom might you turn for counsel and instruction?

You turn to those who are seeking it themselves.

They are troubled and worried about what concerns them.

They may love you and want to help, but they have problems of their own.

Why not ask Me?

I am here for you, loving you more than anyone possibly can.

I will instruct you and teach you in what you should do.

I will show you the way.

My eye is always upon you.

Come to Me and I will counsel you.

Your Father

NOVEMBER 1

CONSECRATE

Who then is willing to consecrate himself this day
to the Lord?

1 Chronicles 29:5 (NASB)

What can we offer God? Consecrate seems like a pious
word to many of us. Maybe we associate it with religion
such as sanctifying the bread and wine for use in the
Communion service. We don't connect consecrate with
ourselves. It sounds holy, but that's not us.

Consecration is an act by which a person or thing is
dedicated or set apart by another for the service of the
Lord. We have the desire to set ourselves apart for God
but don't know how to do that. It is a process. One small
act of obedience practiced regularly, begins our process of
consecration, even if by a slow degree.

We can think of a nagging distraction that distances us
from God, and each day with deliberate, loving surrender,
answer every small call to recognize it and turn from it.
Such a simple and practical submission draws us ever closer
to God.

When we consecrate our will to His, He accepts our gift
of obedience with love. Each small endeavor to please Him
helps us grow and draws us close to Him.

I consecrate my will to You, Father.

NOVEMBER 2
DEDICATED TO HIS WORD

So we fasted and sought our God concerning this matter, and He listened to our entreaty.

Ezra 8:23 (NASB)

Ezra may not be one of the most recognizable biblical names. He was a priest and scribe—a humble, obedient leader. Eighty years after Zerubbabel led the first return to Jerusalem to rebuild the temple, Ezra was sent with a large company of Israelites to Jerusalem by King Artaxerxes of Persia. Ezra had his heart set "to study the law of the Lord, and to practice it, and to teach His statutes and ordinances in Israel" (Ezra 7:10).

When he arrived in Jerusalem, he learned of the inter-marriage of Jews with pagan, non-Jews. He had studied, applied, and obeyed God's commands. He was commit-ted to teaching others of God's Word and the importance of its application to their lives. So he was grieved when he saw how far his beloved nation had strayed from God. He confronted the spiritual disobedience of the people and beseeched God's mercy on their behalf. When hearing his earnest prayer, many wept and repented, confessing their unfaithfulness to God.

It is humbling to read of Ezra's prayer of confession to God on the part of Israel (9:5-15). No wonder the "people wept bitterly" (10:1). This obedient servant was so full of the love of God, just to hear his plea for their forgiveness brought them to their knees.

How important is God's Word in our life? Are we grieved when we recognize the sin in our life? Does our heart weep for the blatant disobedience we practice?

O God! I want to know Your Word. I want as profound a love for it as Ezra had.

NOVEMBER 3

CONFESSION

I fell on my knees and stretched out my hands to the Lord my God.

Ezra 9:5 (NASB)

Yesterday we read of Ezra and his confession to God for the sins of His people. We read it today, relating it to our own sinfulness, both individually and as a nation, and how far we have strayed from Him.

O my God, I am ashamed and embarrassed to lift up my face to You, my God, for our iniquities have risen above our heads and our guilt has grown even to the heavens. Since the days of our fathers to this day we have been in great guilt, and on account of our iniquities we, our kings and our priests have been given into the hand of the kings of the lands, to the sword, to captivity and to plunder and to open shame, as it is this day. But now for a brief moment grace has been shown from the Lord our God, to leave us an escaped remnant and to give us a peg in His holy place, that our God may enlighten our eyes and grant us a little reviving in our bondage. For we are slaves; yet in our bondage our God has not forsaken us, but has extended loving kindness to us in the sight of the kings of Persia, to give us reviving to raise up the house of our God, to restore its ruins and to give us a wall in Judah and Jerusalem.

Ezra 9:6-9

Here we are before You in our guilt, though because of it not one of us can stand in Your presence (v.15).

NOVEMBER 4

I CONFESS

If we confess our sins, He is faithful and just to forgive us our sins and to cleanse us from all unrighteousness.

1 John 1:9 (NKJV)

Dear Father,

I come before You to confess and repent of my sins. Oh that You would cleanse me from all unrighteousness.

That You would restore me to right standing with You.

I am bowed down in sorrow for my sins against You, sins of commission and omission. For I know I don't do as I should.

I do what I don't want to do.

I need You, Father God.

Forgive me and draw me every closer to You.

NOVEMBER 5

LIVING SACRIFICE

> Therefore I urge you, brethren, by the mercies of God, to present your bodies a living and holy sacrifice, acceptable to God, which is your spiritual service of worship.
>
> Romans 12:1 (NASB)

What is meant by presenting our bodies as living and holy sacrifices? In the Old Testament, a sacrifice was a ritual transaction between God and man, physically demonstrating a relationship between them. For instance, an unblemished male animal was brought to the priest by a person who had sinned. He laid his hand on the head of the animal, symbolizing his identification with the animal as his sacrificial substitute. The priest would kill it, cut it up, and place it on the altar. God made it clear that obedience from the heart was His desire, not the ritual of sacrifice. He wants us to be aware of the reason for sacrifice, not the sacrifice itself.

We can get caught up in ritual—going to church, serving on a committee, giving to charity—all are considered being "religious." But God is asking for our heart, a truly repentant heart, given freely with love and obedience.

Christ was the perfect sacrifice, shedding His own blood for us. This immeasurable gift is acceptable to God. By Jesus's death, God's new and perfect sacrifice, we can come to Him in faith and our sins are forgiven.

"The sacrifices of God are a broken spirit; a broken and a contrite heart, O God, You will not despise" (Psalm 51:17 NASB).

O Father, I offer all that I am as a living and holy sacrifice. I am Yours.

NOVEMBER 6

GODLINESS

Godliness is profitable for all things since it holds promise for the present life and also for the life to come.

1 Timothy 4:8 (NASB)

Paul writes about the mystery of godliness. Then he reveals for us how we can be godly.

I write so that you will know how one ought to conduct himself in the household of God, which is the church of the living God, the pillar and support of the truth. By common confession, great is the mystery of godliness:

He who was revealed in the flesh,
Was vindicated in the Spirit,
Seen by angels,
Proclaimed among the nations,
Believed on in the world,
Taken up in glory.

1Timothy 3:16 (NASB)

God doesn't require that we be sinless to come before Him, but He expects us to persevere. While there is sin in us, we can never rest from the battle. He doesn't require that we win but that we fight. And while it is expected we will fall, we are still expected to get back up and continue. It is spiritual combat. If we cease to struggle, if we cease to fight, we can be overcome.

Jesus is the perfect example of godliness. And He makes it possible for us to live a godly life by following Him. He lived to please the Father. Follow Jesus's pattern to serve and obey God in all things.

O God, I strive for a godly life.

NOVEMBER 7
SECOND NATURE

> Lord, You will establish peace for us, for You have
> also done all our works in us.
>
> Isaiah 26:12 (NKJV)

Dear Father,

I want to live only for You so much that it becomes second nature to me.

I want to please You in all I do, resolving to never commit the smallest act

that offends You.

I want it be second nature to me that I am always thinking about You

and my heart continually fixed on You.

Help me to live in the light of Your love that it might become second nature to me, so that my will may be Your will.

NOVEMBER 8
ABOVE THE UNCERTAINTY

The front page of the morning paper can be disturbing. There's so much evil going on. *Don't read it,* I thought. *You should go to the comic section and see if there might be something to laugh about.* But I glanced through the pages, allowing my earlier joy of being in the Word to turn sour. I felt down.

This world of danger and uncertainty leaves me that way. But God's promise ensures me of His presence when I am afraid.

I turn to Psalm 91 and make it my prayer.

> If I dwell in the shelter of the Most High, I will abide in the shadow of the Almighty. I will say to the Lord, "My refuge and my fortress, My God in whom I trust." It is He who delivers me from the snare of the trapper and from the deadly pestilence. He will cover me with His pinion, and under His wings I can seek refuge; His faithfulness is a shield and bulwark.
>
> He will give His angels charge concerning me and guard me in all my ways. I love Him, and therefore He will deliver me, and set me securely on high.

I continue to keep up on the news, good or bad. But most importantly, I continue to be in His Word while He sets me securely on high, above the uncertainty.

It is in Your Word, Lord God, that I rise above the uncertainty.

NOVEMBER 9
THE DISCIPLINE OF PRAYER

But He would go away to lonely places, where He prayed.

Luke 5:16 (NASB)

We cannot mature spiritually without the discipline of prayer. Jesus prayed often, breaking away from the demands on His time to be alone with His Father.

There are times we don't feel like praying and times we don't know how to pray. When that happens, "the Spirit Himself intercedes for us with groanings too deep for words" (Romans 8:26). He doesn't produce these groanings, but sometimes we have emotions which are too deep for expression in articulate language.

We may bear sorrows tucked away in our hearts that others can't see. Hopefully we are blessed to have a close friend with whom we can share. But we might have sorrows that can never be told to anyone; we can't even put them into words and are able only to lay them wordlessly before God. He searches and knows our hearts. And we are assured in His Word that the Spirit assists us, speaking on our behalf. He is our Mediator.

Oh what blessed relief to go into His presence knowing He sees the recesses of our hearts, where we can be with Him to find peace and tranquility.

Have you thought of prayer as a discipline?
Teach me to pray, Lord.

NOVEMBER 10

ACCUSATIONS

In my trouble I cried to the Lord, and He answered me. Deliver my soul, O Lord, from lying lips, from a deceitful tongue.

Psalm 120: 1-2 (NASB)

I felt I had been misjudged. The words were stinging. I tried to take cover, burying my head in my hands. I cried. I was totally unprepared for the animosity that the accuser harbored, leaving my battered spirit with no defense.

It took some time to sort through the hurt and denial. Gradually I began to distance myself from the emotions and focus on God's Word, a healing balm. Time has passed since that day, and the Spirit has lovingly caressed some bruised feelings.

Not by my power, but by His grace, I have been able to forgive my accuser. He did not see my heart, nor read my intentions. But God does, and I have been vindicated by Him. I take solace in His arms, and ask Him to bless those who assume they know me.

We can't always know what others think of us. Even when our intentions are good, there are those who might take issue with our actions or words. It does come as a surprise when their accusatory thoughts become harsh words that hurt us.

Our Father offers us solace and reminds us that no matter how offended we are, we must forgive.

Lord, thank You for the grace that I can forgive. I cannot do it on my own.

NOVEMBER 11

SACRIFICE

Lord, I am ready to go with You, both to prison and to death.

Luke 22:33 (NKJV)

It has been written that Peter was crucified. At his own request he was crucified with his head downward. Tradition has it that his brother, Andrew, was fastened to the cross, not with nails, but with cords to make his death more lingering. He hung there two days praising God. The brothers made the ultimate sacrifice. It is believed that John was the only one of Jesus's original disciples who was not killed for his faith.

We haven't faced death in defense of our faith, but Jesus says there is a cost to follow Him. He laid it out clearly when He said if we want to follow Him we have to take up our cross. We can kill those attitudes and sins that separate us from Him. We can nail them to the cross, cutting off the supply of nourishment that they need to survive. Replace pride with humility, greed with generosity; die to the world of materialism.

Jesus gives some startling measures we must take when He says to cut off our hand, foot, eye—whatever feeds our sinful nature. He uses these illustrations to stress the importance of ridding ourselves of the sin in our lives. It can mean giving up a relationship, habit, or even a job that is nurturing sin. For some, that can be as painful as cutting off a limb or losing an eye. But nothing should stand in the way of following Him. Jesus says we must be determined to remove the sin in our lives or face the unquenchable fire of hell.

Father, I know that I am attached to this world. Help me to die to all it offers, that I might gain my eternal reward.

NOVEMBER 12

CARELESS WORDS

But I tell you that every careless word that people speak, they shall give an accounting for it in the Day of Judgment. For by your words you will be justified, and by your words you will be condemned.

Matthew 12:36-37 (NASB)

Being silent is one of the most challenging spiritual disciplines. Jesus said we are going to give an account for every careless word we speak. The apostle James says to be quick to hear and slow to speak. This helps control the tongue, but he writes that we can't tame it. He calls it a "restless evil."

Jesus gives us the best example of not saying anything when we know it's not going to make a difference. Pilate was amazed to watch this pathetic man standing silently before the chief priests as they shouted trumped up accusations about Him. He asked Jesus why He wouldn't at least answer the charges. Yet Jesus said nothing. He had already said it all. He had taught and healed, proclaiming Himself as the Son of God. There was nothing else to say. Ecclesiastes tells us there's a time to be silent and a time to speak. We should know the difference if we are spiritually disciplined.

We can be drawn into a conversation about someone not realizing we're contributing negative responses concerning them. What do we do? Be silent, or interject something positive. As best we can, we should never use our words to contribute to evil directly or indirectly, but contribute to good.

Someone has said, "Every person you meet today is either a demolition site or a construction opportunity. Your words will make a difference. Will they be weapons for destruction or tools for construction?"

Set a guard over my mouth, Lord. Help me follow Your example.

NOVEMBER 13

GRATEFUL

Jesus said "Were there not ten cleansed? But the nine—where are they?"

Luke 17:17 (NASB)

It has always been a practice of mine to write thank you notes. I learned this courteous expression of gratitude from my mother. I passed it on to my children, and it will be up to them to keep the tradition going.

Expression of gratitude to God for answered prayer is important. I write prayer requests in a journal. When God answers them, in His time and way, I write a thank you next to the request. It is a small token of the grateful praise that resounds in my heart. Our Father doesn't demand a thank you, but He is pleased when we give thanks.

Jesus had healed ten lepers. Yet only one returned to Jesus "and fell on his face at His feet, giving thanks to Him" (v 16). Is our gratitude overflowing so much that that we would kneel at His feet giving thanks?

I like the saying, "An attitude of gratitude." An attitude is more than a mere act of saying thank you to God or anyone else. It's a steady tendency or orientation with regard to our mind.

A grateful heart acknowledges all things, material or spiritual, as gifts from God. The grateful heart expresses thanksgiving with no effort.

I sing praises to Thee, Lord God, with a grateful heart.

NOVEMBER 14

TWO OF YOU

> Again I say to you that if two of you agree on earth concerning anything that they ask, it will be done for them by My Father in heaven. For where two or three are gathered together in My name, I am there in the midst of them.
>
> Matthew 18:19-20 (NKJV)

When thousands gather to pray it is a sight to behold—voices lifted in unison to the heavens with hearts united in petitions to the God of all. You can feel the Spirit move in a mighty way.

But tucked away from the eyes of the world, two followers, Paul and Silas, were placed in stocks in the inner cell of a jail. There they prayed. We are not told what they prayed for, but Acts 16:25 (NASB) says, "at midnight Paul and Silas were praying and singing hymns to God, and the prisoners were listening to them." A great earthquake jolted the foundation of the jail; cell doors opened and chains were broken. The Spirit moved in a mighty way!

Don't wait until Sunday church to pray with others. Join another in sincere agreement, praying according to His will. And feel the Spirit move in a mighty way.

Where there is prayer, You are there, Lord God.

NOVEMBER 15

GRIEVE

Then Joseph fell on his father's face, and wept over him and kissed him.

Genesis 50:1 (NASB)

Jackie Kennedy was admired for her strength during the untimely death of her husband, President John F. Kennedy. His assassination shocked the world. Our nation focused on his widow, a perfect example of composure and grace.

Not everyone can be like that. Mourning the loss of someone we love is personal. Crying and expressing our feelings can be healthy. When we lose a loved one, it is important to take time to mourn. We don't need a clock to tell us it's time to get on with life. Grieving is a process that can't be rushed.

Where can we find comfort when grief overwhelms us? In Luke 7:12-15 we read of Jesus raising the widow's son from the dead. It says, "When the Lord saw her, He felt compassion for her, and said to her, 'Do not weep'" (v. 13). He was there with her. She could find comfort in His presence. Jesus is our Comforter.

When suffering any kind of a loss, we can trust in God to restore our broken spirit.

Lord I am grateful that You are with me. You understand my grief. You are my Comforter.

NOVEMBER 16

FULFILLED

Now when John, while imprisoned, heard of the works of Christ, he sent word by his disciples and said to Him, 'Are You the Expected One, or shall we look for someone else?'

Matthew 11:2-3 (NASB)

John the Baptist sat in a prison cell. Thoughts of the Messiah filled his every moment. When he baptized Jesus in the Jordan, John was overwhelmed when a voice from heaven said, "This is My beloved Son, in whom I am well-pleased" (Matthew 3:17 NASB). But now in the deep recesses of the prison, he heard rumors about Jesus and some of His works, and he was anxious for verification that Jesus was indeed the Messiah.

When John's disciples asked Jesus, "Are you the Expected One, or shall we look for someone else?" He could have said, "Yes I am." Instead He said, "Go and report to John what you hear and see: the blind receive sight, and the lame walk, the lepers are cleansed and the deaf hear, the dead are raised up, and the poor have the gospel preached to them" (v. 4-5).

John was overjoyed. He knew the promised Savior was quoting Isaiah, fulfilling prophesy. "Say to those with an anxious heart, 'take courage, fear not. Behold, your God will come with vengeance; the recompense of God will come, but He will save you. Then the eyes of the blind will be opened and the ears of the deaf will be unstopped. Then the lame will leap like a deer, and the tongue of the mute will shout for joy'" (Isaiah 35: 4-6 NASB).

I too am overjoyed when I see Old Testament prophesies fulfilled in the New Testament. God's Word comes alive for me when I read of His Promises and their fulfillment. I look with anticipation of those fulfilled promises in my life.

Jesus is the Messiah, and He will come again. The promise will be fulfilled as prophesized in His Word.

Thank you for Your Word, Lord. I delight in it!

NOVEMBER 17

MY PROMISE: I AM WITH YOU

When you pass through the waters, I will be with you; and through the rivers, they will not overflow you. When you walk through the fire, you will not be scorched nor will the flame burn you.

Isaiah 43:2 (NASB)

Dear Child,

I don't promise you that there won't be deep waters,

Or that there won't be fire.

I cannot protect you from those circumstances of life that befall mankind.

But I do promise you that you won't drown, and you won't be burned.

For I will be with you through it all.

The water may be deep;

The fire may appear to be all consuming,

But you must know that I am there with you.

Do you know that without a doubt?

If you look beyond Me for help, or try to do it on your own,

I cannot promise you that the water will not overflow,

Or that you won't be scorched and burned.

Remember.

You need Me,

And I am here.

Your Father

NOVEMBER 18

WORRYWART

I trust in You, Lord. I say, You are my God.

Psalm 31:14 (NASB)

Worry is considered the number-one mental health disorder in America. If unchecked, worry can result in mental illness.

Chronic worry puts you under chronic stress. It is like a ticking bomb that is not allowed to explode. Every system in the body is affected by worry. High blood pressure and cholesterol, headaches, back pain, and stomach problems are some of the results of worry. Worry can affect the skin, respiratory system, the immune system, and makes us more vulnerable to viruses and perhaps even cancer.

Jesus earnestly warned His disciples to take no thought about the things of this world. He went so far as to tell them not to even think about what to wear or what to eat. What does that mean for us? Don't we need to provide for ourselves and our families? We need to take care of ourselves, but striving for things must not lead to anxiety. A disquieting and distracting care about the things of life are an indication that the treasure and the heart are on the earth.

When I begin to recognize the results of worry, it is as though I didn't know I was worrying. I think I have it under control, but obviously I don't. I endeavor to practice submission in all things by saying "Thy will be done." It helps. I know it makes no sense to worry about things. But I know I can't do it on my own.

Lord, I will not worry. I will trust.

NOVEMBER 19

IN GLORY

And He was transfigured before them.

Matthew 17:2 (NKJV)

Jesus led Peter, James, and John up on a high mountain. I've read that a mountain was often associated with closeness to God.

And now here they were alone with Jesus on the mountain. What must they have experienced when they saw a supernatural change in Jesus's appearance? It says that His face shone like the sun and His garments became as white as light. And Moses and Elijah appeared to them as they were talking to Jesus. Imagine the disciples shock when a bright cloud enveloped them and they heard a voice out of the cloud say: "This is My beloved Son, in whom I am well pleased. Hear Him" (v.5)! They were terrified and fell to the ground facedown.

It was on the mountaintop that these three fishermen were given a brief glimpse of the true glory of Christ, the King. John later wrote, "we saw His glory, glory as of the only begotten from the Father" (John 1:14 NASB). Peter also wrote of it, "we were eyewitnesses of His majesty… and we ourselves heard this utterance made from heaven when we were with Him on the holy mountain." (2 Peter 1:16-18 NASB).

Yes, they testify as eyewitnesses; they saw His glory. But a promise in Colossians 3:4 tells us that when He comes again, we will be with Him! "When Christ who is our life appears, then you also will appear with Him in glory."

What a glorious promise, Lord. I will be with You when you appear in glory.

NOVEMBER 20

WOULD I?

> The things which happened to me have actually turned out for the furtherance of the gospel, so that it has become evident to the whole palace guard, and to all the rest, that my chains are in Christ.
>
> Philippians 1:12-13 (NKJV)

Paul was under house arrest in Rome for proclaiming Christ as Savior. The Jews had him arrested for spreading the Good News, but that didn't stop him. Even in prison he used the opportunity to reach out to the Roman soldiers who made up the palace guards. He wrote that nothing in his life compared to knowing Jesus Christ as his Lord.

I want to be like Paul—to be so committed to Jesus that no matter what the circumstances, I would tell of the Good News.

On the plane returning from Seattle, I had a haunting thought. It could be that terrorists on board took over the plane. With guns pointed at the stunned passengers and crew, they ordered all who were Christians to stand. We had only seconds to make the decision, knowing we would die.

Paul would have leapt to his feet for the privilege of proclaiming Jesus Christ as his Lord.

Would I?

When all the circumstances are right, it is a privilege to confess You as Lord. Help me that even in the worst circumstances, I would not hesitate to confess You as Lord.

NOVEMBER 21

THE COMMANDING OFFICER

> So the men of Israel took some of their provisions, and did not ask for the counsel of the Lord. Joshua made peace with them and made a covenant with them, to let them live; and the leaders of the congregation swore an oath to them.
>
> Joshua 9:14-15 (NASB)

In Joshua we read of the Israelites as warriors. They had been enslaved in Egypt for four hundred years. Now they marched against great kings and their cities. We can read of their conquests in one sitting, but it took years for them to accomplish the work God had given them.

God had chosen Joshua, who had displayed brilliant military strategy. His commanding officer was God Himself. Joshua could not be victorious in battle without first consulting God.

God had specifically instructed Israel not to make treaties with any enemies of Canaan. But they didn't seek God's guidance when they made an oath with the Gibeonites. Having rushed ahead with their own plans had led them into an awkward alliance with Gibeon.

So many lessons in the Old Testament apply in our lives today. This one makes me think of the many times I've followed my stubborn will, not even considering going to

God in prayer. Not one time has the outcome been one of victory for me. I want to take my orders from Him. I want Him to be my Commanding Officer. He knows what is best for me, and will lead me in the way I should go.

My prayer is that of Joshua; "But as for me and my house, we will serve the Lord" (24:15).

NOVEMBER 22

LONGING

Oh God, you are my God; I shall seek You earnestly;
My soul thirsts for You, my flesh yearns for You.

Psalm 63:1 (NASB)

When I came across the following account, on the web site catholicview.com, I felt such a need to share it that I have included the article here.

> From India there is an ancient story told about a young man who is longing to know and find God. He goes to an old religious man seeking answers and puts this question to him: "How can I find God? There is a longing within my soul and I need to fill it."
>
> The scholar thought for a moment then nodded wisely. He motioned for the young man to follow him to a nearby river and out they waded into

the deep, tepid water. Soon it reached just under their chins. Suddenly the old man seized the young man by the neck and pushed him under the water, held him down until he was threshing mightily in fear and desperation for he did not want to drown. Another minute more and he knew his life would be over. The old man, realizing this, pulled him out and the two came to shore with the young man gasping for air and coughing badly as he tried to expel the water from his lungs.

When they reached the bank the youth cried out, "Why did you do this and what did that have to do with my longing for God?" The old man quietly asked him, "While you were under the water, what did you want more than anything else?" The young man thought for a minute and then answered, "I wanted air! I needed air more than anything else!" The old man replied, "When you want God as much as you wanted air, you will find God."

Are you longing for God? Seek Him.
I long for You, O my God.

NOVEMBER 23

SEA SHELL SUPPLY

Your word I have treasured in my heart, that I may not sin against You.

Psalm 119:11 (NASB)

My seashell supply has dwindled. It seemed I had an overabundance, so for several years I have walked by, only marveling at the sculptured gems lying in the sand. Occasionally I would see one I couldn't resist and added it to my collection.

But after all this time, many of the shells that are kept in the large bowl are brittle and broken. It is time to replenish the supply. This morning I felt like a child in a candy store, eagerly scooping up all I could hold as the beach displayed its treasures along the shore.

That is how I often slip into my quiet prayer corner in the morning. I am eager to replenish the supply of gifts of the Holy Spirit. I gather each gem from scripture taking all I can hold. If I don't open God's Word each day, my spirit grows brittle and breaks under the everyday stress and pressure.

This morning reminded me that I need to check my supply of God's treasures. I don't want to be shorthanded.

O Lord, may I treasure Your Word in my life. Renew my supply each morning.

NOVEMBER 24

THANKSGIVING

All the earth shouts joyfully to You, O Lord.

We serve You with gladness and come before You with joyful singing.

We know that you O Lord are God.

It is You who made us and not we ourselves.

We are Your people and the sheep of Your pasture.

We come entering Your gates with thanksgiving.

and Your courts with praise.

We give thanks to You O Lord, and bless Your holy name.

For You are good, O Lord.

Your lovingkindness is everlasting.

Your faithfulness is to all generations.

Praise the Lord!

Psalm 100

NOVEMBER 25

GIVING UP

> Elijah was afraid and ran for his life… He came to a broom tree, sat down under it and prayed that he might die. "I have had enough, Lord,' he said. 'Take my life; I am no better than my ancestors."
>
> 1 Kings 19:3-4 (NIV)

Elijah experienced times of fatigue, discouragement, and deep depression. This appointed prophet of God tried to run from Jezebel, begging God to take his life. God let him rest and gave him nourishment; then told him to return to the mission He had given him.

I, like Elijah, have wanted only to plop down under the tree. I've wanted to give up. How long was Elijah allowed by God to remain there? I don't know, but I've had to sit there for weeks, resting from the blows and hurts, hiding from the world.

Just as Elijah was ministered to by an angel, I was nourished by God's Word. Touched by grace, I got back up and got with it.

When we are discouraged and depressed, we can stop and literally sit down like Elijah did and allow God's angel to minister to us. Feel the soft, sweet touch of God's love and concern for us. For even in these down times, God is working out His plan for us. We will know when God says, "Now get up and go. Do as I have appointed you to do."

Read about Elijah in 1 Kings 19. Take encouragement from him. Remind yourself that "the Lord will accomplish what concerns me" (Psalm 138:8 NASB).

Teach me to sit and wait on You, Lord. I feel Your touch.

NOVEMBER 26

TEMPTATION

Let no one say when he is tempted, I am being tempted by God; for God cannot be tempted by evil, and He Himself does not tempt anyone. But each one is tempted when he is carried away and enticed by his own lust. Then when lust has conceived, it gives birth to sin; and when sin is accomplished, it brings forth death.

James 1:13-15 (NASB)

Numerous signs are posted along the bluffs that line our beach. "Stay Back! Unstable cliffs!" For years, pounding breakers have relentlessly battered the walls. Shallow caves have been carved into the precipice by the mighty sea.

Yet just below the eroding bluffs, collections of colorful umbrellas jut out of the sand. Wall-to-wall sun seekers lounge under their plastic shade, sipping sodas and reading books. Ignoring the warnings of probable danger, some beachgoers set up their chairs in the caves. Huge falling rocks and dirt have brought death to some who chose to ignore the hazard signs.

There are such signs in our lives. Today's reading tells us of the consequences when we succumb to temptation. It seems clear to us that those beach lovers who ignore the signs put themselves in danger of death. Shouldn't it be apparent to us that if we ignore God's Word, we are subjecting ourselves to the same fate?

When we deliberately refuse to resist temptation, we are willfully going against God.

Seek God's direction in His Word.

Father, by Your power I will resist temptation.

NOVEMBER 27

LIMIT

Before I formed you in the womb I knew you.

Jeremiah 1:5 (NASB)

There is no limit—no limit to God. Don't set one.

We have only to look at the expanse of the heavens to marvel at His limitless wonder. He is almighty. He can do all, and He loves us so much that He wants to do all for us. "He rescued me because He delighted in me" (Psalm 18:19). He delights in us as a father adoringly delights in his child. He grants us our heart's desire, fulfilling all we need.

Call on Him with limitless confidence. "Ah, Lord God! Behold, You have made the heavens and the earth by Your great power and by Your outstretched arm! Nothing is too difficult for You" (Jeremiah 32:17 NASB). You have no limit.

May I never limit You, O God.

NOVEMBER 28

THE CHURCH

> You are fellow citizens with the saints, and are of God's household, having been built on the foundation of the apostles and prophets, Christ Jesus Himself being the corner stone, in whom the whole building, being fitted together, is growing into a holy temple in the Lord, in whom you also are being built together into a dwelling of God in the Spirit.
>
> Ephesians 2:19-22 (NASB)

For as long as I can remember I attended church with my family. It was expected that we go to church on Sunday. For me at that time it meant just that—go to church. It means different things to many of us.

The church is not just a building of bricks and mortar; a small, rural, wooden structure with a rooftop cross or an ornate cathedral with a majestic steeple. It is a household of

God's people, built on the foundation of the first church of apostles and prophets with Jesus as the Cornerstone. Those of us who believe in Him are fitted together becoming a dwelling of God in the Spirit.

We gather in a building for worship commonly bound by our Savior, who died for each of us. For most of us we congregate once a week. But when we walk out the door of our place of worship, do our lives reflect that? We are the church; we don't just go to church.

We can think of ourselves as a family working in harmony with the entire household in serving God. We are called the body of saints. We must live as such.

Lord, I am more than a member of a church. I do more than attend worship services or Bible classes. I am a member of Your household and fitted together with Your saints who love and serve You. We are the body of Christ.

NOVEMBER 29

HEAR ME

But seek first His kingdom and His righteousness, and all these things will be added to you.

Matthew 6:33 (NASB)

Jesus, crowds gathered to hear You. I sit here in this quiet space and listen.

My child,

Don't worry about your life, what you will eat, drink or wear.

Your life is worth more than the birds of the air, yet I feed them.

Have you observed the elegant dress of the lily?

Have you smelled the rich, lush, green grass?

Yet they wither and die.

Their time here is brief.

If you will but turn to Me, fill your mind with Me,

and not be concerned about the things of this world,

I will take care of you.

I know what you need.

I will provide for you.

Just love Me.

The rest will be added to you.

Thank You for Your Word, that I may hear You.

NOVEMBER 30

REACHOUT

If I only touch His garment, I will get well.

Matthew 9:21 (NASB)

I often think of reaching out just to touch His cloak. This woman's faith is an inspiration. She may have wanted an audience with Him, but that wasn't possible, for He was surrounded by the crowds. But oh, just to touch the fringe on His cloak. She said, "I will get well."

Jewish men wore fringe (tassels) on the lower edges of their robes. These were seen as signs of holiness. It was natural if someone wanted to be healed, they could do so by just touching the fringe. This woman knew if she touched Jesus's fringe, she would be made well after twelve years of suffering. She learned that it wasn't touching the fringe that healed her; it was her faith.

Numberless times I need just to reach out and touch Him. He knows when I do. He says, "Daughter, take courage, your faith has made you well" (v.22).

I reach out, Lord, that You may heal me. Not just from physical ailments but from those transgressions that keep me from You.

DECEMBER 1

REFUGE

God is our refuge and strength, a very present help in trouble.

Psalm 46:1 (NASB)

Sometimes we need to escape. When life closes in, we want out.

Do you remember climbing up into the tree house when you were young? We all had our hideouts. We were innocent and most likely didn't have the urge to get away. But it seems we all wanted somewhere we could be alone.

We may not have the same motive as children to climb into our tree house, but we all know of the desire to slip into a serene place and out of those disturbing situations that engulf us.

When I need relief from those things that weary me, I draw on the words of a prayer that I have taken to memory written by E. B. Pusey. I'm always grateful to return from this place of refuge filled with peace and tranquility to meet the headlong challenges that await me.

> Let me not seek out of Thee what I can only find in Thee, peace and rest and joy and bliss, which abide only in Thy abiding joy. Lift up my soul above the weary round of harassing thoughts to Thy eternal Presence. Lift up my soul to the pure, bright, clear, serene, radiant atmosphere of Thy Presence, that there I may breathe freely, there repose in Thy love, there be at rest from myself and from all things that weary me; thence return, arrayed with Thy peace, to do and bear what shall please Thee. 13

Lord, I yield myself to be lifted to this radiant atmosphere, where nothing or no one can disturb me. It is a safe refuge.

DECEMBER 2

IN THE MOMENT

Be perfect, as your heavenly Father is perfect.

Matthew 5:48 (NASB)

Dear Father,

It is a constant battle to stay in the moment.

I want to do the best I can right now.

But I jump ahead to the next task, the next day.

I want to discipline myself to just live in the moment.

There will be time to do what is needed.

If I strive for perfection in little things, I trust the rest will come.

You call me to be perfect as You are perfect.

I know I can't be flawless.

But I can live so as to be more Christ like.

I will live each moment to the fullest.

May my life reflect the perfection for which I strive.

DECEMBER 3

ENCOUNTER OF CHANGE

By the grace of God I am what I am, and His grace toward me did not prove vain.

Corinthians 15:10 (NASB)

"That's just the way I am. I've always been that way, and I can't change." It was the end of another heated argument as the young man slammed the door on his way out.

I think of the Apostle Paul. Talk about change! He was a Pharisee, of Roman citizenship and substantial means; well educated. He was zealous in his persecution of the first Christians, entering their houses where they worshiped, hauling men and women to prison. He was at the stoning of the martyr Stephen and heard him as he prayed; "Lord, do not charge them with this sin" (Acts 7:60). Yet Paul's discrimination continued.

And then he had a personal encounter with Christ on the road to Damascus. He was radically changed. God didn't change Paul's personality; he changed his heart. The same fierce intensity that drove him in his hatred of the Christian movement transformed into his passion to spread the gospel. After his conversion, he found himself the victim of persecution—beaten, stoned, and thrown in prison. Why would he endure such a life? He was changed.

"That's just the way I am," is an excuse. We can dismiss those things about us that we know are undesirable by dismissing the idea that we can change. We can't change on our own. Only He can change us. To get Paul's attention, God knocked him to the ground, spoke to Him from heaven, and blinded him for three days. He probably won't use such extreme measures. But when He wants our attention, it is an encounter of change.

Lord, I am open to change. Only You can change me.

DECEMBER 4
HOPELESS

The sick man answered Him, "Sir, I have no man to put me into the pool when the water is stirred up, but while I am coming, another steps down before me." Jesus said to him, "Get up, pick up your pallet and walk."

John 5:7-8 (NASB)

When visiting Israel in 2008, we stood at the ruins of the Bethesda pool where Jesus performed this miracle. The afternoon sun draped us in warmth as the guide related the details described in John. I stood in awe seeing the gospel come alive for me.

Although ill for thirty-eight years, the man remained by the pool hoping that he might be able to get in when the angel of the Lord stirred up the water at certain times. He believed he would be cured if able to do so. But he was ignored or pushed aside as others rushed ahead of him. He saw his plight as hopeless, and his problem became a way of life after all those years.

It was a feast of the Jews, and the streets of Jerusalem were crowded. Imagine Jesus noticing this particular crippled man out of the multitude of those who were sick, blind, and lame lying by the pool. Jesus approached him and looked on him with compassion. He asked him, "Do you want to get well?" Of course he did, but how? "Get up, pick up your pallet and walk."

It says he immediately got up and began to walk! Then Jesus slipped away into the crowd. Interesting that it was only later that Jesus found him in the temple and told him that although he had been physically healed, he must sin no more. He was to turn from sin to be spiritually healed.

I wonder. Was this man in Jerusalem when Jesus was crucified? Did he know Him to be His Savior and that by Jesus's death on the cross he was truly and forever healed? And did he know that hopelessness became hope because of the greatest gift ever given?

My hope is in You alone, My Lord and Redeemer.

DECEMBER 5

MOMENTARY LIGHT AFFLICTION

For momentary, light affliction is producing for us an eternal weight of glory far beyond all comparison.

2 Corinthians 4:17 (NASB)

Though Paul suffered much as he preached the Good News, he called it momentary light affliction. He looked forward to the day when it would be over and he would be with Jesus.

He tells us not to lose heart, that though the outer man is decaying, the inner man is being renewed day by day.

Paul knew this life is not all there is. He reminds us not to look at things that are seen for they are temporal. We are to look at things which are not seen; they are eternal.

Can we do that? Can we face the trials and believe they are momentary light afflictions? The Holy Spirit continues to renew our inner strength. These afflictions will pass, and we will receive eternal glory—a comparison of which we cannot comprehend.

Lord, help me not to dwell on the momentary afflictions of this life but to look toward the eternal rewards You have promised.

DECEMBER 6

A CHRISTIAN

> Therefore, if anyone is in Christ, he is a new creation; old things have passed away; behold, all things have become new.
>
> 2 Corinthians 5:17 (NKJV)

A Christian is one who believes in and follows Christ. Becoming a Christian is described as a definite act with significant results, which takes place the moment one exercises faith in Christ and is saved. One of these results—the guilt of sin—is removed, and we are no longer under condemnation but righteousness and justification.

When a person becomes a Christian, the Holy Spirit takes up residence and we become members of the family of God. I like how Lewis Sperry Chafer describes us:

> A Christian is not one who does certain things for God, but one for whom God does certain things; he is not so much one who conforms to a certain manner of life as he is one who has received the gift of eternal life; he is not one who depends on a hopelessly imperfect state, but rather one who has reached a perfect standing before God as being in Christ.14

Yes! Being in Christ, the "Anointed One," I am grateful to have received the gift of faith and to exercise that faith by accepting Christ as the Messiah, the Son of God.

Thank You, Lord, that You have given me the perfect gift—the gift of faith! I am a new creation in You.

DECEMBER 7

HEDGE OF PROTECTION

Have You made a hedge about him and his house
and all that he has, on everyside?

Job 1:10 (NASB)

My daughter told me of the narrow miss. She lacked inches
of hitting a car that pulled out in front of her on a busy
street. She was shaken.

Every day I pray for my children and grandchildren that
God place a hedge of protection around them. I release all
concern for them to God, trusting Him completely to take
care of them. "His heart is steadfast, trusting in the Lord"
(Psalm 112:7 NASB).

I may not know of the narrow misses they encounter,
but I am confident of God's protection.

Lord, I pray a hedge of protection around my loved
ones. I know that whatever happens today, You will be
there for them.

DECEMBER 8

HEIRS

> The Spirit Himself bears witness with our spirit that we are children of God, and if children, then heirs-heirs of God and joint heirs with Christ, if indeed we suffer with Him, that we may also be glorified together.
>
> Romans 8:16-17 (NKJV)

How is it that we are heirs of a Mighty King, heirs to the throne, heirs to the love of God, and heirs to His grace yet act as paupers? God's promise says if you are a son, then you are an heir.

In English law, no one is heir of the living. But in Roman law, the moment a child was born he was his father's heir. He didn't have to wait until the father died; he was immediately a participator in family possessions.

As heirs of God, we are given a vivid view of our intimate and eternal union with God, not merely the anticipation of receiving the kingdom; it is ours now. We can claim our inheritance. Why would we live as paupers? He will shower us with abundant blessings.

Abba, Father! Led by Your Spirit, I acknowledge my adoption into Your family and that I am an heir of the Mighty King!

DECEMBER 9

WORDS

Like apples of gold in settings of silver is a word spoken in right circumstances.

Proverbs 25:11 (NASB)

I am in the lab clinic. It is my third blood test this week, and I am weary of it. The small waiting room fills up quickly.

The young woman who has been here the last few times sits behind the reception desk. Patients line up to give her their doctor ordered lab slips. She doesn't look up but says to leave the slips in the wire basket and have a seat. She offers no smile or greeting.

I think of this proverb: "Like apples of gold in settings of silver is a word spoken in right circumstances." Today I will practice this and consider my words to be apples of gold in settings of silver. There are circumstances when my words can make a difference. Hers could.

May the words of my mouth be pleasing unto You, O Lord. May they be as apples of gold in settings of silver!

DECEMBER 10

LOVE

Then Jesus said to him, "Go and do the same."

Luke 10:37 (NASB)

Jesus was using the parable of the Good Samaritan while teaching about loving your neighbor as yourself, when a lawyer seized the opportunity for challenge. "And just who is my neighbor?" Jews hated the Samaritans, a mixed race of inferiority. That a Jew would come to the aid of such a one was inconceivable.

The parable has been a standard for how to behave toward your neighbor since Jesus told that story 2000 years ago. Some countries have Good Samaritan laws to protect people from liability for having come to the aid of others.

I wasn't far from home when my car broke down. A woman stopped and offered to take me home. When she dropped me off at my front door, I asked her if I could pay her or in some way show my appreciation for what she had done. "Do something nice for someone else," she responded. She was saying the same thing that Jesus told that lawyer. "Go and do the same."

We may never come across someone who has been robbed and left for dead as in Jesus's story. But aren't there opportunities everyday to show kindness and mercy?

Lord, help me to do good for others, expecting nothing in return.

DECEMBER 11
PARTICIPATE

All of creation is invited to participate in joyful response to our Maker.

> Shout joyfully to the LORD, all the earth;
>> Break forth and sing for joy and sing praises.
>> Sing praises to the LORD with the lyre,
>> With the lyre and the sound of melody.
>> With trumpets and the sound of the horn
>> Shout joyfully before the King, the LORD.
>> Let the sea roar and all it contains,
>> The world and those who dwell in it.
>> Let the rivers clap their hands,
>> Let the mountains sing together for joy.
>
> Psalm 98:4-8 (NASB)

All of the earth praises You, O God. I participate in wonder.

.

DECEMBER 12
COPING

> I pray that out of His glorious riches He may strengthen you with power through His Spirit in your inner being.
>
> Ephesians 3:16 (NIV)

I was a struggling single mom when I went to work as secretary to a local bank president. Immersed in responsibilities for which I was ill prepared left me overwhelmed as I coped with meeting the daily demands of my job and the needs of my young son.

I had gone to church all my life, but in adulthood I found other matters more pressing. I couldn't connect with the God who was "up there" to what was happening "down here" in my life. I got so caught up in what needed my attention that I gave no attention to my spiritual needs. The further away I got from God, the more I needed Him. My inner man, as the Bible says, was urgently crying out for strength.

When my efforts to do it on my own were exhausted, I turned to the God I had worshipped as a youngster. I felt His presence and His power to meet the demands that were necessary for my survival. It was I who had moved, not Him.

He sustained me when I was alone and has brought me through each difficult time in my life. We don't have to cope on our own. It is not our power but His working in us. We need first to take care of the inner man and the rest will follow.

Help me to draw nearer to You as I cope with daily challenges, Lord. Help me to keep my eyes focused on You.

DECEMBER 13

GLORIOUS SPLENDOR

> I will meditate on the glorious splendor of Your majesty, and on Your wondrous works. Men shall speak of the might of Your awesome acts, and I will declare Your greatness.
>
> Psalm 145:5-6 (NKJV)

A few years ago, a discovery of a large star they call Mira was found to be 350 light years away from the earth. We're told a light year is 6 trillion miles, the distance light travels in 365 days. We cannot wrap our minds around such a wonder.

As unimaginable as that is, our Milky Way galaxy contains 100 billion stars. And if that isn't beyond comprehension, there are 100 billion such galaxies of 100 billion stars each in the observable universe.

My troubles and concerns are minuscule when I meditate on the glorious splendor of Your majesty, my Lord and my God.

DECEMBER 14

CAMOUFLAGE

You are intimately acquainted with all my ways.

Psalm 139:3 (NASB)

It was a holiday evening. Larry and I were sitting in the living room enjoying a glass of red wine, listening to carols, and admiring the Christmas tree. I reached for the wine, spilling it on the white carpet and leaving a huge stain. We tried in vain to remove it. Eventually we covered the area with a rug. Anyone who didn't know what was under the 8' x 11' carpet thought of it as part of the décor. But I knew the ugliness that hid beneath such a beautiful camouflage.

It reminds me of the years I used a camouflage to hide what was really going on inside. It takes emotional energy to hide from others what we think they may find disappointing in us. Such a struggle to suppress the turmoil might be compared to trying to keep a basketball under water. I was exhausted from years of cover up, and I knew it had to be removed.

But I couldn't know the difficult days that lay ahead. One of those agonizing days when I felt overwhelmed, a picture came to mind. I saw myself standing alone up to my knees in a field of manure. No one was in sight—no houses, trees, or animals. There was nothing. The blistering sun scorched the earth around me as the stench invaded my senses. I could not move, nor could I see any way out of the quagmire. I felt hopeless, helpless, and alone. At that moment there was only one sentence available to me. I picked up a pen and wrote: "He subtracts all 'til none is left save Him." As I read the words my heart had given me, Jesus became my All.

When Jesus is our All, there is no reason to cover up. We know that God sees beneath any disguise. He knows our innermost thoughts and from Him no secret is hidden. It is a relief to know that we can cease trying to conceal from Him what He already sees. When we read Psalm 139 we see there is no need for camouflage.

You are my all, Lord Jesus.

DECEMBER 15

ABIDE

Abide in My love.

John 15:9 (NASB)

Jesus says He is the Vine and we are the branches, and without Him we can do nothing. He warns that if we don't abide in Him, we are cast out as a branch, withered, gathered, and thrown into the fire and burned. "If you abide in Me, and My words abide in you, you will ask what you desire, and it shall be done for you. By this My Father is glorified, that you bear much fruit; so you will be My disciples" (v. 7-8).

We must stay as close to Christ as a branch attached to a vine. Joined to Him, we are nourished and nurtured, producing fruit. It is natural for a branch to be attached to the vine, and the more mature the branch, the stronger it becomes. A sturdy vine can't be pulled from the strong branch. It needs to be chopped or cut away. And so it is for us. When we are mature, clinging to the Vine, nothing can separate us.

"Neither death nor life, nor angels nor principalities nor powers, nor things present nor things to come, nor height nor depth, nor any other created thing, shall be able to separate us from the love of God which is in Christ Jesus our Lord" (Romans 8:38-39).

Oh, that I might abide in You Lord, as a strong and mature branch, producing fruit. I cling to You.

DECEMBER 16

SOMETHING FAMILIAR

In quietness and trust is your strength.

Isaiah 30:15 (NASB)

My friend, a young father of three small children, was dying. During that time, his mother continued her daily household chores, washing clothes, hanging them on the line. I recall thinking that she had to do something that was familiar, something routine that could help her cope.

Lord, today when I learned of my loved one having been taken to the emergency room, I couldn't wait to get here with You, my tower of strength. I need to do something that is familiar, something routine to help me deal with the helplessness I am feeling. The peace and comfort I glean from my corner of prayer, is one that abides so deep that I can trust You to take care of it all.

I read this morning "Some of us believe that God is all mighty and may do all; and that He is all wisdom and can do all; but that He is all love and will do all, that is where we fail."

I am so grateful, Lord, that being here with You is something familiar.

DECEMBER 17

SELF WILL

However, he would not listen to her; since he was stronger than she, he violated her and lay with her.

2 Samuel 13:14 (NASB)

The story of the lustful desire by Amnon for his beautiful half-sister, Tamar, is an example of unrestrained freedom.

He was a spoiled son of King David and used to getting his own way. It gives us reason to think that his character was bad in other things, and having forsaken God, surrendered to such vile affections.

The freedom to do anything we want gradually becomes a desire to do everything. Then we are captives of sin. Man's misery comes from his self-will. His blessedness comes from conquering his own will. True freedom comes in obeying God and doing His will, because He knows what is best for us. Children, especially teenagers, can be so certain they know what is best for them. But as parents, we understand the limitations we must enforce in their lives. If left on their own, the result can be disastrous.

Imagine our lives if there was total freedom to do every wonton act our flesh desires. Without surrendering to God's will, we would be lost, bound by sin with no freedom.

The only freedom we can really experience is freedom in Him.

Lord God, help me to die to self, surrender my life to You, and enjoy freedom.

DECEMBER 18
THE CITY OF TRUTH

Thus says the Lord, "I will return to Zion and will
dwell in the midst of Jerusalem. Then Jerusalem will
be called the City of Truth, and the mountain of the
Lord of hosts will be called the Holy Mountain."

Zechariah 8:3 (NASB)

Scripture is clear concerning the second coming of Christ.
This verse was written by Zechariah approximately 520
BC. In the Old Testament, as well as a prophetic sense,
Zion refers to Jerusalem.

In the New Testament Jerusalem is referred to as the
New Jerusalem, "And I saw the holy city, New Jerusalem,
coming down out of heaven from God, made ready as a
bride adorned for her husband" (Revelation 21:2).

We wait for Him knowing His promise is true. Jesus will
come again to rule and reign in Jerusalem, the Eternal City,
described as a place where God will wipe away every tear
from our eyes, where there will be no more death, mourning, crying, or pain. The New Jerusalem is God's future
home for His children.

When we left Jerusalem for the last time while on our
visit to the Holy Land, my husband and I said to each other,
"We will be back." Oh yes, we look forward to returning

with Him to Zion, to Jerusalem, the City of Truth. I don't understand it; I can't comprehend it, but I know it!

I will be there with You in Jerusalem!

DECEMBER 19

RIPE WITH BLESSINGS

A faithful man will abound with blessings.

Proverbs 28:20 (NKJV)

Some days are ripe with blessings, bursting with buds of memories that will only blossom and grow. With time they fade and are pressed and stored in our minds and hearts, looked at occasionally with quiet joy and reflection.

Our heavenly Father delights in giving us days ripe with blessings. In Ezekiel 34:26 (NASB) He says, "I will cause showers to come down; they will be showers of blessings."

And He tell us in Malachi 3:10 (NASB) that He will "Open for you the windows of heaven and pour out for you a blessing until it overflows."

What a generous Father!

Thank You, Father God, for the days that are ripe with blessings. I am Your grateful child.

DECEMBER 20
PRAYER OF PRAISE

Everyday is a new revelation of His almighty power found in His Word.

This morning I find it in Daniel; his prayer of praise when God revealed to him the interpretation of the king's dream. A decree from the king that the wise men were to be killed included Daniel and his friends. They had been unable to interpret his dream.

Daniel approached the king, asking for time. Then he and his friends prayed. God revealed the mystery surrounding the dream to Daniel. I'm sure he was excited and anxious to tell the king, but before rushing in with the revelation, Daniel first gave God the praise and glory.

We can make it our prayer of praise when He responds to our requests.

Daniel 2:20-23 (NASB)

Dear Father,

Let Your name be blessed forever and ever, for wisdom and power belong to You. You change the times and the epochs; You remove kings and establish kings;

You give wisdom to wise men and knowledge to men of understanding.

You reveal the profound and hidden things; You know what is in the darkness, and the light dwells with You.

To You, O God, I give thanks and praise, for You have given me wisdom and power; even now You have made known to me what I have requested of You.

DECEMBER 21

IDOLS

Their idols are silver and gold, the work of men's hands. They have mouths, but they do not speak; eyes they have, but they do not see; they have ears, but they do not hear; noses they have, but they do not smell; they have hands, but they do not handle; feet they have, but they do not walk; nor do they mutter through their throat. Those who make them are like them; so is everyone who trusts in them.

Psalm 115:4-8 (NKJV)

We would deny we have idols. But idolatry is not just bowing before wood, stone or metal. It is putting our trust in what we have made, what we have, and not in God. We trust in the money we have earned, our home, our business, achieved success, even our families and our health. No, we may not bow before objects that have no mouths, eyes, ears, nose, hands, feet, or voice. But we do allow our material goods and successes to come before God.

If all we possess was gone but Him, what would our lives be like? Would we find it empty? If so, then we must evaluate our priorities.

It is possible to have money, a home, business, success, family and health and at the same time to have God. We can worship Him, making Him first in our life.

Lord, I admit to having idols in my life. I seek to rid myself of anything that is more important than You, or anything that takes first place ahead of You. I worship You and bow in humble adoration before Your throne.

DECEMBER 22

BEFORE

> Despite their fear of the peoples around them, they built the altar on its foundation and sacrificed burnt offerings on it to the Lord, both the morning and evening sacrifices.
>
> Ezra 3:1 (NIV)

Today's reading is a great example of "God trusting" preparation. Some of the Israelites had returned to Jerusalem to rebuild the temple. It had been destroyed when Nebuchadnezzar had taken them captive to Babylon forty-eight years earlier.

It was a difficult task, and they were terrified of the people that surrounded them. So they built an altar, symbolizing God's presence and protection, and their commitment to serve God. They had setbacks, delays and enemies determined to stop progress, but God's plan would not be stopped. The perseverance and dedication to the completion of the temple began before the work.

Why would we begin any challenge without God? It is arrogance to think we can do anything without Him. The foundation of any task is prayer. Only then can we depend on God to see us through the difficulties.

It is said, "The task ahead of you is no greater than the power behind you."

No matter the task, minor or major, I am prepared to depend on You in all circumstances.

DECEMBER 23

NEEDING ONE ANOTHER

And all those who had believed were together and had all things in common.

Acts 3:44 (NASB)

For twelve months I was recovering from surgery. Consequently, I had to forfeit many regular times of worship and study with others—Sunday church services, couples Bible study, my women's Bible study, and prayerful times with those whom I serve in ministry.

The early church began by faith in the risen Christ and was enabled to love and serve together through the power of the Holy Spirit. They faced persecution and death because of their zeal to tell others about Jesus. They needed one another, not just for the growth of the church and spreading the Good News, but for encouragement, motivation and courage.

Looking back, the months spent in recovery reminded me of my need for the community of believers in my life. Maybe I was taking that for granted. But now I have an ardent appreciation of being with other believers in worship and study.

Thank You, Lord, for the community of believers in my life.

DECEMBER 24

THE OBVIOUS

Who walks in darkness and has no light? Let him trust in the name of the Lord and rely upon his God.

Isaiah 50:10 (NKJV)

As I came up the driveway from my morning walk, I realized I hadn't taken my house key. I started to panic; then remembered I had left the downstairs bedroom door unlocked. It opens onto a patio surrounded by a four-foot stucco wall, which I eyed skeptically. Several times I attempted to get a foothold on the wall but failed. I spotted a flowerpot on the ledge, turned it over, and stepped on it. Pulling myself up, I jumped onto the tile floor. "Thank you, Jesus," I whispered repeatedly.

Coming up the stairs, I glanced at the front door. It was unlocked! Why didn't I try it before breaking in? How could I have overlooked the obvious? "Pretty typical of me," I muttered.

I thought of the many times in my life when I have tried other ways to fix a situation rather than the obvious. I need to constantly remind myself that Jesus is the solution, not my amateurish attempts at fixing things. I need to try Him.

Oh Lord, help me to realize my total dependence on You and that I may not look for solutions on my own but look only to You, the Obvious Answer!

DECEMBER 25

THE GIFT

The free gift God is eternal life in Christ Jesus, the Lord.

Romans 6:23 (NASB)

As a young mother, I could get caught up in the secular swirl of Christmas, decorating the tree, shopping, and baking. It was time to release the child within! Christmas morning, I loved watching my three little ones, sleepy-eyed and excited, squealing, "Wow, look what I got!" Christmas was about dolls and buggies, plastic tea sets, and new bikes. Eventually their wish list grew more sophisticated.

When several holiday seasons were dimmed by sorrow and loss, the difference between a material Christmas and the true meaning of the birth of our Savior became apparent. Joy was not found in wrapped gifts but in the gifts of peace, comfort, and strength, which He gave to us.

The spirit of Christmas has new meaning for me. It is not all about the gifts, decorating, or shopping. It is about God's gift to me, His Son Jesus Christ, the greatest gift of all. What could I possibly give to Him that could compare to such a gift? I want to give Him my all—my mind, heart and soul.

Can you think of gifts worthy of a King, those that are most valuable to you and pleasing to Him? Might we offer such gifts as acts of obedience, love, self-restraint, and patience?

Release the child within, come before this newborn King, bow down, and worship Him. Jesus came that we might have eternal life. How wondrous a gift is that?

Thank You for Your wondrous gifts, Lord.

DECEMBER 26

VALUABLE

But the very hairs of your head are all numbered.

Matthew 10:30 (NASB)

I am so valuable to You, O God, that You have counted the very hairs on my head.

I am so valuable to You that You have freed me from condemnation forever and made me a citizen of heaven.

I am so valuable to You that You have given me complete access to You through the Holy Spirit.

I am so valuable to You that You have made it impossible to be separated from Your love.

I am so valuable to You that You have established, anointed, and sealed me.

I am so valuable to You that You make it possible to approach You with confidence.

I am so valuable to You that You have made me a temple, and Your Spirit dwells in me.

I am so valuable to You that You have made me Your workmanship, redeemed me, and forgiven me.

Yes, I am of such value to You that You sacrificed Your Son Jesus to die on the cross, that my sins be washed clean by His blood.

I am Your precious child. I am valuable to You!

DECEMBER 27

UNIQUE

You are my God!

Hosea 2:23 (NASB)

I don't know why that particular seashell caught my eye. It rested on the sand along with dozens of others. Some were broken, but others were bigger and more perfectly shaped than this one.

I didn't stoop to pick it up. I paused only briefly, studying it with a cursory eye. As I continued down the beach, I looked toward the rushing sea, keenly aware that I am like that seashell. I live among those who are also God's children and am nothing of significance. However, I am created by His hand, individually crafted by His design. I am His, and He is my God.

I am unique in You, O God.

DECEMBER 28

COMPLACENCY

Oh, that you had heeded My commandments!
Then your peace would have been like a river, and
your righteousness like the waves of the sea.

Isaiah 48:18 (NKJV)

Some friends and I were enjoying our coffee on the outdoor patio of a local café when a car alarm went off in the parking lot. We ignored it. But when it went off again a few minutes later, a friend said, "Why don't they do something about that?" Then we realized that someone might be breaking into a vehicle.

When car alarms were introduced, everyone was aware of them and thought of them as a deterrent to crime. Now we either ignore them or consider them annoying.

Complacency is common. We can be lulled into ignoring the moral issues of our day just as we do other common occurrences. It's easy to become more thick-skinned and tolerant of evil, believing that we are growing older and wiser. But are we thinking only of our own comfort? Is it too much effort to get involved?

Ignoring the major debates in society on moral issues that affect us all will not make them go away. As I watch TV and read the newspaper, I'm aware that so much is out of my control. Sometimes it seems as though everything that affects my life is decided by others. I think, "What's the use. I can't change it, anyway."

Complacency. It is a valuable tool for Satan, knowing that eventually our resistance will be worn down. Isn't there something I can do when I hear the alarm? I can move from comfort and complacency to awareness and action. I have read, "It is not what one does but what one tries to do that makes the soul strong and fit for a noble career."

Lord, I don't want to be complacent. But I need Your help to break out of my comfort zone.

DECEMBER 29

ONLY GOD

> When He came into the house, His disciples began questioning Him privately, "Why could we not drive it out?" And He said to them, "This kind cannot come out by anything but prayer."
>
> Mark 9:28-29 (NASB)

The disciples were put on the spot with this challenge. Christ had given His disciples power to cast out demons, but they were helpless to drive the unclean spirit from the boy. They were baffled, and when alone with Jesus they asked Him, "What happened? We've cast out demons before, why couldn't we use the power on this one?" Jesus explained that this was a major case of demon possession and only prayer could perform the exorcism. Only God could do it.

There were nine of the disciples together before a large crowd. They had become accustomed to performing such exorcisms. This was a humbling lesson for them and reminded them how much they needed to depend on Him. Without Him they could do nothing.

We all need the reminder of our dependence on God. There are things that only God can do. Do we truly understand that, or are we arrogant enough to believe that we can make it alone?

Only by Your power, Lord. Only by Your power.

DECEMBER 30

FOR TODAY, LORD

Dear Father,

> Teach me the way of Your statutes, and I shall observe it all the days of my life.
>
> Give me understanding, that I may observe Your law and keep it with all my heart.
>
> Make me walk in the path of Your commandments, for I delight in it.
>
> Incline my heart to Your testimonies and not to dishonest gain.
>
> Turn away my eyes from looking at vanity, and revive me in Your ways.

Establish Your word to me, as that which produces reverence for You.

Turn away my reproach which I dread, for Your
ordinances are good.

Behold, I long for Your precepts;

Revive me through Your righteousness.

May Your loving kindnesses also come to me, O
Lord,

Your salvation according to Your word.

Psalm 119:33-41 (NASB)

DECEMBER 31

IN HIM

We can ask ourselves am I truly in Him? Can we say in all
honesty that we have come to know Him? It is a simple
question but one that takes deep examination. We can ask
ourselves, do I keep His commandments, and am I walking in the manner in which He walked? John's language
is strong in that he says if we say we do, and we don't, we
are liars.

> By this we know we have come to know Him, if we
> keep His commandments.
>
> The one who says "I have come to know Him,"
> and does not keep His commandments, is a liar,
> and the truth is not in him; but whoever keeps His

word, in him the love of God has truly been per-
fected. By this we know that we are in Him: the one
who says he abides in Him ought himself to walk in
the same manner as He walked.

1 John 2:3-6 (NASB)

While writing these thoughts from here at the water's
edge, I have been immersed in His Word. Maybe writing
the book has been self-serving, giving me the opportunity
to delve into scripture, finding those that have brought
me hope, praise, contrition, tears of love, joy, sorrow, and
much more.

We will never truly know God in this life. But we know
He can perfect our love for Him; it is an ongoing process.

We don't keep all the commandments, and we don't
always walk in the same manner as He walked.

But we must continue to strive to do what He asks of us.
And we will know what that is when we stay in His Word.

I love You, Lord, and one day I will see You face-to-face.
Continue to perfect Your work in me that I may know I am
in You.

ENDNOTES

1   Mrs. Charles Cowman, compiler, *Springs in the Valley* (Grand Rapids, MI: Daybreak Books 1939, 1968) p. 198

2   Mary Wilder Tileston, compiler. *Joy and Strength* (Minneapolis, MN:World Wide Publications 1901) p. 36

3   Mary Wilder Tileston,compiler. Joy and Strength (Minneapolis MN: World Word Publications 1901) p. 137

4   Mary Wilder Tileston, compiler. *Joy and Strength* (Minneapolis, MN:World Wide Publications 1901) p. 105

5   Mary Wilder Tileston, compiler. *Joy and Strength* (Minneapolis, MN:World Wide Publications 1901) p. 105

6   Mary Wilder Tileston, compiler. *Joy and Strength* (Minneapolis, MN:World Wide Publications 1901) p. 180

7 Pope John Paul II, *Crossing the Threshold of Hope* (New York, NY: Alfrede A. Knopf, Inc. 1994) p.125

8 Mrs. Charles Cowman, compiler, *Springs in the Valley* (Grand Rapids, MI: Daybreak Books 1939, 1968) p. 173

9 Mary Wilder Tileston, compiler.Joy and Strength (Minneapolis, MN:World Wide Publications 1901) p. 15

10 Baker Book House, ed., *The Best of C.H. Spurgeon* 1977 (Grand Rapids, MI.: Baker Book House) p. 62

11 Charles Cowman, compiler, *Springs in the Valley* (Grand Rapids, MI: Daybreak Books 1939, 1968) p. 234

12 Mrs. Charles Cowman, compiler, *Springs in the Valley* (Grand Rapids, MI: Daybreak Books 1939, 1968) p. 333

13 Mary Wilder Tileston, compiler. *Joy and Strength* (Minneapolis, MN:World Wide Publications 1901) p. 49

14 The Moody Bible Institute of Chicago, *The New Unger's Bible Dictionary* Revised and Updated Edition 1988 Additional and New Material Copyright 1988 (Chicago, IL: THE MOODY BIBLE INSTITUTE OF CHICAGO) p. 226

ORDER INFORMATION

REDEMPTION
P R E S S

To order additional copies of this book, please visit
www.redemption-press.com.
Also available on Amazon.com and BarnesandNoble.com
Or by calling toll free 1-844-2REDEEM.